Postmodernism and Contemporary
Fiction

AV

REF

Postmodernism and Contemporary Fiction

Edited by
Edmund J. Smyth

B. T. Batsford Ltd, London

© Edmund J. Smyth 1991
First published 1991

All rights reserved. No part of this publication
may be reproduced, in any form or by any means,
without permission from the Publisher

Typeset by Deltatype Ltd, Ellesmere Port
and printed in Great Britain by
Dotesios (Printers) Ltd, Trowbridge, Wilts

Published by B. T. Batsford Ltd
4 Fitzhardinge Street, London W1H 0AH

A CIP catalogue record for this book is
available from the British Library

ISBN 0 7134 5776 7

O 713457759

Contents

Contributors

Hans Bertens is professor of American Literature at the University of Utrecht. He has published *The Fiction of Paul Bowles* (1979), with Theo D'haen *Geschiedenis van de Amerikaanse literatuur* (1983), with Douwe Fokkema *Approaching Postmodernism* (1986), and with Theo D'haen *Het postmodernisme in de internationale literatuur* (1988). He is currently editing a collection on postmodernism.

Michael Caesar is senior lecturer in Italian at the University of Kent. He is co-editor, with Peter Hainsworth, of *Writers and Society in Contemporary Italy* (1984) and editor of *Dante: The Critical Heritage* (1988). He is currently working on the poetry and thought of Giacomo Leopardi.

Thomas Docherty teaches Theory and English at University College Dublin. He is the author of *Reading (Absent) Character* (1983), *John Donne, Undone* (1986), *On Modern Authority* (1987), *After Theory: Postmodernism/Postmarxism* (1989), and of numerous articles on theory. At present, he is working on *Critical Philosophy*, a book exploring the relations between criticism and philosophy in post-modernity.

James Higgins is professor of Latin-American Literature at the University of Liverpool and honorary professor of the Universidad Nacional Mayor de San Marcos, Lima. He is the author of *A History of Peruvian Literature*, books and articles on contemporary Peruvian poetry, and three articles on the Colombian Nobel prize-winning novelist, Gabriel García Márquez. He is currently preparing a book on the work of the Peruvian short story writer Julio Ramón Ribeyro.

Linda Hutcheon is professor of English and Comparative Literature at the University of Toronto. She is the author of *Narcissistic Narrative: The Metafictional Paradox* (1980; 1984), *Formalism and the Freudian Aesthetic* (1984), *A Theory of Parody: The Teachings of 20th-Century Art Forms* (1985), *A Poetics of Postmodernism: History, Theory, Fiction* (1988), *The Canadian Postmodern: A Study of Contemporary English-Canadian Fiction* (1988), *The Politics of Postmodernism* (1989). She is currently working on a book on the ideologies of irony.

John Mepham taught Philosophy in the School of European Studies at Sussex University and, more recently, at Bennington College in Vermont. He has published many articles on philosophy and literature and has translated works by Foucault, Koyré and Jakobson. He is co-editor of the four volume *Issues in Marxist Philosophy* and author of a book on Virginia Woolf's *To the Lighthouse*. He is currently working on a book on Woolf's literary career.

David Seed is senior lecturer in English and American Literature at the University of Liverpool. He has written numerous articles on modern fiction, and has published books on Thomas Pynchon and Joseph Heller. He is currently working on a study of the novelist and film-maker Rudolph Wurlitzer.

Dina Sherzer is professor of French and Comparative Literature at the University of Texas at Austin. Her publications include *Representation in Contemporary French Fiction* (1986), *Beckett Translating/ Translating Beckett* (1987) in collaboration with Alan Friedman and Charles Rossman, *Comedy and Humor in Puppetry* (1987) in collaboration with Joel Sherzer. She is currently working on a book entitled *Play and Display: Verbal Strategies in Twentieth Century French Literature*.

Edmund Smyth is lecturer in French Studies at the University of Liverpool. He has published on contemporary French fiction, drama and film, in addition to comparative literature and autobiography. He is currently working on a book on the *nouveau roman*.

Randall Stevenson lectures in English Literature at the University of Edinburgh. He is the author of *The British Novel since the Thirties* (1986) and of *The British Novel in the Twentieth Century: An Introductory Bibliography* (1988). His other publications include several articles on recent and contemporary fiction and drama, and regular theatre reviews for the *Times Literary Supplement*. He is currently working on a study of modernist fiction.

Introduction

Edmund Smyth

1

It has become fashionable to apply the word 'postmodernism' indiscriminately to a variety of cultural, intellectual and social practices. Several critics in various fields have of course attempted to provide definitions, yet no single definition has gained widespread currency or acceptance. It is evident that no consensus exists regarding either the parameters of postmodernism or the precise meaning of the term.

However, it is possible to identify broadly two distinct ways in which 'postmodernism' has come to be used: first, to designate either negatively or positively the contemporary cultural condition as a whole in all its complexity; or, second, to describe a specific set of textual characteristics which can be gleaned from an analysis of selected literary, dramatic or cinematographic works. In this second sense, it has been applied to a style or a sensibility manifesting itself in cultural productions as varied as fiction (in the work of, for example, John Barth, Salman Rushdie, John Fowles, Alasdair Gray, Alain Robbe-Grillet and the French *nouveau roman*, Umberto Eco, Italo Calvino and Gabriel García Márquez), film (*Providence*, *Blue Velvet*, the work of Godard or Peter Greenaway), drama (Dennis Potter's BBC TV series *The Singing Detective* and *Blackeyes*) – in short, in any creative endeavour which exhibits some element of self-consciousness and reflexivity. Fragmentation, discontinuity, indeterminacy, plurality, metafictionality, heterogeneity, intertextuality, decentring, dislocation, ludism: these are the common features such widely differing aesthetic practices are said to display. In distinguishing between what is or is not 'postmodernist', those works betraying such properties have been labelled as postmodern. However, from common usage it is clear that 'postmodernism' has been adopted by many commentators as a means of describing the contemporary novel in general, whether individual texts exhibit these characteristics or not. Thus, it has come to be regarded as synonymous with the contemporary literary 'period' as a whole, in addition to being used as a synonym for avant-garde experimental writing.

From a literary-historical perspective, it is as a periodizing description that the word has been gaining widespread acceptance. In literary terms, the majority of accounts of the 'development' of postmodernism is couched in historical language: postmodernism is seen both as a continuation of modernism and even, by some, as a rejection of modernism. Frank Kermode (1958) preferred the term 'Neo-Modernism'. Several of postmodernism's literary historians have asserted that postmodernism differs from modernist aesthetics principally in its abandonment of subjectivity: the representation of consciousness is alleged to have been forsaken with the emphasis on the fragmentation of the subject. That the self can no longer be considered a unified and stable entity has become axiomatic in the light of poststructuralism. Also, in distinction from the allegedly 'élitist' dimension of the so-called 'high' modernism of the first half of the twentieth century, it has frequently been stated that such works have absorbed popular cultural forms to a greater extent. Parody, pastiche, quotation and self-quotation have been considered as characteristic features of postmodern textual practice. Brian McHale argues strongly in favour of the 'change of dominant' thesis and speaks in terms of a 'transition from modernist to postmodernist poetics' (McHale 1987: 12). This is even applied to individual texts: William Faulkner's *Absalom, Absalom!* is claimed to contain evidence of just this transformation within its own boundaries. McHale has examined the relationship between postmodernism and modernism as a 'logical and historical *consequence* rather than sheer temporal *posteriority*' (5). Postmodernism is considered to be ontological in the sense that it has abandoned the modernist assumption of the possibility of contact with a reality of some kind: postmodernist fiction therefore foregrounds 'post-cognitive' questions. McHale charts this 'change of dominant' in transitional works by Beckett, Robbe-Grillet, Fuentes, Nabokov, Coover and Pynchon. For Hans Bertens, it is precisely this ontological uncertainty which is central to postmodernism: 'It is the awareness of the absence of centres, of privileged languages, higher discourses, that is . . . the most striking difference with Modernism' (Bertens 1986: 46). Every discussion of postmodernism involves above all the transformation of critic into literary historian. This applies not only to academic critics but to postmodernist 'practitioners' as well: both Robbe-Grillet and John Barth, for example, have had recourse to a narrative of literary history on several occasions when seeking to chart the evolution of avant-garde narrative forms. All accounts of postmodernism become narratives in their own right; this would seem paradoxical in view of Jean-François Lyotard's assertion that what principally characterizes postmodernism is the subversion of totalizing metanarratives of any kind. It may seem curious that commentators have not always been sufficiently conscious of the historicizing nature of their attempts to 'map' the postmodern.

The historicizing impulse of such critics, therefore, must be regarded with some suspicion. It would be false to the pluralizing impulse of postmodernist writing to establish a homogenizing metanarrative of the 'development' of postmodernism as a movement: literary history is a far more problematic area of enquiry than many of these critics suppose. It should always be remembered that literary history is itself a critical discourse fraught with dangers of various kinds, the principal of which must be the establishment of a canon. It is evident from a great deal of recent theory that a postmodernist pseudo-pantheon is in the process of being constructed, however reluctantly. Again, this too may seem contradictory in the light of the caution concerning the establishment of both the realist and modernist canons. As more than one commentator has observed, the evaluative criteria for deciding upon the admission of a work into this postmodernist canon can be applied to almost any literary work from any given 'period': thus, *Don Quixote*, *Tristram Shandy*, *Gargantua* et al. can all be demonstrated to contain postmodern features if one decides to apply a grid of interpretation which privileges well-defined postmodern criteria. A concern with fictionality and self-consciousness has of course been a feature of the novel since its very inception. If these criteria can indeed be applied to such an array of literary works, it becomes necessary to question the nature of the discourse of literary history itself. Clearly, these qualities and characteristics are not exclusive to contemporary experimental fiction. Perhaps not sufficiently recognized is the extent to which postmodernism is an effect of reading: there can be no absolute definition of what constitutes radical textuality. Any discussion of the cultural practice of postmodernism is tied up with the direction of reader response. This should be evident following Barthes's *S/Z* in which he demonstrates how even the apparently most *lisible* texts can be shown to contain those inconsistencies and aporia normally considered axiomatic of modern writerly textuality. Postmodernism must be recognized, therefore, as a condition of reading.

In *History and Value* (1988), Frank Kermode confronts this central question of how value is attributed to certain texts and addresses himself to the formation of a canon. His analysis of a passage from Joseph Conrad's *The Secret Agent* shows a concern in this modernist work for the supposedly supreme postmodernist 'value' of fragmentation. Clearly, other characteristics of the postmodern can be demonstrated to exist in a variety of texts from different 'periods', as Umberto Eco and others have pointed out. Ihab Hassan's schematic 'eleven traits' of postmodernism (Hassan 1987) can be found in several texts not confined to the postmodern period. Postmodernism is a construction of reading rather than a self-contained literary period: it is what the literary institution has chosen to call Postmodernism.

It becomes necessary to examine the role of periodization as a culturally imposed activity dictated by the academy and the dominant ideology. It may well be the case that the endorsement of postmodernism as a cultural process may neutralize and recuperate the radical and subversive impact which postmodern writing can have in contesting and demythologizing the codes of signification which otherwise imprison us. The liberating feature of radical textuality is the extent to which such texts make us confront the ways in which we make sense of the world and how we organize our knowledge of reality. Of course, this interpretative strategy can also apply to what is described as 'classic realist' fiction. It is in fact this supposedly 'liberating' aspect of postmodernism which has been challenged, principally by Terry Eagleton, Fredric Jameson and Hal Foster (in addition to Gerald Graff, Charles Newman and John Gardner), who have been suspicious of the ahistorical nature of postmodern writing and the links with eclectic 'consumerist' popular culture and mass media. It is increasingly evident that they are in danger of occupying the position once held by George Lukács, who was dismissive of modernist writing for its failure to reflect social reality. It is true that postmodern writing can be absorbed, in institutional terms, by the syllabus without any serious threat to the dominant ideology. Although justifiably suspicious of the canon and the means by which it is established, Eagleton and Jameson nevertheless would seem, implicitly at least, to have set up a notional 'approved' canon of their own as an alternative to the 'commodified' and multicultural productions of postmodernism. A whole generation of writers cannot, however, be dismissed in this way. Arguably, they are themselves drawing up a map of literary history and distinguishing between 'positive' and 'negative' writing. As Charles Newman has observed, 'The vaunted fragmentation of art is no longer an aesthetic choice; it is simply a cultural aspect of the economic and social fabric' (Newman 1985: 183). Linda Hutcheon, however, provides a convincing demonstration of the politically liberating effects of postmodern writing as a counterblast to the Eagleton/Jameson position. For her, postmodernism is 'resolutely historical, and inescapably political' (Hutcheon 1988: 4): her postmodernist sub-category of 'historiographic metafiction' encompasses oppositional texts which are both self-reflexive and historical, problematizing the dominant ideology. Hutcheon shows how postmodern writing can challenge the commodification process from within by the parodic use of pluralizing popular forms.

The work of Jean-François Lyotard has been crucial in the elaboration of postmodernism as a means of describing the wider cultural and intellectual condition: the contemporary experience is characterized by epistemological and ontological uncertainty. According to Lyotard, the master and metanarratives which have sustained Western society and discourse since the Enlightenment are no longer considered legitimate and authoritative. What is being challenged are the rationalist and humanist assumptions of our culture. This has led several commentators to suggest that the plural nature of social discourse is, in a sense, reflected in the aleatory forms of postmodernist fiction. It is interesting to note the extent to which several critics have come to rely on this reflectionist and even formal realist argument as a means of explaining the connection between postmodern textual practice and what is supposed to characterize the wider cultural condition. Fredric Jameson, for example, proposes a homology between the cultural form of postmodernism and its economic base. In these versions, the fragmentation and discontinuity of the contemporary experience of reality is deemed to be *reflected* in the plural and mobile structures of postmodern writing. Thus, for Brian McHale and others, epistemological and ontological doubt is conveyed through disjointed formal structures in a work of postmodern fiction. However tempting this view may appear, it is still a totalizing perspective in that it remains predicated on a reflectionist (not to say reductive) description of the complexity of the language of fiction and its relationship to 'reality'. This perspective in fact involves little more than an updating of Erich Auerbach's *Mimesis*, repackaged to encompass the postmodern episteme.

It is evident from several accounts of 'postmodernist fiction' that this can be an all-encompassing term which includes several types of writing, from 'minimalism' through to 'fabulism' and 'magic realism': Beckett can thus be made to rub shoulders with García Márquez and Salman Rushdie. This frequently involves making international links: for example, at a conference on the *nouveau roman* held in New York in 1982, several leading American postmodernist writers were invited in order to discuss the penetration of postmodernism as an 'international' literary style. Much of the debate concerned the viability or otherwise of admitting certain writers (notably Saul Bellow) to the house of postmodernist fiction (see Oppenheim 1986: 195–209). Depending on which definition one is using, several kinds of work have come under the postmodernist heading. Alasdair Gray's novels use both text and illustration as part of the production and subversion of meaning. In terms of syntactical structures, many postmodernist novels have been formally conventional (Muriel Spark's *The Driver's Seat*) or disruptive (Claude Simon's *Histoire*). While it may be common practice to ridicule the discussion of 'influences' in the postmodernist novel, many of the novelists themselves have conceded the influence on their style of previous generations: for example, Claude Simon's writing is immediately evocative of both Faulkner and Proust. In Alasdair Gray's *Lanark* and *1982 Janine*, the author enumerates the intertexts of both these novels. This can also be seen in John Berger's *G.* and John Banville's *Doctor Copernicus*. The question of referentiality is central to any discussion of postmodern aesthetics: the *nouveau roman* has been particularly alert to this theoretical difficulty. We find both the abandonment of the authorial mode and a reinsertion of the author constructed as a discursive entity (as in the work of Martin Amis and Milan Kundera). Postmodernism can include self-reflexive, metafictional novels or more disparate literary forms like the non-fiction novel, essay, autobiography and combinations of realism and fantasy. As metafiction, a novel such as Italo Calvino's *If on a Winter's Night a Traveller* dramatizes the processes of reading in an explicit way: however, many of these novels will contain implicit allegories of reading and writing. Several postmodern novels manipulate the discourses and registers belonging to previous literary periods (John Fowles's *A Maggot*, Peter Ackroyd's *Hawksmoor*). Robbe-Grillet's *La Maison de Rendez-vous* is unmistakably plural in its incorporation of stereotypical representations of Hong Kong in Western culture. The popular form of the detective novel has been used in several manifestations of postmodern writing. Intertextuality is another feature of postmodern aesthetics which seems to illustrate the erosion of 'originality' as a literary value. A novel like William Kennedy's *Legs* invokes both *The Great Gatsby* and *Gargantua* in its construction of the personality of the historical character Jack 'Legs' Diamond. Narrative perspective becomes dispersed and self-consciously unreliable, as in D. M. Thomas's *The White Hotel*. Postmodern writing moves to the very boundaries of fiction: this is apparent in Julian Barnes's *Flaubert's Parrot* and *A History of the World in 10½ Chapters*. History and autobiography meet in Claude Simon's *Les Géorgiques*, and in recent pseudo-autobiography such as Robbe-Grillet's *Le Miroir qui revient* or Philippe Sollers's recent fiction. The evidence of the *nouveau roman* would suggest a dissatisfaction with the formalist Utopian view of the text as pure reflexivity. The 'decentring' impulse of postmodern writing has allowed greater space for marginal and ex-centric discourses. Perhaps the greatest 'liberating' feature of postmodern writing, however, has been the mixing of writings and intertextual referencing: the multivocal, heterogeneous and heteroglossic nature of postmodern writing has broadened the scope of contemporary fiction. The borders between genres have become much more fluid. As Lyotard has commented:

> A postmodern artist or writer is in the position of a philosopher: the text he writes, the work he produces are not in principle governed by preestablished rules, and they cannot be judged according to a determining judgement, by applying familiar categories to the text or to the work. Those rules and categories are what the work of art itself is looking for. (Lyotard 1984: 81)

The text becomes a site of conflicting and intersecting discourses. John Barth's idea of 'the literature of replenishment' (1980b) seems particularly appropriate here.

Such novels may well enter the pseudo-pantheon of postmodern writing in the sense that it is they which most frequently occur in critical works on postmodernist fiction. It is inevitable that a canon will emerge as one begins to discuss which texts are deemed to be most 'representative' of postmodern textuality. Again, the crucial danger is that one can very quickly establish a homogenizing description of postmodernist fiction which is discursively totalizing and totalitarian. As Roland Barthes has warned, a new *doxa* is always in danger of being constructed. Critics are inevitably caught in a kind of double bind when the analysis of postmodernism takes place: in providing a version of postmodernism which rightly emphasizes plurality, multiplicity and mobility, one is valorizing certain critical concepts at the expense of others. As a critical discourse, writing about postmodernism is therefore extremely problematic.

What is abundantly clear is that 'postmodernism' as a description of both the current literary period and the wider cultural and social condition is probably irreversible. In this respect, as a critical term it will remain ill-defined and all-pervasive, despite the numerous attempts which will continue to be made to theorize the concept in a more satisfactory way. 'Postmodernism' and 'postmodernity' will continue to be interchangeable concepts. The discussion will continue to proliferate in several directions. As Ihab Hassan has indicated, 'the question of Postmodernism remains complex and moot' (Hassan 1983: 25) and it is indeed likely to remain so. More 'precise' terms (like Raymond Federman's 'Surfiction' or Jerome Klinkowitz's 'Post-Contemporary Fiction') have not gained wide currency. By studying how postmodernism has been constructed as a cultural and intellectual practice, we are engaged in the process of making sense of our culture.

2

This book provides a comprehensive account of some of the main issues in the debate surrounding the relationship between postmodernism and contemporary fiction. In Part One ('Centres of Postmodernism'), aspects of the contemporary novel in Britain, the USA, France, Italy and Latin America are examined in the context of the evolution of those new fictional forms which have been described as postmodernist. These chapters are not intended to provide an exhaustive analysis of the fiction produced in these countries, nor should it be considered that an international 'movement' of some kind has been identified. The purpose is rather to discuss some of the principal manifestations of postmodern writing without in any way proposing either to establish or to draw from a canon. All the contributors to this section are at pains to emphasize the diversity and multiplicity of writings which exist within distinct cultural configurations.

In Part Two ('The Critical Agenda'), many of the recurring controversies and preoccupations of postmodernism in the wider cultural and intellectual field are examined: the contributors address themselves to those 'common' features of critical thinking on postmodernism which have given rise to intense discussion in a number of related areas. In harmony with the non-totalizing impetus of postmodern writing generally, the reader will not be able to extract from this volume a homogeneous account of postmodernism; but he/she is invited to sample the rich diversity of postmodern writing through which cultural, social and political discourses are articulated.

Part One
Centres of Postmodernism

1 Postmodernism and Contemporary Fiction in Britain

Randall Stevenson

> *I want to emphasize the element of logical and historical consequence rather than sheer temporal posteriority. Postmodernism follows from modernism, in some sense, more than it follows after modernism.* (Brian McHale)

> *So many novelists still write as though the revolution that was* Ulysses *had never happened . . . Nathalie Sarraute once described literature as a relay race, the baton of innovation passing from one generation to another. The vast majority of British novelists has dropped the baton, stood still, turned back, or not even realised that there is a race.* (B. S. Johnson)

'The first impulse of every critic of postmodernism', Ihab Hassan recently suggested, 'is still to relate it to the semanteme it contains: namely, modernism' (Hassan 1987a: 214). As Hassan's comment half-implies, it may in some areas be time for criticism to move on from the task of defining postmodernism in relation to its antecedents. Yet in the British context such a move is probably still premature. The negative views B. S. Johnson expresses above are fairly widely shared: Malcolm Bradbury points to the existence of a general critical assumption that after the work of the modernists, the 'experimental tradition' in Britain may simply have lapsed (Bradbury 1973: 86). This critical assumption, and its origins, are worth examining further. The 'first impulse' Hassan defines, however, remains an essential one. Any study of post-modernism in Britain must first of all establish that there really is something to study; that a literature does exist in Britain which can be seen, in Brian McHale's terms, as the 'logical and historical' consequence of the earlier initiatives of modernism.

For the purposes of tracing their later consequences, these initiatives can be usefully separated into three areas. Firstly, modernist fiction's most obvious and celebrated innovation lies in its focalization of the novel in the minds or private narratives of its characters. Stream of consciousness and a variety of other devices are used to transcribe an inner mental world at the expense of the external social experience most often favoured in the conventional, realistic forms of earlier fiction. Virginia Woolf's demand, in her essay 'Modern Fiction', that the novel should 'look within' and examine the mind thus becomes one of the summary slogans of modernism. In the same essay, Woolf

suggests that the movement within consciousness shows life as something other than 'a series of gig-lamps symmetrically arranged' (Woolf
1919 and 1966: 106): a second distinctive feature of modernist fiction is
its abandonment of serial, chronological conventions of arrangement.
The extended histories of Victorian fiction are replaced in *Ulysses*
(1922) and *Mrs Dalloway* (1925) by concentration within a single day of
consciousness: random memories incorporate the past, rarely chronologically. Time itself becomes inconceivable in terms of clocks and
calendars. Shredding and slicing life, in Woolf's view, menacing it with
monotony and madness, in Lawrence's, clocks provide for modernist
fiction more of a threat than a sense of order and regularity.

A more general sense of difficulty in sustaining order and regularity in
the early twentieth century underlies Lily Briscoe's comments in *To the
Lighthouse* when she remarks that an artist's brush may be the 'one
dependable thing in a world of strife, ruin, chaos' (Woolf 1927 and 1973:
170). Lily's painting also works in the novel as a figurative analogue for the
conduct and conclusion of Woolf's own narrative processes, her own
imposing of order on chaos. Joyce's *A Portrait of the Artist as a Young
Man* (1916), Wyndham Lewis's *Tarr* (1918), and Marcel Proust's *A la
recherche du temps perdu* (1913–27) portray more directly and obviously
the life and artistic commitments of their authors. As these works
illustrate, a third distinguishing feature of modernism is an interest in the
nature and form of art which occasionally extends, self-reflexively,
towards the novel's scrutiny of its own strategies.

This third aspect of modernist innovation is the one whose 'logical
and historical' consequences are clearest and easiest to trace in later
writing. B. S. Johnson's wish to see the baton of innovation initiated by
Ulysses carried forward can actually be satisfied, in this area, by looking
no further than developments Joyce made himself. Even in *A Portrait
of the Artist as a Young Man*, Joyce's semi-autobiographical hero
wonders whether he may not love 'words better than their associations'
(Joyce 1916 and 1973: 167). Competition between love of words and of
the world they seek to represent expands in *Ulysses*. In one way, the
novel is a final triumph of realism, representing character more
inwardly and intimately than ever previously. In another way, *Ulysses*
is at least partly an autotelic novel, its hugely extended parodies raising
as much interest in its own means of representation – and in the
linguistic resources of fiction generally – as in anything which they may
represent. The balance shifts very much further in favour of the latter
area of interest in the 'Work in Progress', with which Joyce followed
Ulysses. Its constant, playful, inventive forging of a self-contained
language can be summed up by the novel's own phrase, 'say
mangraphique, may say nay por daguerre!'. 'Work in Progress' is
primarily 'graphique,' not 'por daguerre': it is writing, writing for itself,
not as daguerrotype or any other semi-photographic attempt to
represent reality. In *Our Exagmination Round his Factification for
Incamination of Work in Progress* (1929), Eugene Jolas comments:

The epoch when the writer photographed the life about him with the mechanics of words redolent of the daguerrotype, is happily drawing to its close. The new artist of the word has recognised the autonomy of language. (in Beckett 1929 and 1972: 79)

The eventual publication of 'Work in Progress', as *Finnegans Wake* in 1939, provides a convenient date – if not for the success of the novel itself, too abstract and esoteric to sustain much attention during the war years which followed – at least for critics and literary historians. Many have followed Jolas in seeing Joyce's 'autonomy of language' and 'new art of the word' as marking a decisive break with earlier epochs of fiction, initiating a postmodernist writing which extends, but into markedly new areas, the initiatives of its predecessor. Ihab Hassan talks of *Finnegans Wake* as 'a "monstrous prophecy of our postmodernity" . . . both augur and theory of a certain kind of literature' (Hassan 1978a: xiii–xiv). Christopher Butler takes *After the Wake* (1980) as the title of his 'Essay on the Contemporary Avant Garde'. Joyce's development towards *Finnegans Wake* also helps confirm the general distinction Brian McHale establishes in *Postmodernist Fiction* between modernism, dominated by epistemological concerns, and postmodernism, focused around ontological ones. Stephen Dedalus's uncertainty about the relations which can be sustained between word and world shows, in *A Portrait of the Artist as a Young Man*, the epistemological concerns of modernism. In *Finnegans Wake*, the breach between word and world is no longer a matter of doubt or negotiation, but of some certainty, even celebration. As McHale suggests, any 'stable world' the text projects is at best fragmentary, and is generally 'overwhelmed by the competing reality of language (McHale 1987: 234). The 'autonomy' of this language establishes *Finnegans Wake* as an almost purely linguistic domain, a self-contained world, ontologically disjunct.

If such developments in *Finnegans Wake* were an augur and a prophecy, what did they prophesy; which literature did they inaugurate? Which authors relayed the baton of innovation that Joyce himself carried forward from *Ulysses* through 'Work in Progress' into *Finnegans Wake*? Two other Irish writers served as intermediaries between Joyce and later developments within Britain. Aware of Joyce's work throughout its progress, Samuel Becket was naturally one of the first to recognize the significance of its 'autonomy of language'. Beckett remarks in *Our Exagmination Round his Factification for Incamination of Work in Progress*, that Joyce's work is 'not *about* something: *it is that something itself*' (Beckett 1929 and 1972: 14), and he goes on in the central part of his oeuvre, the trilogy *Molloy, Malone Dies, The Unnamable* (1950–2), to create a kind of autonomy of his own – as the Unnamable remarks, 'it all boils down to a question of words . . . all words, there's nothing else' (1959 and 1979: 308). Each of the trilogy's aging narrators compensates for failing powers by the endless spinning of evasive artifice in words, yet each anxiously foregrounds and negotiates with the inadequacies of the linguistic medium he employs. Language and the nature of narrative imagination thus become central subjects of the trilogy. Any 'stable world' it presents is further overwhelmed by the progressive revelation that each narrator exists only as an imaginative device of a subsequent one, in a succession of evasions leading towards the unnamable author and the depths of an impulse to articulate, which can neither rest nor ever consummate its desires.

Flann O'Brien's *At Swim-Two-Birds* (1939) follows comparably in the wake of Joyce. Its narrator finds Joyce 'indispensable', and the novel in which he appears is partly a pastiche of 'Work in Progress'. Joyce's material supposedly unfolds in the dreaming mind of a Dublin publican; the story O'Brien's narrator tells concerns a publican who operates his imagination altogether more systematically, locking up his fictional characters 'so that he can keep an eye on them and see that there is no boozing' (O'Brien 1939 and 1975: 35). Unfortunately for his system, they break free while he sleeps and take over his story themselves. Like Beckett's trilogy, though in much lighter vein, *At Swim-Two-Birds* thus becomes a story about a man telling a story about storytelling. Each work extends the 'augury' of *Finnegans Wake*: each work is a postmodernist paradigm, a prophecy of the self-reflexive foregrounding of language and fiction-making which has become a central, distinguishing characteristic of postmodernism.

This is a characteristic which has appeared increasingly widely in post-war British fiction. In *The Alexandria Quartet* (1957–60), for example, Lawrence Durrell's narrator Darley sets up and discusses aesthetic paradoxes, including ones affecting the text in which he figures, quite often enough to justify Durrell's view that, as a whole, 'the novel is only half secretly about art, the great subject of modern artists' (in Cowley 1963: 231). Anna Wulf, Doris Lessing's narrator in *The Golden Notebook* (1962), highlights and demonstrates the problems of writing, dividing the transcription of her experience into various notebooks and commenting frequently on the nature and validity of each. In *The French Lieutenant's Woman* (1969), John Fowles (or a version of him) intrudes famously – or notoriously – into chapter thirteen to discuss his tactics and emphasize that 'this story I am telling is all imagination. These characters I create never existed outside my own mind'. Similar intrusions by authors commenting on their own practice and proceedings, or enacting in their texts problematic relations between language, fiction and reality, also appear in the work of Christine Brook-Rose, Muriel Spark, Giles Gordon, Rayner Heppenstall, David Caute, John Berger, B.S. Johnson, Alasdair Gray, Julian Barnes and others. Alain Robbe-Grillet, admired in *The French Lieutenant's Woman* as a mentor of Fowles's own tactics, once suggested:

> After Joyce . . . it seems that we are more and more moving
> towards an age of fiction in which . . . invention and imagination
> may finally become the subject of the book. (Robbe-Grillet 1965:
> 63)

There is evidence that in Britain this epoch has now arrived. A certain self-reflexiveness even finds its way into otherwise realistic novels, such as Anthony Burgess's *Earthly Powers*, as if no contemporary novel could quite be complete without at least a moment of creative hesitation and self-examination.

This proliferating self-examination, however, has often been seen as an unlikeable, irresponsible tendency in contemporary literature. As Linda Hutcheon suggests, there are now too many critics to list who find postmodernist writing 'a form of solipsistic navel-gazing and empty ludic game playing' (Hutcheon 1988: 206). To such critics, postmodernism's self-reflexiveness seems a renunciation, in favour of a sterile narcissism, of the novel's potential to shape and assimilate the world for its readers. It is sometimes suggested not only that postmodernism scarcely exists in Britain, but that it would not be a good thing if it did: like structuralism, it is seen as a form of literary rabies, to be confined to the Continent for as long as possible. Postmodernism's self-reflexiveness can be defended, even on the grounds of responsibility upon which dismissals of it are usually based. A fuller reply to negative criticism of postmodernism, however, can be made with the further evidence of a brief survey of ways in which postmodernism has followed from modernism's second area of innovation–chronology and structure.

In 1926 Thomas Hardy remarked forlornly of contemporary modernist writing: 'They've changed everything now . . . We used to think there was a beginning and a middle and an end' (in Woolf 1953: 94). Beginnings, middles and ends have become still more problematic, even suspect, in recent fiction. For William Golding, for example, in *Pincher Martin* (1956), they become in a sense almost simultaneous. *Pincher Martin* performs an extreme form of modernism's abbreviation of the span of narrative into single days, reflecting the whole life of its protagonist supposedly within the single moment of his death. Lawrence Durrell sustains in his own way what he calls his 'challenge to the serial form of the modern novel': in *The Alexandria Quartet*, he presents successively three different views of the same set of events, creating a novel 'not travelling from a to b but standing above time' (Durrell 1957 and 1983: 198). Rayner Heppenstall, in *The Connecting Door* (1962), establishes two different eras in which his characters exist simultaneously, and, in a later novel, *Two Moons* (1977), concurrently sustains stories set in two different months, one appearing on all the left-hand pages of the novel, the other on the right. A similar double-narrative tactic is employed in Brigid Brophy's *In Transit* (1969), and something comparable is undertaken by Peter Ackroyd in *Hawksmoor* (1985), which sets alternate chapters in contemporary and in early eighteenth-century London. Two fairly distinct narratives also appear in Alasdair Gray's *Lanark*, whose individual books are presented in the order 3,1,2,4. Somewhere in the middle of the fourth book, Gray includes an Epilogue in which he invites readers to follow the text in one order but think about it in another. Like Gray's protagonist, readers of *Lanark* – readers of postmodernist fiction generally – are likely to get lost in an 'Intercalendrical Zone'. Strange, unstable orders of reading are perhaps most startlingly introduced by B.S. Johnson. His *Albert Angelo* (1964) has holes cut in its pages so that readers may see into the future, while his celebrated novel-in-a-box *The Unfortunates* (1964) is made up of loose-leaf sheets, intended, as a note on the box explains, 'to be read in random order'.

Such random or non-serial ordering thoroughly fragments the middles of some recent fiction: equal irreverence for convention appears, sometimes explicitly, in its beginnings and endings. Flann O'Brien and Samuel Beckett once again appear as transitional figures in this postmodernist direction. Beckett's Molloy expresses it, for example, when he remarks, 'I began at the beginning, like an old ballocks, can you imagine that?' (Beckett 1959 and 1979: 9), while Flann O'Brien's narrator comments, 'one beginning and one ending for a book was a thing I did not agree with' and goes on to offer 'three openings entirely dissimilar' (O'Brien 1939 and 1975: 9). John Fowles, in his turn, invites readers to choose between three different endings to *The French Lieutenant's Woman*. In *G.* (1972), John Berger shuns defining endings, and defining order in fiction generally, remarking that 'the writer's desire to finish is fatal to the truth. The End unifies. Unity must be established in another way' (Berger 1973: 88).

Berger's views relate to a specifically political motivation, variously apparent throughout the novel. The whole text has a fragmentary, indefinite quality. Its vague story is juxtaposed with much historical, even statistical, documentation, in paragraphs whose scant narrative connections are further exposed by their widely separate layout on the printed page. This disjunctive, unfinished quality challenges readers to establish an order which the text does not entirely provide for them. Far from finding, as in conventional fiction, a coherent, structured refuge from the shapelessness of life, readers of *G.* are – as if at a Brecht play – bereft of secure containment within illusion, and forced to take responsibility, conceptually at least, for the reshaping of reality beyond the page. Through the gaping openings between the novel's paragraphs, they are disturbingly re-inserted into the processes of history and power.

G., in this way, helps refute some of the opponents of postmodernism. One of its most powerful adversaries is Fredric Jameson who suggests postmodernism is 'an alarming and pathological symptom of a society that has become incapable of dealing with time and history' (in Foster 1983: 117). *G.*, on the contrary, seems anything but reluctant to deal with time and history, using postmodernism's freedom to challenge literary forms and structures as a means of integrating into the text a much wider challenge to institutionalized forms and structures of power within society at large. Such politically engaged postmodernism is rarer in Britain than elsewhere. Comparable tactics, however, are used by David Caute in *The Occupation* (1971) and in a novel Caute admired as a 'landmark' in 'coherent social comment' (Caute 1972: 252), *The French Lieutenant's Woman*. Fowles takes from Marx his epigraph about emancipation, and, like Berger, uses textual strategies to enforce upon readers an unusually direct engagement with this wider theme in the novel. Separate endings impose, by formal means, a need for freedom and responsible choice, also learned painfully, in personal and social terms, by Fowles's protagonist.

Not all the novels mentioned above are as concerned with political or social comment as *G.* or *The French Lieutenant's Woman*, but few are only empty, ludic or disjunct from history. Fractured, non-serial forms in the texts mentioned suggest a concurrence with conditions of contemporary history, summed up in Italo Calvino's *If on a Winter's Night a Traveller* (1982) which remarks that:

> . . . the dimension of time has been shattered, we cannot love or think except in fragments of time each of which goes off along its own trajectory and immediately disappears. We can rediscover the continuity of time only in the novels of that period when time no longer seemed stopped and did not yet seem to have exploded.
> (Calvino 1982: 13)

Calvino's comments help connect the history of twentieth-century narrative with the wider history of the century itself. Time, for the Victorian age, did not seem stopped, but – for writers such as Wells at least – purposively and positively progressive, a feeling reflected in the chronological continuity, firm resolution and frequent *Bildungsroman* form of their narratives. For the modernists, on the other hand, history seemed not progress but nightmare, and the clock itself a threat. More recent events and technologies have expanded this sense of fragmentation and discontinuity, contributing to a fractured, accelerated, plural life within a wayward, even apocalyptic history. These conditions postmodernist art is often held to reflect. It may not, however, do so as automatically and unhealthily as Jameson's idea of postmodernism as a 'pathological symptom' suggests. Modernism attempted to contain the dark energies of historical nightmare within subtle structures and complex chronologies; that is, by radicalizing form. Postmodernism not only radicalizes forms, but also satirizes them, exposing their incapacities to connect with reality and the possibilities for distortion which result. In one way, as Jameson suggests, this can be seen as evasive, a negation of art's potential to confront the challenges of life and history. In another way, however, it can be seen as responsibly encouraging readers to challenge for themselves cultural codes and established patterns of thought, including some of those which make contemporary history so intractable. An age of consumerism, and of powerful manipulation by mass media, creates the need for what Nathalie Sarraute calls an 'Age of Suspicion'; for scepticism about the means and motives by which the world is constructed and communicated. Postmodernism serves such scepticism. B. S. Johnson's *The Unfortunates*, for example, could scarcely go further in the creation of what Roland Barthes calls *scriptible* fiction. Readers can hardly remain passive consumers, or be seduced by the covert ideologies, of a text they have literally had to piece together, page by page, for themselves. Without going as far as *The Unfortunates*, the forms of all the novels mentioned introduce a comparable questioning of conventional patterns and expectations, often heightened by the novelists' explicit commentary on their own activity. Easily as such writing can, on occasion, include the narcissistic or the vacuously ludic, it has at least the capacity to be seriously – or wittily – challenging, an enabling enhancement of its readers' vision and decisiveness.

   This sort of challenge is, in some ways, further extended by developments of the third area of modernism's initiatives, its internalization of narrative perspectives. Joyce's use of stream of consciousness was often thought at the time to be an achievement so outstanding as to deter imitation: Ezra Pound, for example, suggested, '*Ulysses* is, presumably . . . unrepeatable . . . you cannot duplicate it' (Pound 1922: 625). Some of the authors who have dared adopt Joyce's methods, have done so neither by duplicating nor by radically reshaping them, but by adapting them to reflect heightened or malfunctioning consciousnesses rather than relatively normal ones. The atmosphere of the 'Nighttown', 'Circe' section of *Ulysses* extends further into recent writing than that of, say, Molly's soliloquy in 'Penelope', emphasizing in several novels the warping, unreliable way reality is represented within the mind. Readers of Malcolm Lowry's *Under the Volcano* (1947), for example, are introduced to a herd of buffaloes which quickly turn out to be merely the phantoms of a drink-sodden mind. Beckett's failing narrators manage in their torrents of words only unstably to sustain an existence on a strange edge of death and silence, adrift in 'who knows what profounds of mind' (Beckett 1984: 288). Jean Rhys, in *Good Morning, Midnight* (1939), transcribes a mind strangely unstrung by loneliness, through a mixture of thoughts and memories recorded in a variety of tenses and stream-of-consciousness and interior-monologue styles. Though her technique clearly derives from the modernists, it is adapted into a unique, subtle form of her own. Later novelists have continued to stretch the stream of consciousness in similar directions. Christine Brooke-Rose's *Such* (1966), for example, like some of Beckett's narrative, follows movements in a mind of weirdly diminished vitality, transcribing a whirling chaos of images which invade consciousness at the point of death. B. S. Johnson's *House Mother Normal* (1971) uses the contents of eight minds at, or close to, this point, and one 'normal' perspective, to express a multi-faceted range of interpretative possibilities created by a single event in an old people's home. The impairment of faculties suffered by its inmates is carefully, even graphically, represented by the text – for example, one character who dies, or perhaps falls asleep, leaves only blank pages to represent the extinction of her consciousness.

Though Pound found *Ulysses* 'unrepeatable', he suggests that 'it does add definitely to the international store of literary technique' (Pound 1922: 625). Many later novelists have benefited from this store, and from other forms of modernist facility in rendering individual consciousness. The example of Virginia Woolf's interior monologue has been at least as useful, in this way, as Joyce's or Dorothy Richardson's stream of consciousness, most immediately to Rosamond Lehmann and Elizabeth Bowen in the 1930s, as well as to later writers, women perhaps especially, such as Anita Brookner. It is important, however, to distinguish this work from the fiction of, say, B. S. Johnson and Christine Brooke-Rose. Neither Rosamond Lehmann nor Anita Brookner, for example, should really be called postmodernist, since they follow *after* modernism, adopting something of its idiom and methods, without, as McHale suggests, following on *from* the work of the modernists by not only *adopting* their idiom, but *adapting* it into recognizably new and separate extensions of their own. It is worth trying to retain, in the ways McHale suggests, limits to the meaning of the term postmodernism. Umberto Eco complains, 'Unfortunately, "postmodern" . . . is applied today to anything the user happens to like' (in Hutcheon 1988: 42): as he suggests, the term is increasingly used in the media to signify little more than vague approval of what is new and striking in contemporary culture. Understanding of the nature and variety of this culture is better served by more careful engagement with the 'semanteme' postmodernism contains; by fuller investigation of the 'logical and historical' sources of certain innovations and new fashions. As the survey above suggests, some of the developments in recent British writing can be traced not only generally, but quite specifically, each major area of modernist initiative carried forward through intermediary writers in the 1930s into particular phases of continuing experiment.

The original point of the survey, however, was not, or not only, to suggest how specifically and illuminatingly the term 'postmodernism' can be applied to the British context, but simply as an answer to B. S. Johnson's fear that the baton of innovation had been dropped altogether. On the evidence of the range of writers discussed, this is not the case. Yet such a conclusion may raise more questions than it answers. If postmodernism does exist in Britain, how strongly and significantly does it exist, and why has it often been overlooked? How and why has British writing acquired its 'no experiments, please' reputation? What origins, and what final justice, can be found for the critical assumption that, as Bradbury expresses it, 'the experimental tradition did shift or lapse' in Britain after modernism (Bradbury 1973: 86)?

Bradbury goes on to explain that this 'shift or lapse' is 'usually identified with the thirties, when realism and politics came back' (86). This view of the decade is now very widely accepted, and with reason: political and other stresses at the time did encourage in many quarters a rejection of modernism in favour of documentary, realistic forms more obviously attuned to the contemporary crisis. Nevertheless, several of the experimental novelists mentioned above actually began their careers in the 1930s; Samuel Beckett, Lawrence Durrell, Malcolm Lowry, Flann O'Brien and Jean Rhys each having published at least a first novel by the time *Finnegans Wake* appeared in 1939. The emergence in the 1930s of such writers, in touch with and impressed by the modernists, suggests that any lapse in the experimental tradition at the time was not a complete one. With the partial exception of Durrell, however, none of the writers mentioned carried forward an energy for experiment into a later age by working in Britain. Lowry wrote in Mexico and Canada, hardly completing a novel after *Under the Volcano*, begun in the late 1930s. Beckett mostly ceased writing in English after *Watt*, completed in the early 1940s. Jean Rhys virtually disappeared as an author between 1939 and 1966, and Flann O'Brien's *At Swim-Two-Birds* passed similarly through a penumbra of neglect between first publication in 1939 and a popular reissue in 1960.

The various shifts or lapses in their careers may be the symptoms, or results, of an indifference towards experimental writing within Britain, perhaps understandable enough, during the war and the immediately post-war years. An indifference of this kind is clearer in the 1950s, and can even be seen to have been deliberately fostered. The title of Rubin Rabinovitz's study, *The Reaction Against Experiment in the English Novel, 1950–1960* (1967), sums up part of the mood of the decade. 'Realism and politics' (or at least social issues) came back almost as strongly as in the 1930s, in the work of writers who often dropped the baton of innovation like a hot potato, vehemently rejecting modernism and experiment. William Cooper, for example, suggested that for his contemporaries, 'the Experimental Novel had got to be brushed out of the way before we could get a proper hearing' (in Rabinovitz 1967: 7), and C. P. Snow explained in 1958 that:

> . . . one cannot begin to understand a number of contemporary
> English novelists unless one realises that to them Joyce's way is at
> best a cul-de-sac. (Snow 1958: iii)

These views reflect what has since been recognized as a 'prevailing ideology' in 'the British literary-journalistic establishment' of the 1950s – in which Snow's influence as a reviewer played a considerable part. In his essay 'The Presence of Postmodernism in British Fiction', Richard Todd adds that, although this literary-journalistic establishment emphasized certain quite genuine characteristics in the writing of the time, it conveniently ignored others. Passing over more innovative authors such as Lawrence Durrell or William Golding, it helped establish a sort of myth of the 1950s, to the effect that the complexities and indulgences of modernism had been sensibly rejected in favour of a thoroughgoing return to traditional, realist style, and to the true subject of the novel, class and social relations. Todd points out how limiting this myth, and the literature it supported, have been. As a result of the 1950s' return to:

> . . . naive social realism in a minor key . . . a potentially crippling form . . . it still remains the case that present-day discussion of British fiction is strongly influenced by a widely-held conviction that we are dealing with a literature in decline. (in Fokkema and Bertens 1986: 100)

Though the next decade quickly reversed the conservatism of the 1950s, the notion that British fiction lacks experimental energy, or even just quality, still survives; a partially accurate picture, based upon a lapse in the experimental tradition less complete than suggested at the time.

An important form in which the experimental tradition did survive, during the 1950s and since, is indicated by Todd when he discusses the 'employment within realistic narrative of metafictional or intertextual devices' (in Fokkema and Bertens 1986: 102). Many other critics have noticed this sort of combination. Malcolm Bradbury, for example, points to the existence of:

> . . . a generation of writers the best of whom have taken the British novel off into a variety of experimental directions . . . which have challenged and reconstituted the mimetic constituents of fiction while not dismissing its realistic sources. (Bradbury 1973: 86)

Many members of the current generation of British writers, including older, established authors whose careers began in the 1950s, show, in single novels or at various points of their careers, an attraction towards experiment as well as tradition and realism. The linguistic inventiveness of Anthony Burgess's *A Clockwork Orange* (1962), for example, highlights an admiration for Joyce which its author shows less clearly elsewhere in his work. Much of Iris Murdoch's fiction seems informed by her view that the nineteenth century is 'the great era of the novel' (in Bradbury 1977: 27), yet *The Black Prince* (1973) exhibits a thoroughly postmodernist concern with the process and validity of imaginative writing, its own included. *The Sea, the Sea* (1978) similarly broods upon the capacity of its own language and structure to contain a reality which can be obscured as much as illumined by the illusions of art. Angus Wilson's *No Laughing Matter* (1967) presents a huge family saga much in the manner of Galsworthy or the Victorians, yet it also contains alternating narrators, dramatic interludes, sustained parodies, and frequent reflections on its own narrative technique and difficulties. In *Rites of Passage* (1980), William Golding creates a comparable combination. Though the narrative is broadly realistic, it parodies eighteenth-century styles in ways which extend into a self-reflexive, postmodernist scrutiny of the power and validity of writing itself. Combinations of this sort continue to appear in the work of a younger generation of British novelists. Martin Amis, for example, remarks:

> I can imagine a novel that is as tricksy, as alienated and as writerly as those of, say, Alain Robbe-Grillet while also providing the staid satisfactions of pace, plot and humour with which we associate, say, Jane Austen. In a way, I imagine that this is what I myself am trying to do. (Amis 1978: 18)

Amis's *Other People* (1981) demonstrates the possibilities he outlines. Firmly, satirically based in contemporary London, it also has a fractured time-scheme and an indecipherable, detective story plot which recalls Robbe-Grillet and the *nouveau roman*. In *Shuttlecock* (1981), Graham Swift provides a further example of realistic narrative which also sustains postmodernist anxieties and examinations of the relation between writing and reality.

All these combinations, recent and current, suggest the continuing validity of the picture of British fiction David Lodge presented in 1971. In his essay 'The Novelist at the Crossroads', Lodge sees most British authors hesitating between, or combining in a variety of ways, the possibilities of a main road of tradition – 'the realist novel . . . coming down through the Victorians and Edwardians' – and alternatives offered by modernism and the developments that have followed it (Lodge 1971: 18). This may seem a reassuring picture, a balm to B. S. Johnson's fears. Modernist innovation and the revolution that was *Ulysses*, far from being ignored, continue to expand the range of possibilities for British writers, encouraging new forms and combinations to sophisticate and diversify conventional resources. On the other hand, there are ways in which such a picture is much less than wholly reassuring. Rather than being sustained by a vibrant, developing, experimental tradition, the revolutions of modernism may simply have been absorbed by an engrained, infrangible, realist tradition which rarely does more than appropriate a few of the more alluring additions Joyce and others made to 'the international store of literary technique'. Indirectly, Todd emphasizes this latter possibility by presenting postmodernism as a 'presence', as something amalgamated with more realistic modes in British writing, rather than as a fully autonomous force in itself. This view is developed in a way which partly reduplicates the misleading tactics he identifies at work in the 1950s. Critics at that time excluded authors inconvenient for their picture of a general return to tradition: Todd himself has little to say about authors such as B. S. Johnson and Christine Brooke-Rose, mostly on the grounds that they belong to a counter-cultural avant-garde never identified with the mainstream of British writing. On the whole, this approach is unhelpful. Although they do lie outside the mainstream – indeed, *because* they lie outside it – authors such as B. S. Johnson have at the very least an important exemplary function, keeping open a wide spectrum of possibility, even for authors who may not always wish to go so far in such radical directions themselves.

Nevertheless, although it is not a reason to pass over them as Todd does, a limiting factor in the work of experimental novelists in Britain does seem, as he suggests, to be that they are consistently assigned to marginal rather than mainstream positions. Many of those mentioned above – Rayner Heppenstall, David Caute, Giles Gordon, as well as B. S. Johnson and Christine Brooke-Rose – exercise a very tenuous hold over the attention of the British public. It is only occasionally, as in the case of Fowles or Durrell, for example, that postmodernism has generated the kind of respect and popularity enjoyed by authors such as Thomas Pynchon, Italo Calvino and Gabriel García Márquez. The success of such authors has probably contributed to the view that the inspiration for postmodernism in Britain has often had to come from foreign models rather than a native tradition of this form of writing, or even much of a disposition towards it. The baton of innovation, in this view, may not have been altogether dropped, but sometimes has to be carried by another team before the British outfit can continue its own rather erratic course down the tracks of literary history. The other team in question – the main one, anyway – is that of the French, whose new philosophies and related experiments in fiction have often helped sustain the initiatives of modernism since the Second World War. The example of Alain Robbe-Grillet, who acknowledges a debt to Joyce as well as to Sartre and Gide, offered from the late 1950s onwards a renewed incentive to experiment, at a moment when British writers might have felt themselves particularly distanced from modernism. In John Osborne's *Look Back in Anger* (1956), Jimmy Porter may indicate a real feature of the contemporary scene when he complains that his Sunday newspaper contains 'three whole columns on the English Novel. Half of it's in French'. Since the 1950s there has been a fifth column of British writers who demonstrate and often acknowledge their admiration for French writing, Alain Robbe-Grillet and the *nouveau roman* in particular. John Fowles, a student of French literature while at university, talks in *The French Lieutenant's Woman* of 'the lessons of existentialist philosophy' (Fowles 1969 and 1977: 63) and of working in 'the age of Alain Robbe-Grillet and Roland Barthes . . . the theoreticians of the *nouveau roman*' (p. 185). Christine Brooke-Rose, a bilingual teacher of English at the University of Paris, translated some of Robbe-Grillet's fiction into English and attempted in some of her early novels – *Out* (1964) and *Such* (1966), for example – to transfer into English writing some of the characteristics of the *nouveau roman*. This attempt also informs the work of Rayner Heppenstall, an acquaintance of Michel Butor and Nathalie Sarraute, who employs in *The Connecting Door* the *chosisme* and frustration of conventional orders and expectations of plot which feature generally in the *nouveau roman*. Several other writers were attracted by it in the 1960s and 1970s: Douglas Oliver, in *The Harmless Building* (1973), for example; Muriel Spark, at several stages in her fiction; and Giles Gordon, who follows the second-person narrative of Michel Butor's *La Modification* (1957), making 'you' the protagonist of his *Girl with red hair* (1974). David Caute also records – and shows in *The Occupation* – an admiration for French writing, though his fiction reveals a further strain of influence from postmodernist United States fiction. This also appears widely in the work of other authors: in Thomas Hinde's spaced-out metafiction *High* (1968); in Andrew Sinclair's road-novel *Gog* (1967); even in some of the more conventional writings of David Lodge and Malcolm Bradbury.

At least until recently, however, France has remained the principal external influence on postmodernist fiction in Britain. Even the French language seems to exercise a kind of ownership over the terminology of experiment. Though there is no real reason not to talk of 'the new novel', the term *nouveau roman* has always been retained, perhaps for a certain alluring foreign *frisson*. Similarly, English has never chosen to find an equivalent term for *avant-garde*. There may in this adoption of French terms be some covert assumption that postmodernist writing, like cooking – or rather *cuisine* – is something best left to the French. There may even be an emblematic quality in the image which Fowles records as the inspiration for *The French Lieutenant's Woman*; of Sarah Woodruff poised on an extreme, southerly edge of England, staring across the Channel towards an imaginary lover. Her desires might be seen as figurative of more general feelings among postmodernist British authors, seeking inspiration and affection less often to be found within their own shores.

This tendency to look abroad for inspiration is not new, of course. It is no more a feature of postmodernism than of the modernism which preceded it, very often the work of exiles or displaced persons. Centred around the work of an Irishman living in Trieste, Zurich and Paris, modernist fiction – though strongly an anglophone phenomenon – had relatively few significant practitioners of British nationality and domicile, apart from Virginia Woolf. In one way, this lack of British involvement contributes to a view that, even before the shifts and lapses of the 1930s and 1950s, Britain has *always* had an impoverished experimental tradition, repeatedly needing to borrow from France, Ireland, the USA or wherever, to compensate for a bankruptcy of energies in the domestic context. This view, however, may be to perceive only as a weakness within the British scene something which may more interestingly be considered an incentive to, even a necessary condition of, modernist and postmodernist writing generally. Like many other aspects of twentieth-century thought and culture, both modernism and postmodernism negotiate with the problem that 'we can know the real', as Linda Hutcheon puts it, 'only through signs', and, based on arbitrary relations between signifier and signified, language and sign may sheer away from the reality they seek to represent (Hutcheon 1988: 230). In Brian McHale's model, from the arbitrariness of the signs results an epistemologic anxiety for modernism, which seeks new forms to engage with a problematic, fugitive, but still reachable external reality. Ontologically centred postmodernism largely abandons this quest, highlighting the inadequacies of systems of representation which assume the possibility of valid contact with an ulterior reality. In *either* case, modernist or postmodernist, underlying strains, epistemologic or ontologic, are likely to be particularly focused by experience of foreign language or culture. Immersion in a foreign language environment, confrontation with an alien, yet apparently self-consistent, effective system of words, confirms the sense of arbitrariness in the relation of signifier and signified, encouraging the nature of language and representation to install themselves, self-reflexively, as subjects of enquiry within fiction. More straightforwardly, awareness of another nation's literature helps to create for authors a sense of the particular character and limitations of their own, encouraging the pursuit of alternatives and possibilities for innovation and change. If experimental novelists metaphorically stare across the Channel, it is not only because they hope some valuable contraband –fresh styles from France – may be smuggled through English literary customs. It is because aspects of foreignness itself, of vision focused by contact with other nations and languages, may be a crucial encouragement to the sort of writing they produce.

A peculiarity of the British context – and a possible strength for its future – is that this sort of encouragement may be found without even looking across the English Channel, though generally by looking away from England. A look across the Irish Sea finds Stephen Dedalus defining a particular sort of foreignness in *A Portrait of the Artist as a Young Man* when he meets an English priest and reflects that:

> His language, so familiar and so foreign, will always be for me an acquired speech. I have not made or accepted its words. My voice holds them at bay. My soul frets in the shadow of his language.
> (Joyce 1916 and 1973: 189)

The result of this 'fretting' against the English language and its accepted forms – a continuing experience during Joyce's time in Trieste, Zurich and Paris – appears in the range of parodies in *Ulysses* and the revolutionary linguistic of *Finnegans Wake*. The outstanding inventiveness of Irish literature may be owed in part to a continuing sense of existence in the shadow of an English language and culture which authors may wish to adapt rather than accept. Writers from areas within Britain are likely to experience comparable feelings. Particularly while the affluent, Conservative-dominated South-East grows increasingly apart from the rest of the country, yet retains control over the language and ideology of most of its media, a sense of separateness and of the need for separate forms is likely to result elsewhere. This is especially likely in Scotland where strong feelings of cultural, linguistic and political autonomy have always existed. Alasdair Gray's *Lanark* gives evidence of the evolution of forms which may be the result. Around a core of traditional urban realism, Gray projects a series of fantasies and fractures of convention, as a means of confronting Glasgow's chronic deprivation, economic and imaginative. Ron Butlin's brilliant second-person narrative, *The Sound of my Voice* (1987) suggests Scottish writing may continue to develop a postmodernist idiom. Graham Swift's *Waterland* (1983) shows the appropriateness of this idiom even within the South-East of England, providing a setting can be found which is remote enough to establish the 'contesting of centralisation of culture through the valuing of the local and peripheral', which Linda Hutcheon considers an important constituent of postmodernism (Hutcheon 1988: 61).

Another sort of foreign or peripheral experience may exist for British writers even within London itself. Virginia Woolf, in her Bloomsbury circle, could hardly have been closer to the metropolitan heart of England, yet she, too, found a foreignness within it, deliberately defining herself as an alien. She remarks in *A Room of One's Own* (1929):

> If one is a woman one is often surprised by a sudden splitting off
> of consciousness, say in walking down Whitehall, when from being
> the natural inheritor of that civilisation, she becomes, on the
> contrary, outside of it, alien and critical. (Woolf 1929 and 1977:
> 93)

The 'splitting off of consciousness', and the alien, critical attitudes which result, help to account for departures from convention which are particularly marked in women's writing at many points throughout the twentieth century, and continue to be as a strong area of postmodernist development. *The Golden Notebook* offers a kind of paradigm or anatomy of inclination to innovation created by the particularity, the foreignness, of women's experience. Alternatives to male discourse, particular forms of expression, are sought throughout, and the formal consequences of 'splitting off of consciousness' repeatedly enacted and discussed. Many women authors extend the sort of metafictional self-scrutiny which *The Golden Notebook* so extensively sustains: Eva Figes's novels, for example, often raise self-referential questioning of their own representational validity and Muriel Spark teases several of her heroines with unsettling awareness of the process of their own creation. Doris Lessing's later transition into science fiction writing indicates another complete alternative to realistic conventions, fantasy offering a strategy for escaping altogether the obligation to express a male-dominated world. Fantasy has continued to interest several other contemporary women writers, such as Emma Tennant and Angela Carter, in this way.

Fantasy is also an important component in the work of other writers who occasionally employ a postmodernist idiom: Brian Aldiss in his Joycean *Barefoot in the Head* (1969) or the *nouveau roman, Report on Probability A* (1968); J. G. Ballard in *The Unlimited Dream Company* (1979); Christopher Priest in *The Affirmation* (1981); even D. M. Thomas in *The White Hotel* (1981). Fantasy also figures centrally in the work of Salman Rushdie, its interfusion with more prosaic material demonstrating Rushdie's incorporation into the novel in English of the exuberant magic realism, developed by South Americans such as Gabriel García Márquez. Rushdie's background and career also indicate a further area of foreignness, and of promise, for post-modernist fiction in Britain. Largely as a legacy of empire, the English language has spread very widely across the world. For many of its current speakers – some, like Rushdie, immigrants to Britain – it remains a language foreign as well as familiar, and the culture and conventions it sustains are consequently matters for challenge and reformulation. Culturally and linguistically, Britain offers a nexus of increasingly plural possibilities, a promising ground for a post-modernism which may in the future develop more strongly in Britain than it has hitherto. Increasing cultural complexities suggest that Lodge's image of the crossroads might even be brought up to date – and given, appropriately, a faintly foreign flavour – by the possibility of post-imperial Britain becoming increasingly a sort of spaghetti junction, heterogeneous styles and registers meeting, intertwining, competing or coalescing.

The potential of such a situation is expressed in a different way by Brian McHale through reference to the work of Mikhail Bakhtin. Bakhtin traces the polyphonic nature of the novel – the 'system of languages' which compete within it – back to the practice of popular carnival. McHale sees the parodic, convention-breaking form of postmodernism as the particular heir of such practice; as an essentially 'carnivalised literature' (McHale 1987: 172). Not every critic shares this confidence in the carnivalesque capacities and subversive energies of postmodernism. A. Walton Litz, for example, relates the term postmodernism to the semanteme it contains in a particularly pessi-mistic way, suggesting that 'like post-mortem or post-coital', it implies that 'the fun is over' (Walton Litz 1986: 1142). In Britain, it may not be so. Temporary, partial scleroses in the 1950s encouraged gloomy prognoses, but the British novel is neither as dead nor as indisposed to innovation as its critics have sometimes supposed. Mixing the familiar and the foreign, new and potentially productive connections may be taking place in a number of areas. Much of the fun of postmodernism may be still to come. A new race of novelists may result, making it possible to refute with more confidence than hitherto B. S. Johnson's fear that the British novel has never fulfilled the huge potential created by the irruption of modernism into the literature of the twentieth century.

2 In Pursuit of the Receding Plot: Some American Postmodernists

David Seed

In recent years a critical consensus has gradually been forming as to the nature of postmodernism. Peter Brooks, for instance, insists that there has been a metafictional dimension to the novel since its very beginnings but now finds a new degree of emphasis among post-modernists, 'a greater explicitness in the abandonment of mimetic claims, a more overt staging of narrative's arbitrariness and lack of authority, a more open playfulness about fictionality' (Brooks 1984: 317). The relation of postmodernism to modernism is, in other words, a complex continuity which, in America at least, can be dated with comparative precision. All the novelists who are to be discussed in this chapter began their writing careers in the 1960s and recoiled from the hegemony of naturalistic modes of fiction. They have either demonstrated or explicitly acknowledged influences from Beckett, Nabokov, and Borges, or, within the American tradition, from Kerouac (himself the heir of such modernists as Thomas Wolfe) who opened up new possibilities of voice and open structure. Where André Malraux has stated that modern art is becoming an 'interrogation of the world' (Malraux 1950: 151), the writers under discussion here do not abandon plot as such but interrogate the very means they are using to structure their works. Richard Martin's comment on Walter Abish has a general relevance in this context. Abish's use of arbitrary formal limits in *Alphabetical Africa* (1974) 'becomes the vehicle for an adventurous plot while simultaneously investigating various narrative modes' (Martin 1983: 230). Plot may become a pretext. It may be eroded by comedy or decomposed, but it can never disappear, for it constitutes the 'dynamic shaping force of the narrative discourse' (Brooks 1984: 13). It is typical of the vigour of contemporary experimentation in America, that apocalyptic statements of the novel's demise should be converted into fiction in Ronald Sukenick's *The Death of the Novel and Other Stories* (1969).

Since the early 1970s, Sukenick has emerged as one of the leading practitioners of narration as process. Like Pynchon, he has admitted an influence from Kerouac and the Beats, and, in his 1973 article 'The New Tradition', Sukenick places himself within a late phase of the modernists' 'Revolution of the Word' where verbal and structural experimentation were aimed at coping with the enigmatic nature of the world (Federman 1975: 42). Sukenick has also gone on record as seeing writing as an essentially adversarial activity: 'When I grew up, I grew up with an idea of writing as a form of resistance to the establishment and culture at large' (Sukenick 1985: 139). One focus to this resistance has been realistic plot-paradigms which Sukenick constantly subverts in the interest of getting nearer to the real. 'Things don't appear to happen according to Aristotle any more', he remarks. However, Sukenick has been equally consistent in rejecting the view that such a direction marks a narcissistic introversion of fiction, arguing instead that he has engaged more directly with his culture. The shift in stance away from cultural exile towards critical engagement, for him marks a shift away from the élitism of the moderns towards postmodernism.

The political implications of Sukenick's experimentation can be seen clearly in his second novel *Out* (1973), which sets up a journey as structural metaphor in order to comment on the political temper of the late Nixon years. A backdrop of meaningless shifts in national policy, from 'escalation' to 'deescalation' and back again, foregrounds the 'characters' in this work, who are subversives armed with sticks of dynamite. Sukenick repeatedly draws attention to such underground processes, always as a prelude to comic dismissal: the dynamite is a dud, weapons fire blanks, and so on. Before any line of action can gel, starkly contrasted possibilities are introduced: 'You're either part of the plot or part of the counter-plot' (Sukenick 1973: 1). The novel is mainly devoted to exploring the implications of these propositions for its own form. Firstly, within the atmosphere of conspiracy, ludicrous and later incomprehensible messages are introduced to play games with the reader's capacity to interpret textual data. A particular detail may 'show how events conspire. It indicates a plot. The job of intelligence is to uncover this plot . . . As you can see everything falls into place' (Sukenick 1973: 124). Through a series of strategic puns Sukenick associates the collection of evidence, analysis and causal sequence with political totalitarianism. The threat of 'arrest' becomes the threat of fixity, of stabilized forms, whereas the thrust of the novel is to take us further and further away from such stability. This impulse is figured partly in geographical terms (as Jerome Klinkowitz has noted, '*Out* moves from the clutter and hassle of the East to the pure space of an empty California beach' (Klinkowitz 1980: 137)) and partly by shifting the names of the characters and the nature of their situations, so that travelling ceases to be a realistic indication of movement and becomes instead a metaphor for textual purpose. A journey in a camper shades into a lift with a driver who turns out to be a narcotics agent; the former episode is then repeated, with sado-masochistic variations, until that too shades into a bus journey. The situational shifts prevent a consistent plot-line from forming, making the novel essentially unpredictable, and Sukenick further complicates our sense of sequence by counterpointing a 'count-down' sequence of chapters against the ascending page-numbers. As the novel approaches its end, spaces between its verbal segments grow larger and larger until the text finally recedes into a blank white page.

By politicizing his text in this way Sukenick runs the risk of linking authorial production with political manipulation, but he regularly plays down the privilege of composition by including himself as a minor character within his narratives. In the case of *Out*, a dialogue within the novel articulates Sukenick's engagement with the reader's probable, realistic expectations. A suitably pedagogic figure called Skuul puts the case for cause and effect which is speedily reduced to relativism by an opposing voice: 'You pursue essentials I ride with the random . . . You struggle towards stillness I rest in movement' (Sukenick 1973: 127). As in *Gravity's Rainbow*, Sukenick pairs contrasting voices to raise the epistemological implications of his own novel and to nudge the reader towards an acceptance of indeterminacy. Indeed, Jerzy Kutnik has shown that amorphousness and mobility are the prime characteristics of Sukenick's texts. They constitute 'the ideal condition for fiction but not just for purely aesthetic reasons: they are the natural condition of "things chronic and cosmic", including humanity itself' (Kutnik 1986: 87). The very title of *Out* suggests avoidance, absence, departure (from norms, order, etc.); even the ending of the novel is signalled as an exit. What limits this work is the close association between formal fluidity and a life-style reminiscent of the Beats. It is this underwriting of 'moving on' which Sukenick's next novel brings into question.

98.6 (1975) is divided into three sections. The first assembles a collage of images to confirm the proposition that 'love − power = sadism + masochism' (Sukenick 1975: 7). Sukenick's own composed sequences (revolving around routine violence) are juxtaposed with excerpts from contemporary reports on Hell's Angels, the Manson family, etc. to suggest a picture of conditions. It is as if Sukenick were putting into practice the principles of what he has called the 'architectonic novel' which (and he cites Raymond Federman's *Double or Nothing* as a prime example) works like a jigsaw puzzle: 'the picture is filled out but there is no sense of development involved' (Federman 1975: 38). Having established a context, in the second section Sukenick presents the attempts of a group to set up a commune within the country of Frankenstein (a transparent label for the USA). This section follows the trajectory of an arc in that the attempts gradually fail. The commune attempts to enact its own solidarity through rituals (group sex, baseball, potlatch, etc.), apparently trying to stave off the threats of such hostile outside forces as truckers and bikers. The third section ('Palestine') does not conclude the novel so much as make explicit the narrative implications of what has happened so far. The sequence of composition and decomposition, seen in *Out*'s alternation between meetings and departures, now becomes a textual fact of life: 'Interruption. Discontinuity. Imperfection. It can't be helped . . '. Together for an instant and then smash it's all gone still its worth it. I feel. This composure grown out of ongoing decomposition' (Sukenick 1975: 167).

The narrative base to this section (Sukenick's visit to Israel) represents a journey to a country of spiritual origins as if he is seeking a lost unity antecedent to the modern state of division.

In his more recent works, Sukenick has moved even further away from conventional narrative sequences. *Long Talking Bad Conditions Blues* (1979) makes a virtue out of the condition of 'accelerated shatter' he had located in his earlier novels by attempting to link the diverse aspects of his text within a verbal flow, a 'stream of language' introduced by a twelve-page unpunctuated single sentence. This flux depresses narrative reflection ('. . . it was almost impossible to come to a conclusion about one's own flow and that in fact this was a contradiction in terms since one was precisely one's own flow . . .' (Sukenick 1979: 11)) and also direction, as the title appropriately suggests a spoken improvisation. Characters thus become splintered versions of the dominant voice, examples of what Thomas LeClair has called 'artful ventriloquism' (in McCaffery 1986: 121). Continuity of utterance now becomes an end in itself and lacunae in consciousness, gaps and verbal 'black holes' (linguistic vortices), things to be avoided like the plague. Both this work and *The Endless Short Story* (1986) confirm Peter Currie's general assertion that 'American post-modernism may be seen to endorse a rhetorical view of life which begins with the primacy of language' (in Bradbury and Ro 1987: 64). *Long Talking* is preoccupied with the physicality of utterance, whereas *The Endless Short Story* equivocates about its own length and means. It begins as a mock-documentary on Simon Rodia (architect of the Watts towers) and then shifts through stories-within-stories, digressions, verbal improvisations (explicitly modelled on jazz), and numerous references to the practicalities of narrating. These devices cut across a linear reading of the text, in spite of the early injunction to the reader: 'It doesn't matter where you start. You must have faith. Life is whole and continuous whatever the appearances' (Sukenick 1986: 7). The latter assertion represents no more than a pious belief, since Sukenick's text repeatedly fragments itself into short phrasal units, disparate narrative strands, and oddly shifting 'characters'.

Many of Sukenick's concerns are shared by his friend Raymond Federman. Where both are university teachers, Federman began his career as a critic with a study of Samuel Beckett, *Journey to Chaos* (1965), which played a crucial role in the formation of his attitude towards modern fiction. Federman presents Beckett as a practitioner of perversely inverted narrative values, in effect deconstructing the novel in order to expose the deceits of realism. Beckett's characters 'begin and end their fictional journey at the same place, in the same condition, and without having learned, discovered, or acquired the least know-ledge about themselves and the world in which they exist' (Federman 1965: 4). Federman has fully digested Beckett's influence on him to the point of formulating carefully thought-out positions on the new direction fiction will take. His view of the American situation follows out the formal consequences of earlier complaints by such writers as Nathanael West and Philip Roth, that the American novel can no longer keep up with contemporary reality. Federman sees the post-modern period as one in which the media have taken over the informational role of fiction, drastically reducing its status. The works which are aware of this predicament Federman has called 'surfiction' whose primary purpose 'will be to unmask its own fictionality, to expose the metaphor of its own fraudulence'. Among other casualties in this process will be plot: 'the plot having disappeared, it is no longer necessary to have the events of fiction follow a logical, sequential pattern (in time and in space)' (Federman 1975: 810). Instead, works will progress by digression or circular repetition. Federman's own novels thus revolve around the problematic nature of their own survival.

Federman's first novel *Double Or Nothing* (1971) is a narrative about preparing to narrate, where the different persons named in the text personify different compositional procedures. Many details, such as the reproduction of type-script and the printing of a page askew as if that was how it came out of the type-writer, suggest the fiction that the novel is a draft, a preliminary version, but of course the pages are printed and therefore fixed. There is no final version which they anticipate, and in this respect Federman draws attention to the technology of the text. The novel contains traces of an autobiographical plot-line in which a fictionalized young Federman comes by boat to America and meets his uncle in New York. This sequence is repeated again and again with different emphases, suggesting that the novel is constantly reenacting a threshold experience which becomes a power-ful metaphor of its own formal nature. *Double Or Nothing* mimes out its own liminal qualities, exemplifying Federman's general assertion that, since reading completes a text, 'writing can be considered as a PRE-TEXT . . . Much of literature today . . . functions in the PRE-TEXT conditions, leading towards the potential text' (Federman 1976a: 564). Just as the young Federman arrives in America and will embark on a new series of experiences, so *Double Or Nothing* speculates about the possible shapes it might take. The sections which resemble realistic narrative are either mocked through parenthetical comments, which reduce the passages to pastiche, or are phrased as hypotheses: 'Your uncle will meet you at the boat (with his car – even threw that in). I can see the whole scene already and maybe you'll cry a little . . .' (Federman 1971: 15). The term 'story' becomes an important indicator of what Federman *might* write, although it is impossible to take this at face value. If 'story' suggests a narrative sequence towards which *Double Or Nothing* is gesturing, Federman at the same time questions each fictional possibility so thoroughly that the only reliable sequence becomes the narrative voice which is constantly shifting in person and tone. The novel at times resembles a rambling monologue in which the narrator sometimes performs disconcerting antics, sometimes speculates about the theoretical nature of fiction. Even more than Sukenick's, Raymond Federman's novels repeatedly blur the boundaries between criticism and fiction.

Federman's later novel *Take It Or Leave It* (1976) appears to be even less orderly than its predecessor. Like Burroughs' *Naked Lunch*, it carries a directive that the sections can be read in any order but, unlike B. S. Johnson's *The Unfortunates*, it is not presented as a boxed set. Although pagination has been excluded, the novel is nevertheless bound in a fixed order. Once again the novel repeatedly turns inwards to examine its own nature, presenting itself as a kind of palimpsest. The implications of 'story' have hardened to the extent that Federman constantly refers to the narrative as a 'recitation', as if he were writing over earlier texts such as Beat novels. He now makes a much firmer distinction between plot and story. At one point, quoting Aristotle on catharsis, he reflects: 'Interesting! However, since we are not interested here (what are we a constipated race?) in plot but only travel, it is useless to worry about such problems' (Federman 1976b). Where plot might be jettisoned, story is retained as a principle of connection: 'Once the story is launched it must go on it must follow its course however crooked it may be even if it takes the wrong direction' (1976b). 'Story', 'travel' and 'journey' all blur together, drawing on Federman's study of Beckett, the title of which is incorporated into this text and into *Double Or Nothing*, so that once again traces of realistic action have a metaphorical role to play. This novel draws on a later phase of Federman's life to refer to (but not describe) journeys across America. Travel takes on a multiple significance as geographical discovery, facetious mythical enactment (its resemblance to Alger's stories is mocked), sexual fulfilment, and above all textual sequence. Federman has recognized that this is a staple feature of his works. In an interview he has stated: 'My stories are usually based on a journey of some sort. This doesn't have to be a physical, geographical journey from one place to another – I say "journey" simply in terms of movement' (Le Clair and McCaffery 1983: 129). Travelling can thus indicate the headlong tempo of the narrative or, in its twists and turns, a principle of sequence by digression – not from a 'main action', but simply digression from what immediately precedes or succeeds a particular section. In an epistemological parable, 'The Man who looked into the Future', Allen Wheelis describes a man's attempts to escape from the fluidity of the present and imprint value on his life. He discovers he has a talent for predicting the future, but ironically this privilege only increases his sense of the present. In fact there is no way out of his predicament because he can find no external way of authenticating the present: 'the more clearly the future could be seen, the more evident that it could validate nothing' (Wheelis 1971: 56). He then sinks into a melancholy lethargy. Federman pursues a similar scepticism but with more rubust results. He comically dismisses his attempts to project himself into the narrative future and finds that the past is rendered elusive by the distortions of the means he uses to recapture it. The result is that his narratives collapse time into an extended present where he, like Sukenick's narrators, gleefully rides the random.

Where Federman and Sukenick replace finished story with the process of narrating so that it becomes difficult to say what their novels are 'about', Rudolph Wurlitzer pursues a rather different task in his fiction. One of his earliest pieces was a Western narrative which attempted to avoid the formulaic patterning of Louis L'Amour's novels through parody. Like Sukenick and Pynchon, Wurlitzer has acknowledged an influence from Kerouac which can be seen in the open structure of his first novel *The Octopus* (1969: published in America under the title *Nog*). The narrative has no firm beginning or end. It revolves around a narrator (never named) who is living temporarily on the west coast. He hitch-hikes to San Francisco, lives briefly in a commune, and then sets off on a journey with two of its members, Lockett and Meridith. This journey, which seems to involve a plan to deal in drugs, takes the three to a ghost town where the others become separated from Lockett. Meridith and the narrator drive to Long Beach, join a ship which enters the Panama Canal, and there the narrator is separated again from Meridith. At this point the novel ends. The narrator is a figure in transit trying to live in a perceptual present which avoids fixed relations. Wurlitzer took the openness of 'moving on' from Kerouac but without any of the latter's lyricism. In fact the narrator's language is positively austere as he tries to minimize our sense of recapitulation. Continuity must exclude analysis:

> I am losing the thread. I've done it again. I have to go back, or forward, to another edge. I must keep on forgetting. I must not remember the story I set out to tell. I must not betray myself. It is the only way. This doesn't help, setting it all down, discussing it, unravelling it and rolling it up like a dead tongue. (Wurlitzer 1969: 46)

Story-telling becomes a means of preserving the narrator's protean fluidity and in that respect both of the novel's titles are appropriate. *Nog* is a mysterious itinerant who sells the narrator a foam-rubber octopus, and whose name he adopts as an alias. The octopus, 'literally' a side-show exhibit, represents the narrator's groping towards forms, the perceptual flux as he moves through geographical, residential and sexual space. This sequence is saved from being completely arbitrary by the narrator becoming involved in the plan of others. The road then takes on connotations of purpose but without ever becoming fixed; journeys by land alternate with journeys by water. During the movement of the narrative, space expands and contracts; even the objects mentioned have a fluid status and take their places in shifting strings of signification. Shells suggest vaginas, fossils, bones, and so on.

Wurlitzer has given a geographical explanation of great fluidity. In an interview given soon after the publication of his first novel, he insisted:

> . . . it's a West Coast book . . . Like a lot of people are really nomadic and living outside of cultural definition . . . The East Coast is historical . . . Forms have disintegrated here [in the East] so you're involved in disintegration. But out there forms just *aren't there*. In that sense it's a weird frontier. (Wurlitzer 1970: 36–7)

Wurlitzer originally wrote a quite different last chapter to his novel but threw it away because it seemed too analytical. It was crucial to the consistency of the work that it should not conclude: the narrator simply states that 'there has been no decision except that I'm moving on' (Wurlitzer 1969: 161). All of Wurlitzer's fiction to date has dealt with this felt absence of forms on their breakdown. *Flats* (1970) rules sequence down to an absolute minimum and spatializes the narrative by creating Beckett-like 'characters' who are personified place-names. These figures move slowly around a terrain apparently laid waste by some great disaster. *Quake* (1972) also treats of disaster, this time in a semi-realistic mode, by investigating the cultural breakdown which follows a massive earthquake in Los Angeles. *Slow Fade* (1984) draws on Wurlitzer's own experiences as a screen-writer to set up narratives-within-narratives. One focus for this composition is to discover the fate of a movie director's daughter in India, and the plot-line of that sequence enacts the erosion of cultural certainties by the Orient. Once again, plot is conceived of as compositional process, a bringing-into-being; in other words it is conceived as something quite different from what one of the novel's characters describes as a 'crappy mystical adventure story'.

Although he is one of the most interesting experimental writers on the contemporary American scene, Wurlitzer's novels are not particularly humorous and this would distinguish his works from those of Sukenick, Federman, and Pynchon. All three of these writers introduce low comedy as a safeguard against the fiction claiming the status of high art. Federman has explained this characteristic as 'imagination mocking what it pretends to be doing . . . imagination laughing at its own pretensions' (Federman 1976a: 576). For him, comedy draws the reader into a prolonged act of collusion with the author where both recognize the 'sublime absurdity of the creative process'. Disruption can thus become a means of subverting literary decorum, solemnity, and authorial self-effacement ('fuck MODESTY!' is the succinct exclamation of one of Federman's narrators). One consequence for plot is that composition becomes equated with comic recital. In *98.6*, Sukenick briefly casts himself as an improvising comic on the explicit model of Lenny Bruce and Milton Berle. *Take It Or Leave It* is a much more vocal narrative delivered to a fictional audience with jokes, asides and comments on his own style. Thomas Pynchon has also shown a consistent fondness for slapstick effects in his novels, drawn partly from comic cinema. Like Sukenick, he often refers to the Marx Brothers in *Gravity's Rainbow* and creates a comic dimension to the otherwise sinister phrase 'theatre of war'. Again and again Pynchon suspends the serious implications of his title by transforming the action into pantomime, thereby achieving a staggering variety of tones within the novel. More is involved here than temporary light relief, however. The pantomime analogy draws the reader and characters together into a collective fictional position within an audience, and by so doing counteracts the opposite isolating direction of the forces of war, bureaucracy and totalitarianism. The tension between the two is expressed in terms of imminence at the end of the novel when a V-rocket is poised to land on a crowded theatre.

A writer who has devised a consistently comic vision through formal disruption is Tom Robbins. His first novel, *Another Roadside Attraction* (1971), sets up a ludicrous adventure plot in which two 'heroes' attempt to carry the mummified remains of Jesus (seized from the Vatican) up to heaven in a hot-air balloon. This sequence acts as a base for a whole series of chronological divergences and a parallel plot in which a zoo and hot-dog joint, together, are established as the roadside attraction of the title. Robbins's purpose here is to define theatre as the quality of his narration as well as the subject-matter, and he does this by introducing three author-surrogates. John-Paul Ziller is variously a drugs dealer, magician and con man, personifying – like Rinehart in Ralph Ellison's *Invisible Man* – the flux of narrative stances; Plucky Purcell, as his name suggests, represents the narrator of adventures and Marx Marvellous ('your host and narrator') embodies Robbins's role as narrative compère, constantly leading us into new episodes with an appropriate verbal flourish. At times the effect is reminiscent of a Fieldingesque narrative overlaid with commentary, especially if Robbins indulges in direct address: 'Hello, reader. May the author once again intrude upon whatever mood his narrative might have established long enough to report on current events?' (Robbins 1972: 170). A tacit collusion is set up between narrator and reader not to take the novel too solemnly, but rather to sit back and enjoy the show. Drawing on comic books, the Beatles' *Sergeant Pepper's Lonely Hearts Club Band* and – like Sukenick and Pynchon – the Marx Brothers, Robbins exploits performance and theatricality as ends in themselves. It is not until his second novel that he really develops the implications of this stance.

Even Cowgirls Get the Blues (1976) again takes its bearings explicitly from Kerouac and the Beats but, like the first novel, through a consciously exaggerated plot. The protagonist is one Sissy Hankshaw who uses the fact that she is afflicted with elephantiasis of the thumbs to hitch-hike round America. She becomes drawn into the business dealings of the Countess, a New York cosmetics tycoon, in the course of which she travels to the Rubber Rose Ranch, a Dakota health spa, and takes part in a revolt by the cowgirls. The latter action bears directly on Robbins's statement of purpose within the novel: 'In times such as ours . . . when there is too much order, too much management, too much programming and control, it becomes the duty of superior men and women to fling their favorite monkey wrenches into the machinery' (Robbins 1977: 229). Comic disruption becomes a much needed gesture of resistance to prevailing conditions in America. Where Federman and Sukenick have stressed the specifically linguistic dimensions to such disruption, Robbins once again casts himself in the role of entertainer, trickster and comic commentator. Linear, realistic plot is inseparable from the forces of law and order to him, and so he seizes every opportunity to cut across the plot-sequence with digressions, 'Cowgirl Interludes', commentaries and even a recipe. He controls his expository side by creating a minor, rather scholastic character called 'Doctor Robbins', a psychiatrist who rebels against the prescriptions of his boss. This latter sequence expresses in miniature what the novel as a whole is undertaking. *Another Roadside Attraction* deliberately smothers a simple plot by amassing more and more ludicrous information. Robbins now draws more and more attention to the text itself, by indulging in a dialogue with his projected reader to celebrate reaching his hundredth chapter or by rejecting the claims of traditional literary decorum: 'happily, your author is not under contract to any of the muses who supply the reputable writers, and thus he has access to a considerable variety of sentences to spread and stretch from margin to margin . . .' (124). This comic expansiveness even leads Robbins to insert a chapter (111a) which he then renders as a no-go area, having first defined poetry as an 'intensification or illumination of common objects and everyday events':

> Definitions are limiting. Limitations are deadening. To limit
> oneself is a kind of suicide. To limit another is a kind of murder.
> To limit poetry is a Hiroshima of the human spirit. DANGER:
> RADIATION. Unauthorized personnel not allowed on the
> premises of Chapter 111a. (379–80)

Throughout the novel Robbins has lined up clear oppositions between separations and holism, technology and the organic, restraint and freedom. His joking spatialization of this chapter punningly ('premises') draws attention to the subversive implications of his assertions and ironically contrasts the availability of his text with the proprietary attitudes to property within his narrative. Shortly after this point, the revolt at the ranch is put down in a shoot-out with the police. 'Technology', for Robbins as for Pynchon, becomes a short-hand term for the conditioning and patterning pressures in American life; pressures to be resisted whether in his comic struggle with his Remington type-writer which frames his next novel, *Still Life with Woodpecker* (1980), or, more importantly, through his disruption of narrative illusion and orderly sequence.

It should be clear by now that linear plots are never quite absent from even the most experimental of these novels. They function as a spurious pattern into which the narrative might slide if so allowed. Story then becomes revised into recitation or into a deliberately implausible sequence against which the narrative voice can play. The issue of how story can be preserved is also central to the fiction of John Barth in whose career one event looms large: his discovery of the *Arabian Nights* and other cycles of tales from antiquity. Because these cycles predate by centuries the era of realism, Barth has managed to side-step the issue of narrative truth and retain some notion of the marvellous. Narrating in his works quite literally becomes a kind of fabulation. Barth has referred again and again to this discovery in his interviews and articles, and there is no doubt that the existence of such works as *The Ocean of Story* has helped to form his resistance to the 'modernist notion that plot is an anachronistic element in contemporary fiction'. Barth continues (in an interview of 1971):

> I've never found that a congenial notion; it seemed to me that there were ways to be quite contemporary and yet go at the art in a fashion that would allow you to tell complicated stories simply for the aesthetic pleasure of complexity of complication and unravelment, suspense, and the rest. (in Bellamy 1974: 7)

The second and later major influence on Barth has been, again by his own admission, that of Borges and he has set on record his admiration for that writer in his most famous article, 'The Literature of Exhaustion' (1967), in which he argues that certain literary forms may be used up and so are no longer available to the writer except as parody. Partly irritated by critical misreadings of this piece, Barth published in 1979 a 'comparison and corrective' entitled 'The Literature of Replenishment' in which he sees disjunction, etc. as essentially modernistic and seeks a synthesis between modernism and nineteenth-century realism. Here he elaborates on an argument sketched out a few years earlier, that the label 'postmodern' denoted the quality of being 'free to come to new terms with both realism and anti-realism, linearity and non-linearity, continuity and discontinuity'. Accordingly, he predicts the 'ideal postmodernist novel will somehow rise above the quarrel between realism and irrealism', attaining a new synthesis which might no longer need much commentary (Barth 1984: 129, 203). In spite of some side-swipes at the theories of Raymond Federman, Barth's own fictional practice is not necessarily at odds with that of the latter. His fascination with tales and story-telling is regularly linked to a formalistic relish of complication for its own sake, and Barth has always detached his use of plot from mimesis. His decision to construct a 'fantastically baroque plot' for *The Sot-Weed Factor* (1960) is one example of the creation of pastiche which would not be uncongenial to the theories of Federman and Sukenick. Again like them, Barth has shown an interest in the technology of narrating, in the formal implications of voice, and in the entirely arbitrary patterns of plot. *Lost in the Funhouse* (1968) engages with Beckett-like ultimacies by excluding action and character to the point where narrating becomes self-referential: 'to write this alleged ultimate story is a form of artistic fill in the blank . . .' (Barth 1969: 111). The 'plot' now becomes purely a matter of voice, whereas in such works as *Giles Goat-Boy* (1966), *Chimera* (1972), and in other parts of *Lost in the Funhouse* Barth draws on ancient mythical patterns to write over.

Two recent novels will illustrate Barth's attitude to used-up forms and his move towards a new synthesis. *LETTERS* (1979) must be his most complexly self-referential work to date. It is an attempt to reuse the fictional form which first reached exhaustion, that of the epistolary novel. Barth introduces seven correspondents, or rather *re*introduces them since they are all figures from his earlier works, and Barth himself is projected into the fiction as an updated form of 'Mr. B.', Pamela's seducer in Richardson's novel. *LETTERS* then is a '"2nd cycle" isomorphic with the "1st"', a recycling of Barth's earlier characters whose destinies are expanded and brought to bear on the America of the late 1960s (Barth 1980a: 656). The first of his correspondents is Lady Amherst who records a stormy love affair with one of Barth's surrogates, one Ambrose Mensch. She carries the same name (Germaine) as Madame de Stael, suggesting a further analogy between Ambrose and her lover-author Benjamin Constant. Such correspondences – and Barth underlines the pun – suggest that the novel is a multiple palimpsest with one textual layer over another and the roles of textual producer and fictional character constantly blurring together. The love affair parodies that stock figure of epistolary fiction – the innocent, seduced narrator – in such a way that sexual congress becomes a comic metaphor of composition. Accordingly, Barth plays with multiple notions of plot: love intrigue; a character trying to find the historical pattern in his family's lives; and textual ordering. A computer prints out a 'revolutionary novel' to be called *Notes* – but in numbers! The very proliferation of narrative details and of plots contradicts the historical exhaustion of the form but without ever leaving the parodic. So although vast amounts of historical information are included, as Heide Ziegler has pointed out, 'the facts of history are . . . the premise of other possibilities. They seem to be like texts that allow for various interpretations' (Ziegler 1987: 70). In effect, Barth simultaneously reworks texts and multiplies the dimensions to *LETTERS* so that it becomes a protean work, constantly shifting resemblances. At one point it parodies Richardson, at another it seems to realize the ambition to compose a satirical work called *The Marylandiad* of Ebenezer Cook, the author of another of Barth's proto-texts, the poem 'The Sot-Weed Factor'.

When we turn from *LETTERS* to *Sabbatical* (1982), the latter seems almost to have been written to put into practice the theoretical position laid down in 'The Literature of Replenishment'. The realistic base to the novel consists of a sea-journey by Fenwick Turner, a former CIA agent, and his wife around the Chesapeake Bay. During their voyage a narrative is assembled through a series of flashbacks which reveal a proliferation of connections between the protagonists' families and contemporary political events. The dialogue between Fenwick and Susan establishes a point of origin for the plot since they are both consciously composing their story, drawing parallels with the 'wandering-hero myths' and arguing over the nature of flashbacks (they even throw out a reference to 'something called postmodernism'). As the novel progresses, more and more details (like the protagonists' arrival at an island not marked on any charts) are released which trigger off fears of their being the victims of conspiracy. Such a predicament would be a cue for utter bewilderment or terror in Pynchon, whose characters cannot reliably communicate their fears to anyone else but, in *Sabbatical*, the reaction is a joint decision: 'we must shorten scope on both our paranoia and our writerly sense of plot' (Barth 1983: 53). The conjunction 'and' indicates a crucial aspect of the novel's method since it nicely balances between literary and non-literary reference. The landscape traversed by the Turners is in a sense a literary one (hence indicators like Poe Cove), but Barth is also careful to specify their seamanship with realistic accuracy. The nautical details carry a symbolic significance because they suggest that the protagonists are themselves oriented but, as Barth has said, 'in the troubled and dangerous waters through which they, like the rest of us, necessarily sail . . . no degree of skill in navigation or of seaworthiness in the vessel guarantees that the destination will still be there at our Estimated Time of Arrival' (Barth 1984: 140). Now our perception of the text as palimpsest is far more subdued than in *LETTERS*. We witness the protagonists drawing their own parallels between their story and Homer, Byron's 'Manfred', Poe and thrillers, but in a way which suggests that the act of narrating is not separated from events. Susan's chosen metaphor of bringing *fabula* and *sujet* together is a charac-teristically biological one: 'how could either come before the other, except as one twin happens to get delivered earlier? The doing and the telling our writing and our loving – they're twins. That's our story' (Barth 1983: 365). This metaphor implies that the dynamics of *Sabbatical* are sexual. The Turners' love-making is directed towards bringing their story into being and, in that respect, represents the counterforce to political totalitarianism which causes deaths and rape throughout the novel. Most impressive of all, Barth has built this moving plot on one of the oldest stock properties of literature – the notion of life as a voyage.

Plotting involves by its very nature the establishment of continuity and of interconnections. A postmodernist option, which we have encountered briefly in Sukenick's fiction and now seen in Barth's protagonists composing their story in opposition to political forces devoted to secrecy (to a *silent* plot in other words), is developed to extraordinarily intricate lengths in the novels of Thomas Pynchon.

Plotting is revised into conspiracy and placed *within* the action instead of informing its structure. Pynchon's characters are constantly driven by the impulse to locate themselves within larger schemes which would authenticate their own experience, but waver between the appalling extremes of total randomness (where no pattern is discernible) and paranoia (where *everything* is subsumed into pattern). His first novel *V.* (1963), like his subsequent works, presents a search which gives the work an apparently strong momentum. The particular search is Herbert Stencil's attempts to trace V. through a series of appearances from the 1890s through to the present. Stencil is the personification of a procrustean function rather than a character in any realistic sense, partly a parody of such questing scholars as Robert Graves, partly an imitation of the obsessed protagonist in Nabokov's *The Real Life of Sebastian Knight*. Stencil, in short, pursues a quest the absurdity of which rules out the modernist option of structuring by myth. His search, mocked at every turn by events and other characters, sets up a tenuous connecting thread which links a whole series of episodes set in different places and periods. In each of these episodes, Pynchon releases far more information than Stencil registers, so that evidence proliferates far beyond the latter's tendentious inferences. The initial of the novel's title promises withheld meaning, and is therefore more appropriate than Pynchon's original title for the novel (*World on a String*), but the absurdity of Stencil's activities disqualifies him as an analyst of a hidden principle in modern history, signalled melo-dramatically as the 'Ultimate Plot which Has No Name'. Stencil only demonstrates in a more manic form a common desire to know, to gain certainty, which is enacted through the related figures of penetrating surfaces, interrogation, breaking codes, and above all analysing texts. Pynchon, like Joyce, delights in repeating details in new contexts so as to tantalize the reader into thinking he/she has missed crucial meanings. In fact the two protagonists of *V.* could be seen as contrasting opposite ways of reacting to the modern era. Benny Profane personifies the inertia of modern man, cultivating a passivity towards all experience, whereas Stencil only gains an identity through motion. He apprehends this to the extent that he carefully paces his pursuit of V. to defer ever completing his search.

Plot as theatre emerges in two ways here. Firstly, Pynchon draws on the adventure stories of Conan Doyle and Buchan and on detective fiction to create an absurdist pastiche of these popular genres. And secondly, he stresses the element of impersonation in the action. Behaviour is constantly revealed as imitative of projected stereotypes or to be the result of disguise. Just as Stencil's quest parodies the reader's desire to make sense of the text through interpretative patterning, so his investigation of other periods becomes a ludicrous enactment of an author's creation of characters. One narrator who temporarily takes over from Stencil is Fausto Maijstral, a Maltese poet who has kept a record of the German siege of the island during the last world war. Fausto establishes a crucially sceptical perspective on the rhetoric of texts, since he sees through the 'fiction of continuity, the fiction of cause and effect, the fiction of a humanized history endowed with "reason"' (Pynchon 1975b: 306). His chapter of 'confessions' questions the presumptions involved in causal sequence and acts as a helpful gloss on Pynchon's general method in the novel. Roughly speaking, chapters in the present alternate with chapters from earlier periods, cast in such different styles that they emphasize the novel's formal discontinuity. Both sequences converge on Malta, and the novel seems simultaneously to stop, or – if we have been 'stencillizing' the narrative – to end on a note of imminent war with the Middle East crisis of 1956.

Imminence, this time of ultimate revelation, also characterizes the ending of *The Crying of Lot 49* (1966). Here the sequence begins with an instruction to a typical Californian housewife (typical in all but name, that is), Oedipa Maas, to execute the will of a dead tycoon. This initial impetus is soon deflected into side-purposes, into the desire to explore the extent of the tycoon's estate and – even more thrilling to Oedipa – to confirm the existence of a secret society from the seventeenth century to the present. The more determinedly she hunts for confirmatory details the more the sources and scale of her information multiply, so that she reaches a stage of nervous exhaustion from sheer overload. Drawing once again on the detective genre, Pynchon complicates the linear hunt for information, partly by rendering every detail as ambiguous as possible and partly by having Oedipa literally go round in a huge circle when she is pursuing an 'underground' mail courier. While her investigations take her into history and communication networks, one sequence in particular carries metafictional implications. Attending the performance of a pastiche Jacobean tragedy, she attempts to incorporate lines from this play into the evidence she is piecing together, but then finds it utterly impossible to locate any edition which would confirm the lines she heard. Oedipa's pursuit of this text – yet another diversion from the supposed main plot – thus becomes a comic expression of the reader's own attempts to fix meaning into Pynchon's own inconclusive narrative. Connections prove yet again to be ultimately elusive.

Gravity's Rainbow (1973) marks Pynchon's most complex investigation of the ramifications of plotting to date. With this novel particularly in mind, Richard Poirier has stated that,

> In Pynchon's novels the plots of wholly imagined fiction are
> inseparable from the plots of known history or science. More than
> that, he proposes that any effort to sort out these plots must itself
> depend on an analytical method which . . . is probably part of
> some systematic plot against free forms of life. (Levine and
> Leverenz 1976: 23)

The novelists considered so far have consistently broken away from fixed plot-sequences in the pursuit of authenticity and freedom. Pynchon, however, incorporates within his narrative Manichaean stories in which good opposes evil – the Fu Manchu tales become important in *Gravity's Rainbow* – not simply to mock such narratives out of existence, but to show their inadequacy. In *Gravity's Rainbow*, conspiracies proliferate to such an extent that they beggar description. Using a principle of recession, Pynchon even suggests that historical plotting can be traced back through its superficial manifestations to the grouping of raw matter or to the genetic code itself! One character remarks, '"*everything* is some kind of a plot, man"', and the sentiment is echoed, though less cheerfully, by the novel's main protagonist, an American intelligence officer called Tyrone Slothrop (Pynchon 1975a: 603). It is Slothrop who gives one kind of impetus to the novel in his desire to explain the correlation between his erections and the falling of the V-2 rockets on London (the novel is set mainly in the last months of the Second World War). Slothrop's search, however, has scarcely begun before he realizes that he himself is under investigation. He then joins the ranks of the novel's other characters as a victim, falling casualty to his own search when he uncovers documentary evidence that he was sold to a big business combine as a child. Discovery then leads to a *loss* of self, not a confirmation of identity, and Slothrop's fate only represents the characteristic direction of the forces operating within the novel: to reduce human beings to ciphers, units, or commercial entities.

Through at least the first half of *Gravity's Rainbow*, Pynchon follows a method of pursuing multiple plot-lines around and across Slothrop's search. The criss-crossing between one sequence and another invites the reader to form interpretative connections between them, to assemble a lattice-like text – until, that is, we enter the Zone. On its simplest level the Zone denotes Germany immediately before and after military defeat, but it is much more than that. The Zone is an area of ontological flux where the plots of the novel blur and where texts begin to proliferate. We encounter a string of bawdy limericks, a dream-poem (with woodcuts), a film-script, and the recording of a Kazakh singing duel, among others. In some of these cases Pynchon deals with the political dimensions of cultural representation: print as a means of subjugating an oral culture; direction as a means of implicating actors in roles subservient to the director's fantasy (almost like a miniature history of German Fascism) and so on. The key term here is 'control' whose biological and political connotations are applied to the ordering of Pynchon's text. An important influence here has been William Burroughs's *The Naked Lunch* (1959) which abandons linear sequence in favour of smaller episodes often beginning with pastiches of other texts (detective novels of the 1940s, film-scripts, etc.) which are then broken down. Burroughs anticipates Pynchon with his scientist spokesman for control, Dr Benway, the surreal city called Interzone and in sketching out commercial networks. For Burroughs as for Pynchon, conventional plot sequence would confirm the reader within his/her cultural conditioning, hence the importance of discontinuity, shock tactics and surreally destabilizing images. *The Naked Lunch* does not end so much as tail off entropically into verbal fragments. An 'atrophied preface', typically at the *end* of the boom, contains a mock Whitmanesque statement of stylistic plenty where Burroughs whips up its visual and aural multiplicity: 'This book spills off the page in all directions, kaleidoscope of vistas, medley of tunes and street noises, farts and riot yipes . . .' (Burroughs 1968, 255). Pynchon's tactics in Section IV of *Gravity's Rainbow* are related since he moves further and further from realism. Earlier plot sequences recede into the past of the text; now Slothrop exists only in traces. And scenes are repeatedly dissolving or fading out. Where previously the hiatus between sections acted as an invitation for the reader to cross-relate them, Pynchon now gives individual captions to episodes which emphasize their local autonomy and which attenuate plot continuity almost out of existence. Pynchon is as explicit as Burroughs about the disruptive effects of his method. At one point he inserts the comment, 'you will want cause and effect', as a prelude to a ludicrously far-fetched explanation of what has been happening to a character in one of the text's interstices (Pynchon 1975a: 663). It is as if Pynchon uses his earlier narrative as a pretext for setting up comic or futuristic episodes and then actually begins to deconstruct his text towards the end by separating out frozen images for comment. 'The Counterforce' – the title of this section – becomes a shorthand way of denoting textual disruption and thereby of distinguishing Pynchon's activities from the tainted notions of synthesis and control.

Although the writers discussed here have all turned their back on mimetic realism, they have not abandoned the issue of how their fiction relates to the external world. In spite of being an experimental novelist himself, Charles Newman has recently levelled a fierce attack on postmodernism which he argues 'has come to rely upon its own linguistic awareness of itself rather than plot or character development, to provide its own momentum' (Newman 1985: 98). Expressed in this way, linguistic foregrounding becomes an exercise in self-indulgence, whereas these writers are particularly anxious about how literary discourse relates to other discourses and how literary plotting compares with other systems of ordering. The avoidance of fixed form demonstrates what Tony Tanner has identified as a dream and its corresponding fear:

> there is an abiding dream in American literature that an
> unpatterned, unconditioned life is possible . . . there is also an
> abiding American dread that someone else is patterning your life,
> that there are all sorts of invisible plots afoot to rob you of your
> autonomy of thought and action. (Tanner 1971: 15)

Plotting becomes charged with ambivalence as it may create or impose order. Thus Stephen Wright's *Meditations in Green* (1983) precariously tries to hold together (through the discipline of Buddhist meditation, for instance) a self which is breaking down into hallucination under the impact of the Vietnam War. Sequence is problematic at best, but the novel incorporates within itself sceptical references to alternative means of representation through official military history, collage and a film. One reaction to the latter in effect bemoans the absence of an Aristotelian plot: '". . . I couldn't make any sense out of it at all. I mean, there's no beginning, no middle, no end. There's no coherence"' (Wright 1985: 266). As usual there are metafictional implications in this statement. Wright's character is in effect a projected reader registering bewilderment before an artefact which has abandoned conventional ordering. A broad distrust of previously accepted means of representation has led these novelists to put a high premium on distortion, disjunction and disruption. Let us leave the last words with Walter Abish who declares that 'the innovative novel is, in essence, a novel of disfamiliarization, a novel that has ceased to concern itself with the mapping of the "familiar" world' (Martin 1983: 238). The debate will continue over whether this process involves gain or loss.

3   The *Nouveau Roman:* Modernity and Postmodernity

Edmund Smyth

The *nouveau roman* has played a central role in the debates surrounding postmodernism: the metafictional techniques and strategies associated with the writers commonly identified with this movement have come to be regarded as, in many ways, synonymous with what constitutes postmodernist fiction. It would not be an exaggeration to stress the extent to which the *nouveau roman* has dictated the terms of critical discourse, nor to state that it still acts as the essential reference point in any definition of postmodern aesthetics. The sustained and systematic assault upon the assumptions and procedures of classic realism, vigorously pursued by the leading *nouveaux romanciers*, could almost be said to represent a manifesto of postmodern aims and aspirations; while the emphatic self-reflexivity of their novels is frequently cited as paradigmatic of radical textuality. However, the relationship between the *nouveau roman* and postmodernity is in fact considerably more problematic than most accounts suggest. For instance, it is possible to contend that the *nouveau roman* may be more accurately described as modernist or late modernist when compared with the apparently more subversive avant-garde experimentalism of the *Tel Quel* group, whose claim to be the natural successors of the revolution inaugurated by *Finnegans Wake* would be difficult to refute. Similarly, it would be erroneous to equate contemporary French fiction exclusively with the *nouveau roman*, despite the hegemonic position it has clearly occupied since the 1950s: the work of writers as diverse (and as removed from the *nouveau roman* and *Tel Quel*) as Georges Perec and Michel Tournier also demands the attention of those seeking to map the postmodern. Nor is it by any means the case that the *nouveau roman* is automatically considered in France as emblematic of postmodernism: this remains a largely imported concept, more frequently raised in discussion concerning the wider cultural condition. The *nouveaux romanciers* themselves have been reluctant to embrace the term, which has tended to occur on those occasions when parallels are being drawn with novelists in other countries, as at the New York *nouveau roman* conference in 1982 which many of them attended and which also saw the participation of several leading American postmodernists. Nevertheless, few literary movements have exhibited such an abiding preoccupation with establishing antecedents in order to defend and define their textual practices. This 'self-periodization' has been a constant feature of the *nouveau roman* since the 1950s: literary-historical arguments are frequently deployed by these novelists as a means of both affirming their radical modernist credentials and validating and valorizing their transgressive devices. The development of the *nouveau roman* is often claimed to illustrate the evolution from modernism to postmodernism – a transition which has been perceived and articulated by several of the *nouveaux romanciers* themselves. The postmodernist dilemma of periodization is vividly dramatized by these efforts to circumscribe their location in contemporary fiction.

It is now common in most accounts to begin with the proviso that the designation 'nouveau roman' is merely a convenient quasi-journalistic or even marketing label attached to an otherwise heterogeneous collection of writers, sharing little other than the same publishing house at one time or another (Éditions de Minuit). It has been said to comprise a central group – Alain Robbe-Grillet, Nathalie Sarraute, Claude Simon, Michel Butor, Robert Pinget – with Marguerite Duras and even Samuel Beckett as 'co-opted' members. While it is certainly true that the central core never issued a single agreed programme, a considerable degree of cohesion does emerge from an examination of their critical writings, and an impression of shared novelistic values is suggested by their willingness (to a greater or lesser extent) to appear on the same platform at conferences on several occasions and to accept, however grudgingly, the 'nouveau roman' appellation. During the 1970s, the critic and novelist Jean Ricardou attempted to foster a greater sense of group identity by bringing together Butor, Pinget, Robbe-Grillet, Sarraute, Simon and Claude Ollier at the famous Cerisy conference (1971), in addition to organizing separate *colloques* devoted to Claude Simon (1974) and Robbe-Grillet (1975); however, his endeavour to formulate a theoretical programme met with greater resistance. An analysis of the polemics in which the *nouveaux romanciers* have been prepared to engage demonstrates, at the very least, a concern with *modernizing* the contemporary French novel which they felt had advanced little, formally and technically, since Balzac, as a consequence of the failure to assimilate both the local experiments of Flaubert and Proust and the innovations of Joyce, Woolf, Faulkner and Kafka elsewhere. In Robbe-Grillet's *Pour un nouveau roman* (1963) and Nathalie Sarraute's *L'ère du soupçon* (1965), Michel Butor's essays and Claude Simon's conference papers, articles and interviews, all of these writers have had recourse to a modernist canon as part of an impetus of literary self-justification.

The explicitly polemical nature of the attack on the persistence of Balzacian realism was perceived as 'historically necessary' if French fiction was to progress in a positive way. Implicit in the arguments produced by the *nouveaux romanciers* was the assumption that the presence of causality, linearity, plot and characterization in the novels of their reactionary contemporaries rendered them redundant, both in literary-historical and in formal realist terms. The adoption of the superannuated forms of nineteenth-century fiction did not adequately reflect the epistemological and ontological uncertainty characteristic of the contemporary experience of reality. Nathalie Sarraute's condemnation of plot and character in *L'ère du soupçon* is based firmly on the conviction that traditional narrative cannot convey the experience of incoherence and discontinuity in modern life, nor the dissolution of the personality. The fixed categories of the character-based fiction of the nineteenth century had to be abandoned in favour of structures permitting fluidity and instability. The modern reader had also become distrustful of the authority of the act of narration and of the narrative voice, hence the condemnation of omniscience in particular. For Robbe-Grillet, there was also a direct correlation between Balzacian realism as a literary form and the society which produced it. In his lucid and highly combative essay, 'Sur quelques notions périmées' (1957), he stressed that the formal components of the realist novel reflected the dominant ideology of bourgeois society:

> Tous les éléments techniques du récit-emploi systématique du passé simple et de la troisième personne, adoption sans condition du déroulement chronologique, intrigues linéaires, courbe régulière des passions, tension de chaque épisode vers une fin, etc – tout visait à imposer l'image d'un univers stable, cohérent, continu, univoque, entièrement déchiffrable. Comme l'intelligibilité du monde n'était pas mise en question, raconter ne posait pas de problème. L'écriture romanesque pouvait être innocente. (Robbe-Grillet 1963: 31)

It was therefore necessary to introduce narrative forms which would more accurately mirror the unintelligibility of the world: the problematic nature of reality had to be more suitably translated. Claude Simon has also indicated that he considered the causality and confidence of the traditional novel as perpetuating a misrepresentation of reality. Their reading of Balzac was of course extremely distorted – the Balzacian novel was made to encapsulate in a convenient way everything which the *nouveaux romanciers* considered to be deficient in any *modern* representation of reality. It is significant that in the light of Roland Barthes's *S/Z* (1970), critics would subject even Balzac to the kind of analysis usually reserved for the more oppositional novels produced by the *nouveau roman* (see Jefferson 1983): poststructuralist and deconstructive readings could transform the 'readerly' into the 'writerly'. The classic realists could be shown to be just as transgressive and problematic as the modernists. By default rather than by design, therefore, the *nouveaux romanciers* inadvertently encouraged this interpretative transformation.

The *nouveau roman*'s 'map of misreading' is also apparent from its writers' confrontation with more immediate predecessors. In establishing their ancestry, little reference is ever made to the surrealists, who obviously contributed a great deal to the contestation of realism – this seems to arise mainly from a dislike of the practice of automatic writing. On the other hand, a writer like Céline becomes an 'approved' forerunner on account of the liberation of literary language which he effected in *Voyage au bout de la nuit* (1932). Existentialist fiction was considered to be insufficiently experimental. Sartre in particular was especially reprehensible as a consequence of his advocacy of 'la littérature engagée' – such a delineation of a social and political function for the writer was at direct variance with the formalist prerequisites of the *nouveau roman*. Demonstrating in a tangible way the 'anxiety of influence', in Robbe-Grillet's *Le Miroir qui revient* (1985) and Claude Simon's *Discours de Stockholm* (1986), Sartre is castigated for having failed to follow through the innovative *La Nausée* (1938) by writing *Les Chemins de la Liberté* (1945–49), which seemed unambiguously political in conception and, as a consequence, axio-matically non-modernist. However, their arguments rest purely on Sartre's intentions rather than his practice in the latter novel: Sartre in fact adopts a whole range of modernist devices throughout the three volumes, deriving precisely from the narrative experiments of Joyce, Dos Passos, Faulkner and others. Arguably, Nathalie Sarraute's career benefited enormously from Sartre's famous preface to her first novel, *Portrait d'un inconnu* (1947), which he claimed placed her in the alternative tradition of the 'anti-roman'. Sartre had initially been attracted to her work because it seemed to demonstrate his own concern with the inauthenticity of human relationships, yet he would later reject her fiction simply on the basis that her novels are set in an upper-middle-class Parisian milieu. Camus's *L'Etranger* (1942) is also marred (at least for Robbe-Grillet) by the unwelcome intrusion of a 'metaphorical' vocabulary in the second part of the novel: in his landmark essay 'Nature, Humanisme, Tragédie' (1958) and in *Le Miroir qui revient*, Robbe-Grillet had condemned this unfortunate lapse from 'le degré zéro de l'écriture' almost as a kind of betrayal of modernism, and as deficient in phenomenological terms by establishing a complicity between man and the world. If we accept J.-F. Lyotard's definition of postmodernism as the subversion of metanarratives, then the *nouveau roman* can be said to have rejected the totalizing metanarrative of existentialism, even if only to have replaced it with a literary-historical metanarrative of its own. Significantly, it is the metaphysical dimension of Samuel Beckett's writing which places him, strictly speaking, outside the confines of the *nouveau roman*, despite the similarities in formal experimentation. André Gide's *Les Faux-monnayeurs* (1926), a novel characterized by self-reflexivity and self-consciousness, in which the device of *mise en abyme* (or internal duplication) is especially conspicuous, has perhaps not received from them the kind of attention that could be expected. Gide was perceived as having been too closely allied to the psychological novel in the

French tradition of the *roman d'analyse*. Marcel Proust's *A la recherche du temps perdu*, however, is recognized as an important technical achievement, especially by Claude Simon and Robbe-Grillet. Simon's syntactical and thematic discursiveness and preoccupation with memory and time are clearly reminiscent of Proust. For Nathalie Sarraute, Proust's psychologizing had to be refined and transformed in order to convey the mobility and fragmentation of consciousness. Proust's use of the anonymous first-person narrator was to be adopted in several *nouveaux romans*.

All of the *nouveaux romanciers* have paid tribute most notably to Flaubert: Robbe-Grillet has explicitly credited Flaubert with the departure from realism in favour of a more self-consciously modernist writing; the title of Nathalie Sarraute's essay 'Flaubert le précurseur' itself underlines the indebtedness of the *nouveau roman* towards Flaubert's work. In a series of overtly periodizing comments by these novelists, Flaubert's *œuvre* is deemed to constitute a 'turning-point' in French literary history. Flaubert's use of *style indirect libre* in order to voice the consciousness of his protagonists, is regarded as the fore-runner of the stream of consciousness technique popularized by Joyce and other twentieth-century modernists. It is, of course, the Joyce of *Portrait of the Artist as a Young Man* and *Ulysses* who attracted the *nouveaux romanciers* rather than *Finnegans Wake*, whose verbal and linguistic inventiveness did not receive many enthusiasts, except for a period during the 1970s when both Robbe-Grillet and Simon were influenced by the theories of Jean Ricardou, who stressed the productive nature of work on language in order to counter representation. Ricardou was particularly guilty of attempting to establish an officially sanctioned list of approved modernist precursors: the criteria he used were based on a simplistic and over-schematic distinction between writers who accepted a mimetic function and those for whom the materiality of language could be shown to be paramount. In general, what the *nouveaux romanciers* would jettison from modernism was the privileging of interiority and the portrayal of the awakening artistic sensibility: although writer figures occasionally appear in the fiction of Robert Pinget and Nathalie Sarraute, we find a rejection of the élitist preoccupation with the artist as a unique individual possess-ing a heightened awareness of reality. The concern with anonymity and alienation, present in the metaphysical novel of the twentieth century, is absorbed most obviously by Robbe-Grillet, although devoid of an overtly philosophical content. It is clear from his critical writings that, to some extent, he considers himself to be the successor of Kafka and Camus: this influence emerges in his novels, *Dans le labyrinthe* (1959) – whose very title evokes Kafka and Borges – and his first work, *Un Régicide* (1949; published 1978) in which the atmosphere is very tangibly that of the absurd-cum-behaviourist novel (see Smyth 1983), even if in both cases the metaphysical is subjected to parody.

It is evident from the comments made by the *nouveaux romanciers* that they considered themselves to be developing and integrating the formal experiments of writers drawn from a carefully selected modernist canon, suggesting that they judged modernism to have been incomplete in the French novel before their arrival. The attack on the norms of classic realism was of course aided and abetted by the emerging school of structuralist critics, most notably Roland Barthes, who, in *Le degré zéro de l'écriture* (1953) and in *Essais Critiques* (1964), espoused the efforts of the *nouveau roman* (or, more exactly, of Robbe-Grillet) in overturning the Balzacian bourgeois novel and its attendant retrograde ideology. The deconstruction of narrative as a natural or unproblematic activity was to be amplified by several other literary theorists. The decentring of the author as the source and guarantee of his/her discourse, and the increasing preoccupation with the operation of intertextuality in the novel could be demonstrated to be reflected in the work of the *nouveaux romanciers*. Structuralism was able to use the *nouveau roman*'s denial of an autobiographical motivation and its allocation of an apparently more active role to the reader as an illustration of the 'death of the author' criterion, while the difficult question of referentiality would be echoed by many of the novelists themselves in critical debate. This collusion between writers and critics was not deliberate, let alone coordinated in any systematic fashion, yet, in cultural and intellectual terms, the principal outcome was to revolutionize the literary landscape by initiating new, evaluative criteria to chart the movement from realism to modernism: Flaubert is also considered by Barthes to be the pivotal figure in this transformation towards an apparently less transparent writing. Both the *nouveau roman* and structuralism were able to find nourishment and encouragement in their parallel activities and in the polemical tactics both movements employed as a means of furthering their broadly similar aims. If it is in any way meaningful to speak in terms of a 'cultural dominant', then arguably the *nouveau roman* could not have achieved this without the support of like-minded critics. Indeed, in the 1970s, the theoretical influence of Jean Ricardou, who was aligned to both movements, extended even to the actual fiction produced by Robbe-Grillet and Claude Simon at that stage, and several of the concepts he formulated were regurgitated in critical interventions by these writers.

The *nouveaux romanciers* have used not simply formalist, but explicitly formal realist arguments to explain their departure from traditional narrative structures: the form of the novel itself had to reflect the changing perception of reality as fragmentary and discontinuous. For Robbe-Grillet in particular, this was also a philosophical and quasi-sociological necessity, mirroring the dehumanization and alienation of man in modern society – a critique which would later be adapted by the Marxist theorist Lucien Goldmann – in *Pour une sociologie du roman* (1964) – who was able to use the concept of reification as a means of explaining the *chosisme* of Robbe-Grillet's early novels and the subversion of character in the *nouveau roman* generally. Even as recently as 1982, Robbe-Grillet would explain his transgressive narrative techniques by relying on the Sartrean concept of contingency (see Oppenheim 1986): the disruptive narrative syntax conveys the fragmentation of man in the world, the absence of meaning in his novels can thus be said to correspond to the gratuitousness of existence. With the exception of the Ricardou-dominated 1970s, Claude Simon would adopt a similar set of epistemological and phenomenological pretexts for his textual practices. 'Rendre la perception confuse, multiple et simultanée du monde' was the title of one of the interviews given to coincide with the publication of *Histoire* (1967), in the course of which he described his narrative strategy in the novel as an attempt to convey, in formal terms, the incoherence of perception and memory. Nathalie Sarraute has consistently defended the narrative structures of her texts as the only possible means of representing, in fictional form, the psychological interactions between consciousnesses which she describes as 'tropisms' – the depiction of subtle intersubjective activity involves the creation of a more fluid narrative discourse. The linearity and chronology of the conventional novel had to be abandoned in order to achieve this: the minute movements of attraction and repulsion towards other consciousnesses, language and objects could not be accommodated within the character-centred novel of classic realism. It is clear from *L'ère du soupçon* that Sarraute is arguing from a position which considers psychological realism of the traditional kind as a falsification of mental experience. Michel Butor's justifications for the devices used in his early novels are also grounded in the language of mimetic realism.

Although the attack on the forms of classic nineteenth-century fiction was pursued in the interests of modernity, it is evident from the defences provided by the *nouveaux romanciers* that they were in fact relying to a considerable extent on a revised concept of realism. It is certainly the case that the arguments they employed were partly designed in order to make their work appear more *lisible*, in response to the frequently voiced objections about the difficulty of their novels. In this respect, their rhetoric had the principal aim of facilitating the reader's response to these otherwise 'incomprehensible' texts whose erosion of conventional contours impeded the reader's access. The retrievability, or recuperability (as it came to be known), of the *nouveau roman* depended to some degree on the reader being convinced of the necessity for modernity.

The issue of recuperability itself became a key factor in critical debate with the publication of Bruce Morrissette's *Les Romans de Robbe-Grillet* (1963). Roland Barthes's preface to this volume warns against the attempt made to 'naturalize' Robbe-Grillet's fiction by adopting such a markedly humanist approach. Before Morrissette, Robbe-Grillet had appeared to accept the *chosiste* label attached to him by Barthes on account of the supposedly flat and neutral representation of external reality and the minute descriptions of objects in his early novels, which seemed to be in accordance with the phenomenological position outlined in *Pour un nouveau roman*. Morrissette's interpretative strategy was derived from Robbe-Grillet's own departure from this standpoint in favour of a more 'subjectivist' view. Thus Morrissette was able to perform readings of his work which concentrated on the psychological realism of the texts in question. He argued that, in each of Robbe-Grillet's first three novels, the narrative discourse is focalized around the consciousness of the central protagonist, so the recurrent objects (the rubber in *Les Gommes*, the cord in *Le Voyeur*, the centipede in *La Jalousie*) connote some sexual or criminal obsession and the presence of an interiority. Far from being neutral, the objects and descriptions become in fact suffused with meaning when attached in some way to a centre of consciousness. Robbe-Grillet showed himself to be willing to embrace this psychological/subjectivist mode of analysis as readily as he had previously accepted Roland Barthes's imprimatur as the model *chosiste*. It was not uncommon for critics at this time to be engaged in character study and reconstructions of plot and chronology. Under Ricardou's encouragement, Robbe-Grillet's compliance with such 'naturalizing' endeavours would be abandoned for a textual materialist perspective, focusing on the self-referentiality of the practice of writing. This, in its turn, would be replaced by the novelist's insistence on the ludic nature of his fiction. Barthes's caveats against recuperation have been most convincingly demonstrated by Stephen Heath (1972) who is critical of the tendency towards naturalization: the radical experience of the *nouveau roman* is undermined when the novels are subjected to reductive readings of the psychologizing variety enacted by Morrissette, however much these may be encouraged by the novelists themselves. For example, despite her attachment to an extra-textual and pre-linguistic domain of mental activity, Nathalie Sarraute's work, according to Heath, should not be limited by interpretative strategies which are fundamentally referentialist in orientation. In his highly influential critical works, Jean Ricardou was particularly adamant in his condemnation of readings of *nouveaux romans* which suggest a mimetic motivation of any kind.

In support of the proposition that the development of the *nouveau roman* corresponds to the transition from modernism to postmodernism, it can certainly be shown that the early productions of the *nouveaux romanciers* are susceptible to readings which to some extent meet the criteria of psychological realism so important in modernist aesthetics. The subsequent evolution towards an apparently less recuperable writing would seem to bear this out.

In Robbe-Grillet's fiction, this movement may seem most tangible. In *Un Régicide* (1949/1978), the narrative oscillates between two apparently distinct, fictional universes: a 'prosaic' world (recounted in the third person), in which a character named Boris is socially, metaphysically and politically alienated in the manner befitting an existentialist hero, intersects with the 'poetic' world of an anonymous first-person narrator who inhabits an isolated farming and fishing community. These competing discourses struggle to achieve hierarchy in diegetic terms. However, the text invites us, as a result of the parallels and correspondences between the two worlds, to consider the first-person sequences as occurring oneirically in Boris's mind: thus the disruptions in the narrative could be interpreted as the symptom of his distorted ordering of experience. In *Les Gommes* (1953), Robbe-Grillet adopts a mock-Oedipal detective story format: the detective Wallas, at the end of a period of 24 hours, kills the man whose 'murder' he had been sent to investigate. His investigations are accompanied by a search for an india-rubber, about which he remembers only that it contained the two letters 'di' in the middle of its trade name (hence 'O*edi*pe'). This novel becomes 'readable' if we accept the psychologizing interpretation that Wallas is a kind of victim of Oedipal obsessions which he projects onto the objects around him. In *Le Voyeur* (1955), the intense preoccupation with specific objects which the travelling watch salesman displays – the figure-of-eight patterns, the girl's neck, the rope, the cinema poster – is contrived to function as an index of his guilt: Mathias is incriminated by the narrative, although his guilt is never proved conclusively. The sado-sexual crime is not described, yet everything in the text points to Mathias as the perpetrator. In *La Jalousie* (1957), the disjointed chronology, the use of the present tense, the repetition of scenes, the recurrence of certain details – features which initially perplex readers – become explicable if an identifiable narrator is postulated. If we accept that the narrative discourse represents the consciousness of the unnamed 'jealous husband' of the woman known as A . . ., then the ambiguities and contradictions in the text can be related to this narrator's obsessive fascination with the possibility of his wife's adultery. According to this reading, the repetition of episodes and the lack of a linear structure can be regarded as being in keeping with the formal realism of a narrative which is being conducted by someone whose overwrought state of mind colours his perception of the world around him, and who is no longer able to distinguish between imagination and reality. The central gap in the text is the narrative perspective; however, by accepting the proposition that this is indeed a first-person narration, with the first person conspicuously omitted, then the novel becomes understood in psychological terms as a radical example of stream of consciousness writing. In all of these novels, the disorders and inconsistencies can be justified as the attempt to convey the limited viewpoint of an incompetent or unreliable narrator, or the workings of a confused and obsessed consciousness.

Similarly, in what seemed a particularly unconventional technique at the time, Michel Butor, in *La Modification* (1957), employs a second-person narrative as a means, apparently, of voicing the monologue which Léon Delmont is conducting with himself as he travels from Paris to Rome to join his mistress, explaining to himself the history of his affair and anticipating how it will resolve itself. In Robert Pinget's *Le Fiston* (1959), the grief of the drunken narrator clouds his view of the world. Claude Simon's fiction provides for the possibility of retrieval, if we accept the mimetic claim that the form of the novel must be dictated by the incoherence and instability of memory and perception: in *Le Vent* (1957), *L'Herbe* (1958), *La Route des Flandres* (1960), *Le Palace* (1962) and *Histoire* (1967), the fragmentation and discontinuity of reality is conveyed in the narrative syntax itself. The arguments adduced by Simon reveal a concern with representation: the partial and subjective nature of perception and the flux of experience necessitate an equally disruptive formal structure. These novels can be read as attempts to reconstruct the fragmentary apprehension of the past. As Simon himself has stated, there is a striking incompatibility between the discontinuity of perception and the continuity of writing: it is central to Simon's aesthetics to bring to the novel the non-linearity of painting.

Many of Simon's novels dramatize the attempts to impose order and meaning on the chaos of reality and history, hence the appearance in his fiction of tumultuous events such as war and revolution. His work is intimately concerned with epistemological questions. In stylistic terms, the long and digressive sentences, the accumulation of parentheses, the sustained use of the present participle, the increasing lack of conventional paragraphing and punctuation are all deployed in order to convey simultaneity of perception, in a manner reminiscent of both Proust and Faulkner. In *Le Vent*, there seems to be a reconstitution of the past in which perception, memory and imagination all play equally important roles: the central protagonist Montès provides the narrator with a disordered version of events. In *L'Herbe*, Louise is another unreliable narrator; indeed, the perspective changes from sharing Louise's point of view to a wider lens. The theme of disintegration in the novel (Louise's Tante Marie is lying comatose in an upstairs room on the verge of death) is suggested formally by the disjointed narration and chronology. In *La Route des Flandres*, the fluctuations between first and third person mean that it is not possible to contend that the novel's discourse is organized entirely around the consciousness of the central character Georges, who otherwise seems to be re-creating his experiences in the course of a night in bed with the widow of his commanding officer, some time after the wartime conflict. The principal theme of this novel is again decomposition in all its aspects, so the formal disintegration of the text mirrors the dispersal of Georges's subjectivity. Using the *débâcle* of the Flanders campaign as a basis, a reconstruction of the fragments of a chaotic experience occupies the narrative. Simon's decision to dispense with normal syntax implies that stylistically the intention is to render the real more satisfactorily than the conventional novel would allow. *Le Palace* presents a reconstruction of the events of a day, a night and the next morning during the Spanish Civil War, apparently in the mind of a student – into this narrative is imbricated the 'Récit de l'homme-fusil' by an Italian who has committed an assassination. In *Histoire*, the narrator is engaged in the elaboration of descriptions which are suggested by a set of postcards: he attempts to evoke and organize these fragments of the past, aware that it is ultimately unknowable and that reconstructions are inevitably incomplete and distorted by the passage of time. The chaotic narration is therefore in harmony with such a fractured representation: conventional syntax and punctuation would only conceal the discontinuity of experience. It is evident from these examples that Simon wished to compose novels whose structure and language would reproduce the confusion of perception, the discontinuous and simultaneous aspect of memory and the fragmentary nature of knowledge. Simon's own statements made at this time betray a strong representational intent: while rejecting the forms of classic realism, the novel nevertheless retained its mimetic role. His subsequent development, however, may be said to demonstrate an autonomous and self-referential orientation: his later works confirm the anti-representational and non-recuperable trend in postmodernist fiction.

Nathalie Sarraute, however, has never deviated from her conviction that her novels must be considered as attempts to reproduce, in formal terms, the domain of the interpersonal, pre-verbal psychological reality of tropism. It is to facilitate the translation of the dramas of sub-conversation and activity below the surface of consciousness that she abandons the conventions of linear narrative, normal chronology, plot and characterization. The 24 texts which comprise her first work, *Tropismes* (1939), are in fact closer to prose poems than traditional narrative. The representation of psychological states in formation demanded the expansiveness offered by the full-length novel to depict the psychological sub-surface in all its complexity: the experience of tropism should be created in the reader. In *Portrait d'un inconnu* (1948) and *Martereau* (1953), anonymous first-person narrators, hypersensitive to the power of tropism, provide the narrative focus. In *Le Planétarium* (1959), however, although it is possible to attribute some of the sequences to the consciousnesses of the 'characters' involved, we are presented with conflicting narratives and interpretations of events emanating from insufficiently individuated figures. Her subsequent novels confirm this development towards a narrative discourse in which it is increasingly difficult to situate a perceiving consciousness. Sarraute's aim is to stress that tropistic movements are interchangeable: movements of attraction and repulsion towards or away from other human beings, and the frequently clichéd and stereotyped language they employ, demand representation in a more flexible narrative structure. She has repeatedly emphasized that her novels are linguistically self-conscious explicitly in order to translate the apprehension of the problematic area of language. The subject of *Les Fruits d'or* (1963) is a novel which is itself entitled 'Les Fruits d'or'; this situation acts as a catalyst for tropistic interactions amongst a set of predominantly anonymous figures who are trapped within the fixed patterns of social discourse. *Entre la vie et la mort* (1968) depicts the drama of a writer's struggle with language and the processes of creation, aware as he is of the potentially enslaving power of words. In *Vous les entendez?* (1972), an art object is the topic of discussion: it becomes a kind of totem whose aesthetic value is upheld by a father and contested by his children. In the short texts which make up *L'Usage de la parole* (1980), the traumatic reactions to particular words and phrases are once again dramatized in all their intensity. Although eschewing the analysis prevalent in the traditional psychological novel, Sarraute's work nevertheless combines representation with reflexivity.

Rejecting realism as a literary form, the *nouveaux romanciers* are still prepared to adopt the mimetic impetus, while jettisoning the conventional devices of plot, character and linear chronology. The obvious validity of recuperable readings of many of these *nouveaux romans* by applying criteria derived from psychological realism cannot be denied. It is evident from a perusal of the 'legitimizing' commentary provided by the novelists themselves that the reader is being encouraged to 'naturalize' the texts along the lines suggested. The subsequent evolution towards the production of fiction from which no coherent narrative perspective emerges would seem to demonstrate a measure of discontent with previous textual practice. It is certainly not the case that this can be discerned in the work of all the *nouveaux romanciers* at the same time; however, that such a development did indeed take place suggests that a new poetics was being tacitly formulated.

Ricardou has been credited as the instigator of this development, although his contribution to the *nouveau roman* was principally to articulate and systematize this new aesthetic. Coming from the *Tel Quel* camp, which, under Philippe Sollers's leadership, was pushing experimentation even further, Ricardou sought to contest the referentiality of the *nouveau roman*. The importance of *Tel Quel* in setting the new agenda should not be underestimated: from the point of view of periodization, the writers and critics associated with this journal (the most influential since Sartre's *Les Temps Modernes*), in addition to espousing the 'classic modernists', also resurrected from literary history non-canonical writing which they considered to have been neglected. Lautréamont, Raymond Roussel, Céline and Joyce's *Finnegans Wake* all benefited from this redrawing of the map of subversive discourse. It is vital to emphasize *Tel Quel*'s perception of the implicitly political nature of avant-garde writing: Ricardou shared the group's belief in the 'critical function' of oppositional works. He also attempted to import *Tel Quel*'s conviction, derived from semiotics, that the *hors-texte* did not exist. This critical language favoured the free play of the signifier at the expense of the signified, hence the importance of word-play and the exploration of the properties of language in the elaboration of the text. According to this version, the materiality of the text should replace the evocation of the workings of consciousness. In this respect, the emergence of a *nouveau nouveau roman* was said to have evolved which was deemed to be characterized by this emphasis on textual productivity, instead of on reference and representation. Ricardou refused to countenance any vestigial mimetic input, such was his preoccupation with a view of the 'authentically' radical text, as defined by work in and on language. If it had become axiomatic that the author (or 'scriptor' in Ricardou's terminology) had become decentred and that the novel could not represent any psychological or social reality, then the origins of a text could only be found in the self-generating aspect of language itself. Ricardou contested the 'referential illusion' that the text could refer to anything other than itself: the myths of expression and representation, propounded by the (historically superannuated) literary movements of Romanticism and realism, had to be excised from self-reflexive modernist practice. He distinguished between 'l'aventure d'une écriture' and 'l'écriture d'une aventure': this precluded the existence of a pre-verbal, pre-textual domain.

The fiction of Robbe-Grillet and Claude Simon can be said to approximate most closely to these new literary values. *Dans le labyrinthe* (1959) was the first of Robbe-Grillet's novels not to have a tangible focalization, unless we accept Morrissette's interpretation that it dramatizes the attempts of a delirious narrator to construct a text from objects around him. Developing even further the *gommage* technique of his previous novels, this novel presents permutations and combinations of a set of elements subject to revision, repetition, and repetition with variation. *La Maison de rendez-vous* (1965) and *Projet pour une révolution a New York* (1970) continue in this vein, except that the 'content' of these texts is provided by clichéd representations of the cities of Hong Kong and New York, respectively, in popular mythology. Robbe-Grillet has chosen these stereotypical exotic and erotic images precisely in order to prevent the reader from constructing a 'meaningful' world. In his work of this period, Robbe-Grillet increasingly abandoned the cohesion and narrative hierarchies of his earlier fiction: the ontological status of the text is problematized. The novelist has himself referred to the self-generating quality of these works: he seems to provide the reader with a metaphor of the construction of narrative. His highly playful *Djinn* (1981) – originally written as a French teaching text – demonstrates the limitless power of narrative to combine and fragment in ever-changing patterns. Robbe-Grillet appeared to be illustrating the poetics of the *jeu combinatoire*: the novels reflect their own processes of composition, and the interpretative strategies which the reader brings are encoded within the text. These novels are full of gaps and contradictions of various kinds.

Claude Simon's fiction at this time is particularly amenable to the criteria established by Ricardou. In *La Bataille de Pharsale* (1969), *Les Corps Conducteurs* (1971), *Triptyque* (1973) and *Leçon de choses*

(1976), any trace of an interiority has been elided. The texts seem to have been composed as a result of work in and on language. Simon explores the properties, associations and connotations of words in order to form the thematic basis of the novel. The opening of *Leçon de choses*, significantly entitled 'Générique', can almost be said to provide a poetics of the autonomous, self-referential text, such is the emphasis upon the creative power of words: a description is composed which will generate the text as a whole and which also acts as a self-reflexive commentary on this process. The following extract from the preface to *Orion aveugle* (1970) conveys the importance he attaches to the exploitation of both signifier and signified:

> Chaque mot en commande (ou en suscite) plusieurs autres, non seulement par la force des images qu'il attire à lui comme un aimant, mais parfois aussi par sa seule morphologie, de simples assonances qui, de même que les nécessités formelles de la syntaxe, du rythme et de la composition, se révèlent aussi fécondes que ses multiples associations.

The descriptions can be generated almost endlessly by means of this productive view of the activity of writing. These texts lack a fixed centre: the narrative perspective is always shifting, and what remains of 'plot' is subject to continual fragmentation. The descriptions, far from gesturing to an external or subjective reality, merely affirm their own status as verbally constructed artefacts. There is a concerted desire to destroy what remains of the referential illusion: what seems 'real' is immediately transformed into another representation in the form of a painting, a postcard or a film. Robbe-Grillet's contemporaneous work exhibits similar characteristics: in *La Maison de rendez-vous*, for example, a 'real' person turns out to be a dummy, or a narrative sequence is revealed as a theatrical representation or a description of a magazine cover. The textual practices of these *nouveaux romanciers* reveal a much greater similarity than was previously the case: under Ricardou's stewardship, a new aesthetic programme seems to have been in operation. The linear and temporal progression of the narrative is disrupted by the non-stratified discourse of the text. The proliferating, non-hierarchized narratives impede recuperable readings from occurring. They present the reader with the autotelic novel, sufficient unto itself and the fruit of the endless play of language. Many of these texts can be read as elaborate commentaries on the nature of writing and reading. It would be difficult to find more suitable candidates for postmodern metafictionality than the novels of Simon and Robbe-Grillet at this time. These plural, heterogeneous and non-totalized novels vividly proclaim their metafictional status, referring constantly to the processes of their own production. They would seem to demonstrate the proposition that a text can only ever designate its own activity, that textuality is inherently narcissistic.

While this blatant metafictionality is most evident in Robbe-Grillet's and Simon's novels of the period, it is less noticeable in the work of Sarraute and Butor. *Degrés* (1960) is in fact the last of Butor's works to be labelled a novel; the remainder of his output is difficult to classify in generic terms, as his writings seem to eschew any narrational impulse. Indeed, in many of these later works, coherent and sequential narrative patterns seem to have been abandoned in order to be more representational, as in *Mobile* (1962), *Réseau aérien* (1962) and *6 810 000 litres d'eau par seconde* (1966). It has already been indicated that Nathalie Sarraute has always remained committed to the depiction of psychological states, despite the apparently 'narratorless' trend of her fiction since *Le Planétarium*. The chasm between her and the other writers is most apparent in comments she made at the 'Nouveau roman: hier, aujourd'hui' conference at Cerisy in 1972, in which she clung resolutely to her conviction of the existence of a pre-verbal, extra-textual reality in mental life. This was obviously anathema to Ricardou, in particular, and a fairly acrimonious exchange erupted during the conference sessions surrounding this question of referentiality. It is evident that Ricardou had established a new *doxa* of reflexivity from which no deviations could be permitted, such was the extent to which he saw himself as the custodian of a radical modernity. For a text to be described as a *nouveau roman* it had to exhibit self-reflexive and metafictional features as well as foreground the exploration of the semantic and phonetic properties of language. Nathalie Sarraute's novels could be claimed to display autonomy and reflexivity, despite her preoccupation with such a mimetic project.

An analysis of Ricardou's theoretical rhetoric, accompanied by readings of the later fiction of Robbe-Grillet and Simon, would amply support the proposition that a 'change of dominant' in favour of a postmodern aesthetic had occurred. Recuperative readings grounded in psychological realism could no longer be effected. The removal of a centre of consciousness to which the narrative discourse could be attached and the self-conscious preoccupation with both the linguistic/verbal origins of the text and the status of the reading and writing of fiction suggested that a new aesthetic had been evolved. However, as many of the novelists have themselves pointed out, the presence of transgressive and subversive features could be shown to exist in their earlier works.

While it is undeniable that Robbe-Grillet's early novels are indeed capable of being read as essentially modernist texts whose narrative strategies consist in the representation of a distorted perception of reality, nevertheless, 'retrospectively', they can also be considered to demonstrate reflexivity. The use of *mise en abyme* and the presence of an element of word-play would seem to align them with the apparently more transgressive works initiated – if the literary history of the *nouveau roman* is correct – by *Dans le labyrinthe*. Equally, the existence of alternative and proliferating versions of 'events' of dubious ontological status anticipates the more radical disruptions of narrative syntax carried out in the later novels. Even *La Jalousie*, which had become assimilated into the 'great tradition' of the French psychological novel, could be described as an exercise in serial composition, as its author himself would claim. All of these texts can be read equally well as examples of the *récit lacunaire* paradigm in poststructuralist criticism, such is the extent to which they seem to be generated by a gap or an absence. In these earlier works, there are traces of the *glissements* in narrative structure which are so common in the later works. Robbe-Grillet's insistence upon the essentially ludic dimension of all of his fiction (and cinema) was also a means of escaping what might be termed the prison-house of reflexivity; it was not uncommon to find him distancing himself from Ricardou, even during the conference devoted to his work in 1975, at which he claimed that even his supposedly 'theoretical' utterances over the years should be construed as attempts to maintain plurality and mobility. Ricardou is accused (like Morrissette before him) of ironing out the contradictions and tensions in his novels. It is only by stressing the element of play that the imposition of totalitarian meaning of any kind can be avoided. This emphasis on an aesthetics of textual pleasure provides a convenient way of confronting the adventure of meaning present in Robbe-Grillet's *œuvre* as a whole. Of course, it could be argued that ludism is, in its way, another interpretative strategy launched by the novelist: while conceding the liberating effect of viewing the literary text as an open and democratic discourse, Robbe-Grillet is again allocating a new role to the reader. The novelist's justification of ludism is usually couched in pseudo-political language: all meaning is seen to be implicitly ideological, therefore playful and experimental writing becomes a means of subverting dominant ideologies. Just as the novelist considered the deconstruction and demythologizing of carefully selected cultural stereotypes to be a politically liberating activity, so, in the same way, he appears to be propagating an idealistic and positivistic view of the literary text which he was so quick to criticize in Sartre's aesthetics.

Claude Simon's *Les Géorgiques* (1981) was seen by several critics as a rejection of the extreme textual materialism of his more recent fiction, as if Simon had finally shaken off the pernicious influence of Jean Ricardou. However, although there seems indeed to be a return to 'History' (in Simonian terms) and an apparent abandonment of the scriptural narcissism of the self-generating novels he produced in the 1970s, this view also rests on a historicizing version of the development of Simon's fiction. Again, it can be demonstrated that Simon's apparently more mimetic works also exhibit the linguistically self-generating features typical of his later fiction. In *La Route des Flandres*, for example, there is ample evidence that many of the fictional sequences emerge as a result of an exploration of the properties of certain words: the inherently fertile nature of language can be shown to have generated the subsequent text, and, through the use of metaphor and metonymy, the associations of both memory and language work together in the production of the text. The dispersal of the narrative voice in this and other novels can be claimed to illustrate poststructuralism's preoccupation with the disintegration of subjectivity. *Histoire*, whilst at one level a transposition of the discontinuity of experience, can at the same time be considered as providing an implicit commentary on the nature of fiction and writing: the text can be said to be formed from a meditation on a collection of postcards which the narrator is sifting through. The process of description triggers off the narrative sequences. Both of these novels contain in their opening pages a narrative sequence which acts as a kind of generating cell for the rest of the text – the process of textual production foregrounded in *Leçon de choses*. Disturbing further the historicizing account of Simon's writing, *Les Géorgiques* commences in a similar vein. Thus, the existence of both mimetic and autonomous features in Simon's novels proves that the two are not incompatible, as Ricardou claimed and which the novelist himself had been willing to endorse for a time. It is evident that earlier *nouveaux romans* do contain, although less conspicuously, many of the radical features of the later works. This observation raises the crucial question of precisely what kinds of criteria are being used to chart the evolution from a modernist to a postmodern aesthetic. The example provided by the *nouveau roman* directly contests any strict application of many of the versions of this transformation. If it is claimed that a poetics of textual production and reflexivity replaces mimetic strategies of any kind, then the early *nouveau roman* can also be made to conform to this new postmodern aesthetic. Similarly, if subjectivity and interiority are deemed to be essentially 'modernist' characteristics, then it has to be said that these are also challenged in a number of ways in novels such as *Le Voyeur* and *L'Herbe*.

The increasing discontent of the *nouveaux romanciers* at being imprisoned in an interpretative mode of exclusive autonomy is witnessed in their attacks on Ricardou. Nathalie Sarraute had never been prepared to accept his insistence on pure textuality, and both Robbe-Grillet and Claude Simon sought to distance themselves from the increasingly over-rigid application of his theories. Robbe-Grillet stated that it was the tension between reference and reflexivity which characterized his works, and described as naive the belief (which he admits to having encouraged) in the self-generating text devoid of a controlling subjectivity (see Robbe-Grillet 1984: 10–13). Claude Simon would become vociferous in his condemnation of Ricardou's 'terrorism' (see Oppenheim 1986).

The major disadvantage of the textual materialist perspective is its complete failure to confront the autobiographical dimension in more recent examples of *nouveau roman* writing, which has proved to be increasingly fertile in the 1980s. In *Les Géorgiques*, letters and documents attributed to the figure L.S.M. are in fact extracts from a bundle of papers belonging to a real ancestor of Simon. Investigating the life of this 'ancestor', the narrator is led into an account of his own experience. Representation is called into question: the fictional status of the text being produced is repeatedly acknowledged. In his most recent work, *L'Acacia* (1989), Simon again approaches, from another angle, many of the locations and themes of his previous novels. As in *Histoire*, the narrative framework is provided by a kind of meditation from a window: again, the text is generated from an exploration of both the processes of memory and the fertility of language. Ricardou's exclusively self-reflexive interpretative grid was never able to incorporate the presence of actual historical/autobiographical 'truth' (however fundamentally relative Simon acknowledged it to be): a consideration of *La Route des Flandres* which is not afraid to examine the referential data can result in potentially valuable readings of the text. Robbe-Grillet's two volumes of autobiography (*Le Miroir qui revient* (1984) and *Angélique* (1988)) merge conventional accounts of 'real' events with obviously fictitious sequences (based around the mysterious activities of a character called Henri de Corinthe), in addition to reflections on the *nouveau roman* generally and his own textual practices. By stating provocatively, at the beginning of the book, 'Je n'ai jamais parlé d'autre chose que de moi' (1984: 10), Robbe-Grillet could not be more ostentatiously exhibiting his departure from a textual materialist perspective. However, the disruptions in chronology and the mixture of writings suggest that this is far from being a reactionary return to a more traditional form; indeed, these two works are grouped under the title *Romanesques*, further contravening the reader's conventional expectations of an autobiography as a revelation of some truth.

Nathalie Sarraute's *Enfance* (1983) also foregrounds hesitations concerning the legitimacy of the autobiographical temptation: generically, this work is not categorized as either novel or autobiography. The structure of the work takes the form of a dialogue between an 'autobiographizing' narrator persona and an interrogative voice which raises reservations about the validity of the whole enterprise: at various points throughout the text statements and versions of events are contradicted and contested, thus inscribing the anticipated response of the reader in a manner reminiscent of the technique she used to great effect in her previous book, *L'Usage de la parole* (1980). Such interjections are clearly ironic as they are likely to be those of the 'trained' *nouveau roman* reader who has come to regard the decentring of the author as paradigmatic of contemporary experimental fiction. The problematics of selfhood and subjectivity become the focus of many of the autobiographical texts produced by the *nouveaux romanciers*. Robert Pinget's fiction is frequently inhabited by authorial personae. It was mistakenly assumed that this trend represented a return to more traditional literary values; an examination of such works reveals a postmodernist contestation of the conventional boundaries between genres and an intertextual mixture of writings, of which the fragmented subjectivity of the writer was itself a discourse capable of being plundered in order to generate text. This is very much in evidence in Marguerite Duras's *L'Amant* (1984), which began as a commentary on an album of family photographs and which dramatizes the fragility of identity and the textualization of recollection. In Philippe Sollers's most recent works (*Le Coeur absolu* (1987) and *Les Folies françaises* (1988)), the playful exploration of the drama of the male subject's sexual psyche is frequently the central theme: these texts hover between the categories of fiction, literary essay and autobiography. This does not suggest that a return to psychological realism or a romanticization of the author is taking place; rather, the auto-biographical trend in recent writing demonstrates an attempt to maintain the plural and unrestricted nature of writing. Far from privileging authorial discourse, such writing submits the figure of the author and his/her subjectivity to intense scrutiny.

A frequent accusation levelled against the *nouveau roman* and, indeed, both modernism and postmodernism is their apolitical nature. Even during the phase of rampant textual materialism, Ricardou and others were still able to claim that avant-garde writing was inherently political by its very existance. By subverting conventional forms of representation and by foregrounding the reflexivity of the text, the dominant ideology could be in a sense unmasked. This view involves an updating of what is essentially a Brechtian formulation: self-conscious-ness in formal terms will induce a socio-political *prise de conscience* on the part of the audience/readership, making it hostile to repressive ideological discourses. Whilst not all the *nouveaux romanciers* would embrace this perspective with the enthusiasm of the *Tel Quel* group (whose combination of Marxism, psychoanalysis and radical semiotics made it particularly receptive to this positivistic role for avant-garde writing), Robbe-Grillet has always upheld the validity of this critical function. The contestation of meaning can be regarded as a funda-mentally transgressive practice which can have a liberating effect on the reader – hence his emphasis on the value of the ludic aspect of fractured narrative which had a 'carnivalesque' role (almost in the Bakhtinian sense) of freeing the reader. In his Nobel Prize acceptance speech, Claude Simon also considered marginalized writing to be subverting totalitarian political control at least implicitly. In this speech, Simon has recourse to the theories of the Russian Formalist school of criticism to support many of the arguments he puts forward on behalf of the inherently political viability of a formalist aesthetic. Univocal meaning could be suppressed by evolving texts which are heterogeneous, polyvalent and thus, by their very nature, interrogative and oppositional. The plurality and mobility of the modern experimental text was therefore, by its very rejection of the techniques and assumptions of the classic, realist, bourgeois novel, contravening the ideology on which such novels rest. The major difficulty, however, with this view is that it stems again from a misreading of realism.

The modernity or postmodernity of the *nouveau roman* resides not only in the degree to which the novels in question are transgressive in narrative terms, but also in the extent to which they call into question the legitimacy of the practices they install. It can be demonstrated that they go beyond mere autorepresentation, and that they contextualize in a variety of ways, as the recent autobiographical texts demonstrate. Parody, self-quotation, the mixing of writings and culturally defamiliarizing strategies place the *nouveau roman* firmly within postmodernism. It could be argued that there can be no more suitable example of the 'epistemic break between the modern and the postmodern' (Hutcheon 1988: 51). The pluralizing nature of texts as varied as Robbe-Grillet's *Le Miroir qui revient* and *La Maison de Rendez-vous*, Claude Simon's *Triptyque* and *Les Géorgiques*, Pinget's *L'Apocryphe* and Sarraute's *Enfance* places them firmly within the postmodernist camp. Claude Simon's novels disprove the proposition that the *nouveau roman* is 'dehistorical': almost all of his novels engage directly with the epistemological and ontological status of the encounter with history. Marguerite Duras's *L'Amant* and *La Douleur* bear witness to real, historical events; indeed, her fiction as a whole is particularly susceptible to politicizing readings because of the presence of feminist and colonial concerns. If a definition of postmodernism rests on the removal of subjectivity, then several of the *nouveaux romans* cited demonstrate forcefully that the subject is a site of contradictions. As Linda Hutcheon has stated:

> Postmodern discourses both install and then contest our traditional guarantees of knowledge, by revealing their gaps or circularities. They suggest no privileged access to reality. (Hutcheon 1988: 157)

It would be difficult to find a better description of precisely those textual practices in the later manifestations of the *nouveau roman*.

An examination of the development of the *nouveau roman* displays exactly those difficulties with periodization which have beset postmodernist poetics, calling into question the legitimacy of literary history as a critical practice itself. It has been central to the *nouveau roman*'s poetics to establish a literary-historical metanarrative as a legitimizing strategy. Postmodernism has created a reading community with specific expectations and evaluative criteria of its own. It is important to take into account how this readership has been constructed and to recognize the danger implicit in the formulation of a totalizing version of literary evolution.

4 Italian Fiction in the Nineteen-Eighties

Michael Caesar

The terms 'postmodern', 'postmodernism' and their affiliates have not so far been accepted in Italy, except, for the most part, vaguely, in reports from overseas. They are acknowledged to have a specific connotation in architecture; particular moments of contemporary Italian culture, though bearing a local label – that of the 'trans-avant-garde' (*transavanguardia*), coined for the visual arts by Achille Bonita Oliva (1984), or the philosophical notion of 'weak thought' (*pensiero debole*), theorized in a series of books and essays by Gianni Vattimo, Pier Aldo Rovatti and their colleagues (cf. Vattimo and Rovatti 1983, Vattimo 1985, 1987) – are recognized as possessing at least a family resemblance to the more general phenomenon of 'postmodernism'. In literary criticism, the idea of the postmodern has scarcely taken hold at all. That is not to say that such an idea, or something like it, is not necessary in Italy. Insofar as the 'post' of postmodernism points to a lack, an emptying of a previous content, an absence of positive connotations to the present, then the term might do quite well to describe the current mood of dissatisfaction in Italian literary culture. Simply used as a marketing term, to designate a fashionable commodity, it might also have appealed to publishers, had it been available at the time, as a packaging for the wave of fiction that followed in the tracks of Eco and Calvino in the early and mid-1980s, and for which no better epithet could be found than 'new' or 'young' (despite a number of its representatives being somewhat less than youthful).

I would not wish by the foregoing to convey any sense of a lack of seriousness on the contemporary Italian literary scene. On the contrary, what is happening, and has been happening over the past ten years or so, raises very serious questions indeed. There appears to have been a return to narrative, with more titles published and more copies sold (although it must always be borne in mind that the Italian literary market is a relatively small one). The reflowering of narrative has taken place without reference to one particular school or movement, to one genre or style. Old certainties – the idea of a fundamental division between 'realism' and 'experimentalism', for example – have been superseded by a new pluralism. Italian fiction, for a long time predicated on an absolute distinction between 'high' or 'quality' writing and 'popular' writing, and, with few exceptions, limited in its 'higher' forms to an alternation between social observation and psychological introspection, has changed its shape: the detective story, the thriller, the Gothic fantasy, science fiction, the romance, all now occupy an honoured place in what is accepted as 'serious' fiction. The result is a sense that a great deal is going on, although how good all this writing is and, even more significantly, what the make-up of the new public and the social function of its reading are are matters for debate.

Beyond the obvious success (relative) of much recent Italian fiction, from Calvino to Tabucchi, from Eco to De Carlo, there surfaces from time to time the obstinate question, What can we now ask of literature, fiction in particular? There was a time when its readers expected the novel to inform or to instruct, to contribute to the definition of a direction for society. As recently as the late 1950s when Pasolini wrote his two novels of, and largely in, the language of the Roman slums, at least part of his purpose was to stun his reader into recognition of a hidden social reality. That purpose might be challenged, as it was by the neo-avant-garde of the early 1960s (cf. Hutcheon 1977 and Wagstaff 1984), in the name of a radically different literary project, wherein the text draws attention not to the outside world, but to its own procedures. But now the question is whether anything can be asked of fiction at all. It exists, in a variety of discrete forms, being everything and nothing. It seems not theoretically mistaken, but simply anachronistic, an error of praxis, for Goffredo Fofi to complain about the lack of writing which confronts the terrible realities of Italian public life in the 1970s, 'that tells who we are, that is immersed in the lives of everyone' (Fofi 1985: 13). Such a book, or books, might exist or come into being, but there is no reason, in the present literary economy, why they *should*. The critic, no longer speaking for a collectivity, if he/she ever did, cannot summon writing forth. Never as in a time like the present – of radical social change in Italy as in other European countries, of the transition from an industrial to a service economy (Italy's second major economic revolution in 30 years), of the questioning of many social values, above all in the matter of social relations (between the sexes, between friends, between producer and consumer), of profound uncertainty about the future, commingled with fear, anxiety and even expectation – never has the impotence of literature been so apparent, its inability to say the word which, in Montale's phrase, 'squares us off on every side' (Montale 1977: 47). Yet one understands and sympathizes with the reader who urges for that word to be said (even as he/she understands that it cannot be), and no amount of earnest preaching that this is the way things are, that no certainties can be reached, will attenuate the sense of frustration that accompanies our contemplation of the ruins.

1 Calvino and his contemporaries: De Carlo, Del Giudice, Celati

Italo Calvino's last complete book, *Mr Palomar* (1985), opens to the movement of waves and the look of a solitary observer whose gaze attempts to follow the progress of one single wave in its passage, separated and isolated from that of all the others, from open sea to shore. Mr Palomar, the observer, is a nervous man, living 'in a frenzied and congested world' (Calvino 1986: 4): congested not only with other humans like himself, crowding preferably into places which seem to reflect back at them mute incomprehension of their triumphant ubiquity (the zoo, the garden of rocks and sand of the Ryoanji of Kyoto), but criss-crossed furthermore with signals and signs, simultaneously requiring and resisting interpretation. Mr Palomar's attempt to isolate the wave is a difficult and repeatedly unsuccessful one. But where does the difficulty lie? In the things themselves? In Mr Palomar? Neither of these, strictly, is the territory of Calvino's fiction, which focuses rather on the relation between the two. Mr Palomar is aware that the words we use to ask the questions and phrase the answers determine the very reality which they are intended to interrogate. The little waves 'strike' the shore, the high part of an advancing wave is a 'hump'; looking to another portion of creation, it would surely be better, but impossible, just to 'observe' the behaviour of migrating starlings than to try to understand it through the conflicting 'explanations' that have been proposed for it. Visiting the ruins of Tula in Mexico, Mr Palomar is torn between interpretation and non-interpretation, between the explanations of his knowledgeable friend, who transforms each mysterious stone into 'a cosmic tale, an allegory, a moral reflection', and the attitude of the teacher with his little party of schoolchildren who resolutely refuses to speculate on meaning, preferring simply to show his pupils the thing that is there. Not knowing whether to interpret or not, and trying to decide between two impossible alternatives, is a characteristic problem for the 'nervous' Mr Palomar who, 'to defend himself against the general neurasthenia . . . tries to keep his sensations under control insofar as possible' (4).

In his precisely delineated observation of the world, Calvino's Palomar is an emblematic figure of recent Italian fiction. Neither a sociological nor a psychological type, he represents an assemblage of mental attitudes, providing a kind of vade-mecum and at the same time an ironic counterpoint to the anxieties of a public that is presumed by the book itself to have lost faith in totalizing explanations and englobing narratives. In the face of such a generalization, it is worth pausing for a moment to take stock of the kind of observer that Palomar is *not*. Stefano Tani has already pointed out that Calvino's idea of observation, within his wider poetic of 'seeing', is a different matter from the 'impassive and indifferent, basically *blind*, gaze that we have inherited from the *nouveau roman*'. Calvino's, and Palomar's, gaze, on the contrary, is interrogatory, teasing out the meaning of things, impartial but never impersonal or 'inert' (Tani 1986: 122, 124). This is true of some of the younger Italian writers too, but not of all: Andrea De Carlo, for example, puts much more 'personality' into his observing heroes and heroines than the *nouveaux romanciers* ever did, but it is a very different personality from that of Palomar. It is true that, as Calvino himself declared in his generous presentation (on the back cover) of De Carlo's first novel *Treno di panna* (*Cream train* 1981), the book recounts a youth made up, among other things, of sharp-eyed observation and an 'insatiability of the eyes'. Giovanni Maimeri wants to see, certainly, and gradually assembles the kind of equipment that a modern, young observer needs, a second-hand Ford to cruise the Los Angeles freeways in, a telephoto lens. His alertness, however, hardly resembles the quizzical interrogations of the puzzled but essentially self-effacing philosopher Palomar; it is the wide-awakeness of a picaresque hero on the make. The narrating self not only sees, but wants to be seen to be seeing: the registration of detail, also praised by Calvino, and the reproduction of objects, gestures and expressions are conscripted into a form of obsessive and narcissistic display on the part of the observer. What is seen takes second place to the act of seeing. Much of what is seen, furthermore, the 'reality' of the narrator's experience, conveys the impression of having been seen already. For all his doubts and self-irony, Palomar still wants to penetrate the secrets of the world and, to this end, what is seen acts only as a means of activating the thoughtfulness of language. Whether the explorations of language, with all their risk of being self-defeating, are successful is another question. But compared with the world of De Carlo's first novel, where the information garnered by the eye leads to no critical interrogation of reality, Palomar's, and Calvino's, project seems almost hopeful.

Mr Palomar can be read as a series of representations of the world, attempted reproductions and descriptions of the out-there being constantly modified in the light of new experience and new information. The observer's readiness to modify is admirably honest (Mr Palomar is a *nice* man) and ultimately exhausting: the process of adjustment can go only so far before atrophy threatens. Each of Palomar's observations is a quest and each, in itself, a failure (even though the book, taken as a whole, conveys no sense of waste or disappointment but, on the contrary, of something rather noble and achieved).

Quests and questions of a distinctly Calvinian kind are the stuff of the two very intelligent novels published to date by Daniele Del Giudice: *Lo stadio di Wimbledon* (*Centre Court* 1983) and *Atlante occidentale* (*Western atlas* 1985), both of which also have a metaliterary dimension which links them to Calvino's other influential late novel, *If on a Winter's Night a Traveller* (1983). The first follows the attempts by the first-person narrator to reconstruct the life and inner motivation of the Triestine man of letters, Roberto ('Bobi') Bazlen (1902–1965), whose literary ambitions were realized solely through the promotion of other writers and never through a completed work of his own. From the tracking of this 'non-writer', Del Giudice proceeds, in the second novel, to the portrait of a fictional novelist who, on the brink of receiving the Nobel Prize, acknowledges with joy that he has passed beyond writing:

I do not think that I am claiming any particular credit if it seems to me that I have traversed writing in all forms, as best I could. Now I have emerged from it, just as happy. I have always been waiting, all my life, for writing and story-telling to be transparent to me as well; that moment has arrived . . . (Del Giudice 1985: 30)

The metaliterary component is not so much in the existence of characters who discourse on the state of the art, even obliquely, through the exploration of writing's other – through non-writing or no-more-writing – as in the project of the central characters, which is an essentially dramatic one: that of trying to imagine themselves into the world of another. In *Lo stadio di Wimbledon*, the young researcher is drawn in search of his elusive quarry by the few traces that remain: the occasional photograph; a few letters and other writings; the memories of surviving contemporaries. The effect of his successive encounters and discoveries – which are very sparse – is that things become more complicated, or rather, that they become increasingly difficult to describe, to 'capture'. At a certain point in his investigations, at the harbour in Trieste, the narrator imagines the pleasure felt by the midshipman who at that moment is explaining the lay-out and workings of his ship to two visitors, giving all the parts of the ship and all the instruments their proper names, which 'have no synonyms' (Del Giudice 1983: 44); and muses further on his own dreams of navigation, envying the midshipman 'the way in which he concentrates on the angle and the height, and his habit of considering himself in relation to something', above all 'the exactitude of the chart' (45). He envies too the regularity, the normality of a life at sea and the unique relation of those who work it with the element by which they are surrounded: 'The water opens and closes continuously, and only those who are on board know that they have really passed through. Just the act of passage is a complex one' (46). This is an important recognition for the narrator, for gradually in his quest for Bazlen he too comes to accept that he is 'passing through', and that the truth of which he is in pursuit is not an object fixed in time and space. He cannot approach it by superimposing successive and ever more accurate (more informed) mental approximations to the real thing; he cannot name it, like an object, without fear of equivocation; but rather it lies here, in the moment through which he is passing, and the important thing is to see that.

The dialectic between 'passage' and 'approach' is played subtly in both novels. Simply to pass risks a sense of purposelessness; but the purposefulness of approach requires delicacy and tact. In *Atlante occidentale*, the writer Ira Epstein meets the particle physicist Piero Brahe after a near collision in mid-air between their two light aircraft in the skies above Geneva. Brahe works on the CERN accelerator (which the novel assumes to be completed and functioning); his experiment involves close and constant watching of the monitor which will tell him when the 'event' has taken place. This is not, however, a novel about two cultures, but about two people, about friendship. The approach of the two men to each other is conducted like a ritual, a crucial moment of which comes when they go up in a plane together for the first time. Brahe 'shows' Epstein his work – that is, he flies him around the 30-kilometer circumference of the accelerator which is buried deep underground, pinpointing the surface features and describing their relation to the features concealed below the surface. Epstein then insists that Brahe should 'tell' him about his work, but that he must use the right words, the words that he would use with his scientific colleagues. Brahe complies, and they enter into a description of the accelerator and the experiment, the details of which are covered for the reader (not for them) by the engine noise:

> Epstein as he listened leant towards Brahe, and Brahe as he spoke leant towards Epstein, and they were so involved with each other, and in any case the engine noise was so continuous and enveloping, like the air, that no-one, behind them, could have heard anything! (Del Giudice 1985: 120)

This small but central incident might serve as a model for Del Giudice's representation of knowing – the broad sweep, an outline superimposed on a subterranean reality; the naming of things in a concentrated and satisfying way; these as the preparation for meetings that are both intellectually passionate and composed, without possibility or need of further elaboration.

There is a passage in *Mr Palomar* which plays on the dialectic between speech (or communicative language) and silence and which might be taken to foreshadow the structure of the book as a whole. Curiously enough, it is introduced by Palomar, yearning for the knowledge provided by precise denomination: every summer he listens to the birds in the garden and does not know what birds they are. But it is not Palomar's regrets at not having cultivated 'precise nomenclature and classification' that concerns us here.

> After a while the whistle is repeated – by the same blackbird or by its mate – but always as if this were the first time it had occurred to him to whistle; if this is a dialogue, each remark is uttered after long reflection. But is it a dialogue, or does each blackbird whistle for itself and not for the other? And, in whichever case, are these questions and answers (to the whistler or the mate) or are they confirmations of something that is always the same thing (the bird's own presence, his belonging to this species, this sex, this territory)? Perhaps the value of this single word lies in its being repeated by another whistling beak, in its not being forgotten during the interval of silence.
> Or else the whole dialogue consists of one saying to the other 'I am here,' and the length of the pauses adds to the phrase the sense of a 'still,' as if to say: 'I am here still, it is still I.' And what if it is in the pause and not in the whistle that the meaning of the

message is contained? If it were in the silence that the blackbirds speak to each other? (In this case the whistle would be a punctuation mark, a formula like 'over and out.') A silence, apparently the same as another silence, could express a hundred different notions; a whistle could too, for that matter; to speak to one another by remaining silent, or by whistling, is always possible; the problem is understanding one another. Or perhaps no one can understand anyone: each blackbird believes that he has put into his whistle a meaning fundamental for him, but only he understands it; the other gives him a reply that has no connection with what he said; it is a dialogue between the deaf, a conversation without head or tail. (Calvino 1986: 22)

These reflections do not come at the end of the piece – Palomar then goes on to make analogies with human communication – but they do encapsulate its essential spirit and that of many other pieces in the book. Observation is at a certain point self-effacing; interrogations cancel each other out. Inquiry reaches a point of maximum tension, then cannot proceed further. Impasse is reached. The tension is resolved, the impasse broken, by pushing on, to the next moment, the next story or reflection. But there is no interconnection between these moments: although there is a recognizable Mr Palomar throughout, operating in a recognizably similar environment from one piece to the next, there is no attempt to construct a coherent and consistent account from his scattered observations. What the reader comes across are events, flashes, brief encounters, steps on a journey, though what the shape and direction of the journey itself might be is hard to say.

A similar structure may be discerned in Del Giudice's novels (which tend to the episodic), but is decisive in another important book of the mid-1980s, Gianni Celati's *Narratori delle pianure* (*Story-tellers of the plains* 1985), a book with which Celati returned to writing after seven years of 'silence' and critical and theoretical reflection. The 'plains' in question are the flatlands of the Po Valley, stretching from the region around Milan in the west to the river-delta in the east, and the 'story-tellers' are the anonymous sources of the tales that Celati relates. Each of the 30 stories in the book bears a relation, sometimes strong sometimes tenuous, to a place on the schematized map with which the reader is presented when he/she opens the volume. This map and the sense of movement from one place to the next form the frame of the book, equivalent to Boccaccio's paradisiacal garden to which his story-tellers have fled from the plague-infested city, and it ensures that *Narratori delle pianure* is read not as a collection of stories, but as a succession. That said, it is also true that each of these stories is self-contained and, like each of Palomar's two or three-page reflections, suggests concentration. The stories read as distillations of the life or experience of ordinary people (working people, lower-middle-class and also the 'emarginated', the young, the unemployed, the old) plucked from a grey background where nothing appears to be going on.

The stories themselves do not, however, recount an exceptional event, indeed they seldom focus on a single event at all. Rather, they represent (in very few pages) the continuities of people's lives through and beyond the ordinary accidents of birth, marriage, death, fortune and misfortune. A hairdresser believes he sees the ghost of a fellow-soldier; spends some years in a mental hospital; on his release is rejected by his wife who he believes is 'denying him his existence'; begins to think that everyone else is denying him his existence, perhaps because he was once shot at by a German and they all think he is dead; spends his Sundays looking into the river for the bullet which missed him; after his death, his wife discovers she is pregnant; she lets it be known that the hairdresser has spoken to her by night and told her 'he was very happy that she had recognized the child as his, because that way she had stopped denying him his existence'; when eventually she moves away from Piacenza, the hairdresser stops speaking to her by night. A woman spends many years charring in Cremona; she saves all her money to buy an apartment for her son when he gets married; her no-good husband, the boy's father, reappears after years and demands assistance; she refuses; when the son is engaged, she relents and negotiates subsidies to her ex-husband, for a suit, a car, a wedding-present; she organizes a big reception to which she invites all her former employers; nobody comes except a tennis-star; there is no sign of the husband; her lawyer tells her that the girl her son is marrying is her husband's mistress and that he had already taken over the apartment; she reflects a moment and decides to carry on with the reception, everything is all right, 'if no one notices anything, it is as though nothing has happened'; passers-by are invited to join the wedding-party, which they happily do because the tennis-star is present; the husband turns up in his new car; no one takes any notice of him because no one knows who he is, except for the dealer he sometimes does jobs for, who tells him all new cars lose half their value as soon as they are bought and end up on the scrapheap anyway.

These tales are told with an extraordinary lightness: the frequency of the present or the perfect as narrative tenses; the adoption of a simple but precise vocabulary; the sparing use of adjectives; the composition of short, essential paragraphs added one to the other, not like bricks, in the conventional metaphor of story-building, but more like transparent balloons lifting the story off the ground – with all of these techniques, Celati has created a mode of story-telling which shakes off the weight of narrative in what is a conscious and consistent effort to pare away the superstructure of ideology and 'that homogeneous and totalizing continuity that is called history' (Celati 1975: 14; cf. West 1986: 70). In his travel across the plains, Celati has created a space which may be filled with meanings, but where no single or definitive meaning can be imposed. Neither origins nor ends predetermine meaning, which for the reader may rest as much in the gaps between the stories as in the stories themselves, in their continuity and succession as in their uniqueness and completion. Indeed, at a certain point the stories come to seem almost like pauses, moments of reflection perhaps, in a wider discourse that envelopes the written word, such as to make the readers of Celati's narrative acknowledge something in common with Palomar listening to his blackbirds, uncertain which part of their communication is language, which silence.

2 Metaphors of space and time

Mention of the transversal space explored by Celati provokes a more general consideration of place and time in contemporary Italian narrative, starting from the marshy area where fiction borders with reportage. Italy has at the moment no Bruce Chatwin or Paul Theroux, and the history of Italian travel-writing belongs more to the sixteenth and seventeenth centuries than to the nineteenth or twentieth, but it is possible to discern an interest in the imaginative and expressive possibilities of travel-writing in the work of some contemporaries who are not travel-writers as such. I would particularly mention two books by Antonio Tabucchi: a collection of 'fragments' centred on the Azores entitled *Donna di Porto Pim* (*Woman of Porto Pim* 1983) and a quest-novella whose protagonist moves the length and breadth of India, *Notturno indiano* (*Indian nocturne* 1984). In *Donna di Porto Pim*, the archipelago is represented by a variety of means: the memory of the narrator and the inhabitants; stories; legends; document; biography; a map; a historico-topographical description; fiction; what the author calls 'guided fiction', that is, a story based on an overheard conversation; dreams and, finally, a bibliography of the impressions of earlier writers, those 'honest travel-books' which 'have the power to offer a theoretical and plausible *elsewhere* to our overwhelming, inescapable *where*' (Tabucchi 1983: 9). From none of these can the reader derive any composite picture of the Azores. The place is experienced as an accumulation of its pasts, a wreck like those whose flotsam litters its shores and provides the walls and furniture and windows of one of its villages, described by the English travellers Joseph and Henry Bullar in 1841 and revisited by Tabucchi 140 years later (29). It is experienced by the narrator as a place where he, the cultivated, Portuguese-speaking, well-read foreigner, must tread with care; an old man, who is paid to sing typical local songs for the tourists, recognizes the narrator as something different from them but also as different from himself:

> You are curious, you are looking for something else, because this
> is the second time that you have invited me to have a drink, you
> order *cheiro* as though you were one of us, you are a foreigner and
> pretend to speak like us, yet you drink little and then you stay
> silent and wait for me to speak. (78–9)

The old man does tell the visitor the story of the woman of Porto Pim (and his own), but there remains something menacing about the silence of the listener-narrator, as though he were taking something away with no intention of giving anything in return. The closest thing to an acknowledgement of what this might be comes at the end of the splendid description of a whale-hunt, which has all the care for technical precision of a Del Giudice (71–7), when the old whaler asks the narrator why he wanted to join the expedition that day, whether it was just out of curiosity (76–7).

As against this oblique and moving meditation on last things, departure, relics, abandonment, the quest of *Notturno indiano* adopts a different metaphor: that of the journey as mirroring or reflection. While in *Donna di Porto Pim*, the writer, having sailed for many days and nights, has understood that 'the West has no end but continues to move as we move, and that we can follow it as far as we like and never reach it' (Tabucchi 1983: 13; the notion is echoed in the title of Tabucchi's later novel, *Il filo dell'orizzonte* (*The horizon's edge*, 1986)), the Indian journey proceeds, not always straightforwardly, towards an end of a sort. The stages of the journey are so many acts of self-questioning and self definition; its end a moment of self-recognition which is, however, also a reversal of the narrator's image, as in a mirror (Roux the pursuer is identified with Xavier the pursued, the first and last letters of their names are switched, Xavier is now Mr Nightingale, or *rouxinol* in Portuguese). The ending of the novel is too pat and contrived, but in the course of it Tabucchi has created an India which is constantly surprising and challenging to the European traveller/narrator/reader without ever allowing its mysticism or its exoticism to run away with it, for the sub-continent is also an ironically observed tourists' India of hotels, buses, taxis, sights and restaurants.

While the other, the elsewhere, is used by Tabucchi to measure the self, the 'where', his narrator is not in awe of the other. Otherness is not so much something to be frightened of, a threat to the stability of the self, as something that can be added to or incorporated into the already existing. *Notturno indiano* tends in fact to a conciliatory posture. In other contemporary Italian fiction, widely contrasting realities are juxtaposed to more dramatic effect. Two novels, for example, which in other respects are very different, Claudio Piersanti's *Charles* (1986) and the first of Aldo Busi's three novels published to date, *Seminar on Youth* (1988), have this in common: they both veer between an urban setting whose contemporaneity is underlined by its fashionableness and topicality (Busi) or which is vaguely futuristic (Piersanti) and a rural, provincial past which, though overtaken by the modern world, still remains extraordinarily alive. There is no sense of development between these two spatial blocks, no continuity. It is as though, in literary terms, the peasant world, defined by neo-realism, and the disembodied, technocratic environments of the neo-avant-garde had been lifted out of their historical context and plastered together in a sharply disjunctive collage.

The crisis of identity suggested by this violent displacement is reflected in the themes of the two novels. In *Charles*, the rural past plays a more traditional, but still surprising, part than in Busi's novel. The story centres on Giorgio, a successful eye-surgeon working in Paris and his *alter egos*: his much younger brother Piero, who is caught up in the obscure 'manoeuvres' going on in Sicily (it will turn out that he has sabotaged an American helicopter and is on the run), and Charles, a 12-year-old boy who is at the centre of the whole story. There is a strong thriller element to the novel, particularly in the last part, in which Piero is tracked down by the agents of what is portrayed as something close to a police or military state in the underground corridors of the prison-like block of flats where Charles lives and the fugitive has been hiding. It is from this forbidding, inhuman Paris, projected into the not-too-distant future, that Giorgio returns to his childhood haunts in the Abruzzi. What is surprising is not that the rural past should be called up, but that the writer should invest it with the imaginative and emotional power that he does. The countryside has a dignity in Piersanti's novel which keeps it from becoming a mere object of nostalgia. Given the assertiveness and self-advertisement of modernization in Italian life across all forms of culture, from literature to political and social theory, during the 1960s and early 1970s, this return assumes something of the force of a revenge or, at any rate, a restitution. Written by a 32-year-old who had already published in the libertarian vein of the student movement which erupted in Bologna in 1977 (*Casa di nessuno*, *No one's house* 1981), such a move might seem like a premature return to order. But the plot takes us back to Paris and its police for the dénouement of the story, and it is there that the real and menacing power is seen to reside. The patriarchal values of the countryside seem unthreatening by contrast, much as they do in Francesco Rosi's film *Three brothers*, in which a similar transaction between city and countryside is followed through.

The rural patriarchy is anything but unthreatening in the autobiographical novel by Aldo Busi (but on autobiography, Busi warns: 'I contain my book, my book does not contain me': Mondello 1984). On the contrary, it represents the backdrop of repression and barbarity against which the young Barbino proclaims his homosexuality and on which he contemptuously turns his back. *Seminar on Youth* (and its sucessors) is a novel which in many ways goes against the grain of recent writing in Italy: quite at odds with the studied poise of Tabucchi, the selective precision of *Narratori*, or the deceptively balanced complexities of Calvino, Busi's language is rich, extravagant and, to use the adjective which so irritated Gadda, 'baroque'. It is a gargantuan language spilling out from the talker who once he opens his mouth has no intention of shutting it again. The art of vituperation comes naturally to Busi, and, although the picture of Northern Italian provincial life (in the vicinity of Brescia) which the author paints occupies only a small part of the novel, which takes his picaresque hero on to greater things in Milan, Paris and London, it is a memorable picture, and provides the necessary underpinning to a writing that spares no effort to make the reader understand the nature of the social and sexual domination.

These two novels suggest in their different ways that the relation between province and metropolis, countryside and city, periphery and centre, ever potent themes in modern Italian writing, is open to reinterpretation and reorganization into new narrative and symbolic combinations. One example is the combination of a rural petty-bourgeois ancestry and the children of those parents, who live a very different life in a future which is already upon us, as in the two novels already discussed and, to some extent, in Marco Lodoli's *Diario di un millennio che fugge* (*Diary of a millennium in flight*, 1986); the protagonists of these fictions seem to belong neither to the past nor to the future, but to be caught in between, in some time-slip between the nineteenth and the twenty-first centuries. The sense conveyed here of transition, of one age giving way to another, of an approaching end, a decadence, an *Untergang* – veering violently in its emotional response between nonchalance and terrible fear – is in some ways more disturbing than the resolutely futuristic or science fiction settings of the very talented Stefano Benni, who has been compared, not without reason, to Vonnegut (Tani 1986: 134–8), or the sub-human dystopia created by the Sienese poet Attilio Lolini in his only novel to date, *Morte sospesa* (*Suspended death* 1987), in which a man stumbles through the aftermath of what Loloni describes as 'an ordinary apocalypse', trying to confess to a horrible and long-forgotten crime of which no one will believe him guilty.

In discussions of the recent Italian novel, however, most attention has been focused on its treatment not of the future, but of the past. There has been in the 1980s in Italy, as elsewhere, a revival of historical narrative in which, however, the reader is not allowed to take the authenticity and authority of the historical material for granted. Umberto Eco's magisterial novel *The Name of the Rose* (1983), for example, plays on the dialectic between the reader's curiosity about the medieval world and his/her almost total ignorance of it (funnelled, as Eco explains in his *Reflections* on the novel, through the observations of the novice Adso (Eco 1985: 33–4); between the sense that the historical world (the abbey and the cultural and religious context of the time) is a world of its own and the sense that it is connected to the world of the reader. The real protagonist of the novel is knowledge – the knowledge of the late-medieval philosophers and scholars about the natural and spiritual universe; the knowledge of the investigator, William of Baskerville, about human nature and the politics of the religious orders; the knowledge gradually acquired by the reader of an unfamiliar subject. The novel proves that knowledge is possible, but also that it is in a sense artificial: it does not come *from* the past, historical knowledge in particular cannot simply be uncovered, laid bare and put out to view (or rather, the novelist can no longer create the illusion that the past is speaking for itself); it is a construction *of* the past, and the reader is conscious of, and in compliance with, the careful disposition and organization of the disparate elements that go to make up the whole edifice. Whereas in the classic Italian historical novel, Manzoni's *The Betrothed* (1827), much admired by Eco, the omiscience of the author consists in his ability to probe at will into the psychology of his characters and, at the same time, to link this to broad historical movements and even some sense of a providential 'plot' in history, in Eco it is closer to the power of the master craftsman who can make what he will with the materials to hand, and unmake it too. This is perhaps what is most satisfying about the conflagration at the end – the child/builder/master mason has knocked down his tower of bricks. And it is from this point of view that I would endorse the observation made by Gian Carlo Ferretti about this and other historical novels (by Saltini and Mancinelli, for example), that:

> In these novels, 'history' no longer (as in the past) provides illusory certainties nor is a gallery of misleading models; but neither is it a moment of critical verification or problematical comparison. For better or worse, it is a de-historicized 'history': a reservoir of literary and cultural materials that can be drawn on precisely for the purpose of making novels; a reservoir, more exactly, of cultures, themes, characters, rhetorical forms, stereotypes and structures . . . (Ferretti 1981)

A fascinating example of the dehistoricization of history is provided by the two novels published to date by the poet Roberto Pazzi, *Cercando l'imperatore* (*Looking for the Emperor* 1985) and *La principessa e il drago* (*The Princess and the Dragon* 1986), both set in the last years of Tsarist Russia. The first in particular is an accomplished piece of work. Two separate but converging stories are recounted in alternating chapters: the story of the White Russian Preobrajensky regiment under the command of Prince Ypsilanti, which for two years, cut off from contact with the outside world, marches through Siberia trying to reach the Tsar, and that of Tsar Nicholas II himself and his family in their last months, especially during their confinement at Ekaterinburg. The forced march through Siberia becomes increasingly desperate and hallucinatory (in fact Ypsilanti is, from the outset, clear in his own mind that they will never find the emperor): when the regiment comes to cross the *tajga* in July 1918, the forest takes on the appearance both of a paradise regained and of a place of horror, endless in extent, haunted by marauding tigers and ghostly tribes. In parallel, the inner life of the Tsar and that of the two most visionary of his children, the haemophiliac Tsarevich Alexis and the daughter Tatiana, becomes increasingly burdened and tormented by visions. The two stories are linked towards the end by reciprocal dreams (in which the protagonists dream of each other) and by the symbolic flight of hundreds of birds, the migrating souls of the dead soldiers and the doomed imperial family.

The novel exercises considerable power over the reader, perhaps because of this duality, because, as Giovanni Raboni suggests in his Preface, it articulates two typical and basic forms of the narrative imagination, 'the claustrophobic fascination of imprisonment, exile' and 'the adventurous-picaresque fascination of the journey, of a search across hostile and uncertain spaces' (Pazzi 1985: x); because of its capacity, to paraphrase Angelo Guglielmi, to tell a story of life while it is telling a story of death (Guglielmi 1985). But despite the fact that at first sight the novel looks as though it is going to offer a fairly conventional, though well-written account of an actual incident, this is not a book from which to learn about Russian history. No doubt the evocation of a specific and well-known moment of the twentieth--century past corresponds to the needs, not only of the author – whose reactionary views are amply documented in his frequent interviews – but also to a public that does not necessarily share those views, but appears to be fascinated by the spectacle of a culture in decline or at its end. Contrary to the process in Eco's novel, Pazzi effects a caesura between past and present in a way that is disturbing – the fascination of his novel is also a morbid one. His past is made up very largely of futures – plans, expectations, anxieties, fantasies, dreams and visions– but they are futures which are closed: every forward thought is stalked by death. If the present, our present, has a place in the novel, it is as something that is looked to and not seen; we do not exist.

3 Genre and the market

It is not only its intrinsic qualities which have guaranteed Umberto Eco's novel its prominent position in the Italian literary scene. With the uncanny sense of timing which has characterized Eco's writing career, *The Name of the Rose* epitomizes, almost in counterpoint to Calvino, certain conditions of the contemporary novel. The knowing use of the conventions of the detective story to write something that is not quite a detective story not only follows a rather well-established practice in post-war Italian writing, of which the novels of Gadda and Sciascia are the best-known examples (cf. Tani 1984), but is part of a more recent trend on the part of 'serious' fiction to incorporate what hitherto tended to be regarded as 'popular' genres: the detective story (*giallo*) in Stefano Benni's *Comici spaventati guerrieri* (*Comic frightened Warriors*, 1986) and in Gianfranco Manfredi's two novels to date; the thriller in De Carlo's *Uccelli da gabbia e da voliera* (*Cage Birds and Aviary Birds*, 1982) and, in a form largely hidden by the luxuriance of the language, in Aldo Busi's most recent book *La Delfina Bizantina* (*The Byzantine Dolphin*, 1987); science fiction (Benni's *Terra!*, 1983); the fantastic, with its recurring topic of 'doubles', in another novel published by the enterprising Ancona firm Il Lavoro Editoriale, Claudio Lolli's *L'inseguitore Peter H.* (*Peter H. the Shadow*, 1984). A special *frisson* seems to be guaranteed for readers who think they are readers if the object of the mystery is itself a literary (or artistic) artefact – the manuscript in *The Name of the Rose*, the novel in Francesca Duranti's *The House on Moon Lake* (1987), the unwriting writer in Del Giudice. Laura Mancinelli's *Mozart's Ghost* (1986) combines two rather donnish mysteries: the protagonist is pursued by 'anonymous' telephone calls which consist of nothing but music by Mozart; when she is spared further harassment by the entire Turin telephone system seizing up, she goes off in pursuit of the concealed manuscript of Plato's last dialogue. Along with the mingling of the genres go the other stylistic features of a rather modish postmodernism: pastiche; montage; paraphrase; parody; allusion; quotation; often adding up to no more than a cultivated *divertissement*. While a number of writers have profited from Eco's example, they seem less exercised by the specifically creative problems with which, if we are to follow the *Reflections*, he was faced as a working author, not least the problems of how to say anything about anything without sounding unbearably false:

> Is it possible to say 'It was a beautiful morning at the end of November' without feeling like Snoopy? But what if I had Snoopy say it? If, that is, 'It was a beautiful morning . . .' were said by someone capable of saying it, because in his day it was still possible, still not shopworn? A mask: that was what I needed.
> (Eco 1985: 19)

There is a carnival spirit abroad in contemporary Italian writing, with a lot of masks being worn, but a depressing sense that a few of them have much to hide. It is perhaps because of an effort to buck the trend towards an insufferable and market-conscious cleverness that we are witnessing an attempt amongst more committed narrators to seek out a way of dealing directly with the emotions, without all the paraphernalia of intrigue and description that has accumulated over the past few years. Celati's unadorned 'tales from the plains' is one example; the second novel of a talented young writer, Enrico Palandri, is another. Already in his first novel, *Boccalone* (1979), widely recognized as the best to come out of the youth movement of the late 1970s, Palandri had shown an extraordinary ability to create sufficient space for his characters, 'enrico' and 'anna' and their friends, to speak for themselves without being overwhelmed by the surrounding clutter or by the pretensions of 'literature', pretensions from which the narrator keeps his distance: 'I don't want to make big speeches, I never did when I was with anna and I was better off; I just want to recount incidents and let the rest come out of that, if there actually is anything' (Palandri 1979: 124). In *Le Pietre e il Sale* (*Stones and Salt* 1986), Palandri tells a story of adolescent love and adult corruption in a manner which generated mixed notices in Italy, many seeing it as simply a return to the 'shopworn'. But while some moments, particularly settings (the school, the petty-bourgeois home, the professional home) and situations, seem highly formalized, even stereotypical, the deliberately paced dialogue and unhurried tone of the narration allow the novel to achieve a rare psychological density.

The idea that the only way of coping with the desuetude of the age, its profound certainty that everything has been said already, is by openly proclaiming this fact as itself the new fact, the idea that the only way of selling your article as original is to declare that it is repro, seems to run up against an ethical objection in a writer like Palandri, however sophisticated his own literary apparatus undoubtedly is. The notion of pastiche is now a guiding thread in critical discourse, to the extent that Palandri's novel can be put forward as 'a disturbing attempt to write a kitsch novel' (De Michelis 1986a), and the argument be made – referring to Piersanti's *Charles* – that no novelist born in the 1950s can return to 'traditional narrative' without being aware that he/she is 'holding an old toy which might look fine in an antique shop, or might be an ornament or a collector's item, but is no good for playing with any more'; if they do use it (but why should they if it is no use any more?), it is with a mixture of pleasure and melancholy, 'like someone repeating a game which once gave pleasure for years and years and now gives none, only the memory of the joy it once gave' (De Michelis 1986b). These are 'novels squared, novels of novels', a formula which tells us little about the actual narrative rendition of the works in question, but a great deal about the unhappiness of the critic.

Authors, readers and critics, however, are no longer the only actors on the stage. Publishers have come to assume an ever more prominent role. It is not perhaps since Romanticism that there has been so much discussion, and underlying uncertainty, about the market of literature, and it is no accident that recent years have seen an expansion of the sociology of literature as an academic discipline, alongside increased research into reading habits, the best-seller and how to write it, and the levels of writing that appeal to different strata of the public. Perhaps the only firm conclusion to emerge from this continuing debate is the recognition that the literary scene has become pluralistic. In particular, the traditional, if untheorized, distinction between serious literature and 'rubbish' has broken down; as Franco Fortini said, the occasional slummings of the aristocratic writer of the past have given way to a situation in which we all live off the 'guano' which our society produces day by day (Cadioli and Peresson 1984: 85). American (and, to a lesser extent, British) criticism has tended in the past to be less hierarchical than Italian and at the same time more alert to very minute differences in the type of product and the type of consumer being aimed at by the literary market. Italy is moving rapidly in that direction, in pursuit of something that is 'enjoyable' at the same time as being 'not escapist' , that magic formula which Eco believes to have been the discovery of the American postmodernists (with Barth as their prophet) and to which in his own best-seller he aspired (Eco 1985: 65–72).

5 Spanish America's New Narrative

James Higgins

Recent decades have seen a remarkable flourishing of Spanish-American fiction. The emergence of the so-called 'new narrative' presupposes the existence of an 'old narrative' which it superseded and, in effect, the early 1940s may be regarded as a watershed. The preceding decades had been dominated by the old-style realism of the regionalist novel, which reached its high point in the 1920s with the publication of José Eustasio Rivera's *The Vortex* (1924), Ricardo Güiraldes's *Don Segundo Sombra* (1926) and Rómulo Gallegos's *Doña Barbara* (1929) and produced its last major work, Ciro Alegría's *Broad and Alien is the World*, in 1941. The new narrative itself falls into at least two phases. In the 1940s and 1950s a new kind of fiction began to be cultivated by the likes of Borges, Onetti, Sábato, Asturias, Carpentier, Rulfo, Arguedas and Roa Bastos. Properly speaking, therefore, the new narrative pre-dates the so-called 'boom', a term which is sometimes erroneously used as a synonym but which in fact refers to a process which took place in the 1960s and continued into the 1970s, when Spanish-American fiction won increasing recognition outside Latin America itself and achieved unprecedented commercial success. Essentially, the boom revolved around four figures who rapidly became international celebrities – Cortázar, Fuentes, García Márquez and Vargas Llosa – and, in the wake of their success, other writers such as Lezama Lima, Donoso and Cabrera Infante came to prominence. At the same time, as a result of Spanish-American fiction's growing popularity, the work of the earlier writers mentioned became more widely known and some of them went on to enhance their reputation by producing new works in the 1960s and 1970s. Finally, towards the end of the 1960s, a second wave of successful new writers emerged in the shape of younger figures like Puig and Bryce Echenique. The following table, though by no means exhaustive, lists the major writers and their principal works.

1 The pre-boom (1940s and 1950s)

Jorge Luis Borges (Argentina): *Fictions* (1944); *The Aleph* (1949)
Juan Carlos Onetti (Uruguay): *A Brief Life* (1950); *For a Nameless Tomb* (1959); *The Shipyard* (1961); *Body Gatherer* (1964)
Ernesto Sábato (Argentina): *The Outsider* (1948); *On Heroes and Tombs* (1961); *Abaddon the Exterminator* (1974)

Miguel Angel Asturias (Guatemala): *The President* (1946); *Men of Maize* (1949)

Alejo Carpentier (Cuba): *The Kingdom of This World* (1949); *The Lost Steps* (1953); *Explosion in a Cathedral* (1962); *Reasons of State* (1974)

Juan Rulfo (Mexico): *The Burning Plain* (1953); *Pedro Páramo* (1955)

José María Arguedas (Peru): *Deep Rivers* (1958); *All Bloods* (1964); *The Fox Above and the Fox Below* (1971)

Augusto Roa Bastos (Paraguay): *Son of Man* (1960); *I the Supreme* (1974)

2 The boom (1960s and 1970s)

Julio Cortázar (Argentina): *The Winners* (1960); *Hopscotch* (1963); *62: A Model Kit* (1968)

Carlos Fuentes (Mexico): *The Death of Artemio Cruz* (1962); *A Change of Skin* (1967); *Terra nostra* (1977)

Gabriel García Márquez (Colombia): *No One Writes to the Colonel* (1961); *Big Mama's Funeral* (1962); *One Hundred Years of Solitude* (1967); *The Autumn of the Patriarch* (1975)

Mario Vargas Llosa (Peru): *The Time of the Hero* (1963); *The Green House* (1966); *Conversation in the Cathedral* (1969); *The War of the End of the World* (1981)

José Lezama Lima (Cuba): *Paradiso* (1966)

Guillermo Cabrera Infante (Cuba): *Three Trapped Tigers* (1967)

José Donoso (Chile): *The Obscene Bird of Night* (1970); *A House in the Country* (1978)

Manuel Puig (Argentina): *Betrayed by Rita Hayworth* (1968); *Heartbreak Tango* (1969); *Kiss of the Spider Woman* (1976)

Alfredo Bryce Echenique (Peru): *A World for Julius* (1970); *So Many Times Pedro* (1977)

The regionalist novel represented a kind of literary discovery of America, in that it revealed to an urban public the conditions of life in the remote, underdeveloped areas of the continent's interior: the plains; the jungle; the Andes. In the main, it was a documentary type of novel which aimed to be an authentic depiction of a particular environment, and as such it tended to continue the tradition of nineteenth-century realism. It was also a didactic novel that set out to expose social injustice, to diagnose problems of national development or to vindicate local cultures. In fairness, it should be said that the best of the regionalist novels were considerably more complex and accomplished than they are usually given credit for, but, nonetheless, the regionalist novel as a whole came to be identified with a type of writing against which later writers reacted, one which, in its concern to document and to convey a message, was artistically clumsy and simplistic in its presentation of reality. What distinguishes the new novelists from their regionalist predecessors is, above all, their attitude towards the writer's craft. As has been implied, the motivation of the regionalist novelists was often extra-literary, the novel being used as a vehicle to draw a particular situation to the eyes of the world, to influence public opinion and, thereby, to bring about social change. In contrast, the new novelists consider themselves first and foremost to be creative artists whose main obligation is to produce a well-crafted work of art that stands up in its own right as an autonomous reality. Indeed, in reaction to the documentary pretensions of regionalist fiction, they sometimes insist on the fictionality of their work. A case in point is Gabriel García Márquez's *One Hundred Years of Solitude*, on whose closing page the last of the Buendía family finally succeeds in deciphering the hitherto incomprehensible manuscript presented to the family by the mysterious gypsy Melquíades, only to discover that it is an account of the history of the Buendías written 100 years before, that they will cease to exist when he finishes reading it and that he is, in effect, no more than a creature of Melquíades's imagination, with no existence outside the pages of the manuscript. Such an ending serves, among other things, to warn the reader that the novel is, in David Gallagher's words, 'a fictive construct, a creation, and not a mirror that meticulously reflects reality' (Gallagher 1973: 88).

Another major difference between the new novelists and their regionalist predecessors is that, whereas, by and large, the latter were men of limited cultural formation, the former are generally much more widely read, more cosmopolitan in outlook, more in tune with developments on the international literary and intellectual scene. One only has to note the impressive erudition manipulated by the likes of Borges, Cortázar, Carpentier or Fuentes or the intertextual references that abound in the new narrative to realize that the Spanish-American writer has long since ceased to be a provincial and is now very much a citizen of the world. Moreover, while the new narrative has un-doubtedly been influenced by European and North-American fiction, and by Joyce, Faulkner and the *nouveau roman* in particular, the new novelists have had the maturity and self-confidence to assimilate influences and to develop their own distinctive literary voice, and thus to make their own original contribution to world literature. Spanish America's new narrative has therefore to be seen not only in its local context, but in wider terms as part of the evolution of modern fiction generally.

Like most modern literature, the new narrative reflects the onto-logical uncertainty of contemporary man. Emblematic in that respect are the short stories of Jorge Luis Borges which debunk man's intellectual pretensions and express scepticism about his ability to understand his world. 'Death and the Compass', for example, parodies the detective story to satirize the faith in reason which that genre epitomizes. The story may in fact be read as an allegory in which the detective's attempt to solve a series of crimes by the use of logic represents man's efforts to decipher the meaning of the universe, but he himself ends up as the final victim, undone by his misplaced confidence in his intellect and baffled by a confusing world that makes a mockery of his pretensions to explain it. The afore-mentioned tendency of writers to insist on the fictionality of their work is to be understood partly in the context of the attitude here expressed by Borges. When, in *One Hundred Years of Solitude*, the last Aureliano Buendía tries to persuade others of the truth of his version of certain events, he runs up against the scepticism of the local priest who, ironically, is conspicuously lacking in the certainties which he is supposed to embody:

> The priest measured him with a pitying look. 'Oh, my son,' he sighed. 'I'd be satisfied if I could be sure that you and I exist at this moment.' (García Márquez 1978: 330)

Effectively, García Márquez is here waiving any claim to be 'telling it the way it is', for the new novelists no longer share traditional realist fiction's confident assumption of man's ability to understand and describe the world. Scepticism with regard to the writer's power to translate reality into words is taken even further by Guillermo Cabrera Infante in *Three Trapped Tigers*, where endless word-games, irreverent discussions of literature and parodies of various literary styles all point to an acute sense of the treachery of language. Indeed, one of the characters even goes so far as to advocate an aleatory literature which, abandoning all pretence of saying anything, would provide the reader with dice and a random list of words and leave him/her to make of it what he/she may.

In a whole variety of ways, the new narrative challenges the traditional perception of an ordered and coherent world which underpins realist fiction's pretension to reproduce reality in literature. One procedure, favoured by Mario Vargas Llosa in particular, is to abandon a linear plot in favour of a disconnected narrative which confronts the reader with a world that is confusing, shifting and elusive. Thus, the fragmented structure of *The Green House*, which changes in form, style, time, place and protagonists every few pages, conveys an image of Peru as a disunited nation, divided by geography, levels of development, culture, race and class, and of the world as a chaotic labyrinth in which disoriented individuals struggle in vain to find some coherence. Other writers undermine conventional notions of reality by blurring the frontiers between the real and the imaginery. A favourite device of Borges, for example, is to toy with the reader by sprinkling his fictions with references to real people and places, a technique used to good effect in 'Tlön, Uqbar, Orbis Tertius', whose realistic trappings lend credibility to the story of a non-existent world which is the reverse of our own, while the fictional world in its turn calls into question the reality of the one in which we live. However, the work which most dramatically highlights the unreliability of the world and of literature's portrayal of it is perhaps José Donoso's *The Obscene Bird of Night*, whose schizophrenic narrator/protagonist experiences modern man's ontological insecurity as a psychological condition. In recounting the story of his life, he assumes a variety of identities and gives multiple conflicting versions of events in a contradictory attempt to acquire the sense of identity he has always lacked and to conceal himself from a world by which he has always felt persecuted. As Pamela Bacarisse explains:

> Many pieces of information given to the reader are subsequently contradicted, many of the events recounted are then said not to have happened, there are conversations which may or may not have taken place and characters are themselves then someone else, or themselves *and* someone else. (Bacarisse 1980: 19)

The end result is a novel in which it is impossible to be sure of anything.

Such scepticism about literature's power to duplicate reality leads the new novelists to shun the stance of the traditional, omniscient narrator with a total overview of the world he is describing. In some cases, the author seeks to disguise his presence and distances himself from the narrative by employing techniques such as interior monologue, dialogue and intermediaries, which simultaneously highlight the subjective nature of the material presented and create the impression of an autonomous narration. An outstanding example of this type of narrative is Vargas Llosa's *Conversation in the Cathedral*, which pivots around a four-hour conversation between two characters, the whole novel being made up of dialogue and narrative units generated in waves by the central conversation, as the two men's review of their past lives sparks off inner thoughts and recollections and conjures up other conversations and dramatized episodes. In contrast, other writers abandon all pretence of detached objectivity and deliberately flaunt their presence, thereby foregrounding the subjective nature of their narrative. Cabrera Infante, among others, repeatedly draws attention to his role as author, while the narrator of Alfredo Bryce Echenique's *A World for Julius* not only maintains a running dialogue with the reader, but also involves himself with his characters, putting himself in their shoes, addressing them directly as if they were there alongside him and, like a supporter at a sporting event, siding with some against others. A consequence of the demise of the traditional, omniscient narrator is that the new narrative invites, and requires, the active participation of the reader, who, in the absence of authorial guidance, must disentangle the complexities of the text for him/herself to arrive at his/her own understanding of the world described. The new role assigned to the reader is defined in Julio Cortázar's *Hopscotch* by the writer Morelli:

> Better yet, give him something like a façade, with doors and windows behind which there operates a mystery which the reader-accomplice will have to look for . . . What the author of this novel might have succeeded in for himself, will be repeated . . . in the

reader-accomplice. As for the female-reader, she will remain with
the façade . . . (Cortázar 1975: 408)

The reader for whom the new novelist is writing, in other words, is not
the traditionally passive figure who is content to accept and, indeed,
expects a straightforward narrative expounding a clear-cut view of the
world, but an accomplice who will collaborate with the author in the
search for a deeper understanding of a complex and confusing world.

Yet the passage quoted above implies a continuing belief in the
meaningfulness of literature, and it would be fanciful to conclude from
the new narrative's questioning of realism that the novel has been
reduced to a formalistic game, without reference to anything outside
itself. It is true that there is a considerable element of self-referentiality
in the new narrative, in that many novels contain reflections on the
nature of fiction and the problems of writing. It is also true that several
novelists, such as Carpentier and Fuentes, delight in weaving elaborate, formal patterns. And it is also true that much contemporary
Spanish-American fiction has a distinctly ludic quality, with Borges and
Cabrera Infante, in particular, taking pleasure in playing games with
the reader. Yet one text at least makes an explicit profession of faith in
the act of writing. José Lezama Lima's *Paradiso*, a kind of portrait of
the artist, recounting the childhood and adolescence of a young poet,
elaborates a poetics in which words are the tools to understand the
world, to make sense of history and even to achieve transcendence. As
the work of a man who is not only a poet but a Catholic poet, *Paradiso* is
hardly a typical case, but the sheer volume of fiction produced in
Spanish America in recent decades – and continues to be produced –
scarcely betokens a general collapse of confidence in the written word,
and it is noteworthy that Cabrera Infante's *Three Trapped Tigers*, for
example, re-creates the atmosphere of pre-revolutionary Havana even
as it casts doubt on the feasibility of such an enterprise. Most of the new
novelists, in fact, set out to portray in their works the social reality of
their respective countries, and some novels – notably Carpentier's
Explosion in a Cathedral, García Márquez's *One Hundred Years of
Solitude* and Vargas Llosa's *The War of the End of the World* – are
continental in scope, reflecting the reality of Latin America as a whole.
In effect, despite their questioning of the assumptions of realism, and
despite their awareness of the enormity of the task confronted by the
writer, Spanish America's new novelists still aspire, by and large, to do
what novelists have always sought to do, namely, to depict the world in
which they live.

In practice, the new narrative is based in large part on what might be
described as a broader concept of realism, one which takes account of
the complex, multifaceted nature of reality. The fragmented narrative
cultivated by Vargas Llosa, for example, is intended to replicate the
way in which we experience real life, in that events and information are
presented to us in a disjointed fashion and it is only when we have lived

through the reading experience that we are able to piece it all together with the benefit of hindsight. That is not to say that the novels are unstructured, of course. Indeed, montage plays a crucial role in enriching the reader's view of reality, for narrative units are arranged in such a way as to create an interplay, so that they bring fresh perspectives to bear on one another and are mutually illuminating. Another favourite technique is the use of multiple narrators to give differing views of the same reality. Vargas Llosa's *The Time of the Hero*, which is set in a Peruvian military academy where the cadets assume an ostentatious machismo as a survival strategy, oscillates between third-person narration and monologue (interior and spoken) to bring out the gulf between the boys' public personae and their sensitive and vulnerable inner self, and to highlight how social intercourse distorts their personality by conditioning them to suppress their softer feelings. This gulf is shown most dramatically in the surprise ending, which obliges us to re-evaluate our reading of the novel by revealing that the anonymous, timid and sensitive lad who has been narrating the story of his early life in the first person is none other than Jaguar, the aggressive bully we have seen ruling the roost in the school. One of the most impressive examples of multiple narration is Carlos Fuentes's *The Death of Artemio Cruz*, in which the story of a dying ex-revolutionary turned corrupt capitalist magnate is recounted in alternating sequences of first, second and third-person narrative. The third-person sections narrate the main events of his life in a more or less objective manner. His interior monologues convey the thoughts that pass through his mind as he lies on his deathbed and reviews his past life with a mixture of pride and guilt. In the second-person sequences, he is addressed by the voice of his subconscious which, speaking in the future tense, takes him back to relive the moments of truth when he made the choices which were to determine what he later became. This multiple view of Cruz not only gives an insight into the conflicting forces that have been struggling to control his soul, but also reflects his loss of integrity as a man and his disintegration in face of his approaching death. The overall effect is that the morally indefensible opportunist appears as a very human figure, a man who would have liked to have had his cake and eaten it and who, forced to make choices, alternates between self-congratulation and a sense of self-betrayal.

The new narrative also extends the scope of realism by according to the world of the mind the same status as to that of the physical and social world. Subjective reality is treated as no less real than so-called objective reality, and what is thought, felt or imagined is recorded as if it were literally true. The events narrated in Donoso's *The Obscene Bird of Night*, for example, are largely a working-out of the fantasies and obsessions of the narrator/protagonist, Humberto Peñaloza, who, as secretary to Don Jerónimo Azcoitía, lives on the fringes of the privileged world of the oligarchy, and whose dreams of joining the ranks of the upper classes are counterbalanced by a humiliating sense of social inferiority. In one of the central episodes in the novel, Humberto not only cuckolds his employer, but fathers on his wife the heir whom the oligarch himself has never been able to engender, and it is only subsequently that it becomes clear that what has been narrated as a factual account of events is, in reality, no more than a fantasy in which he simultaneously avenges his social humiliation and effects the incorporation of the humble Peñaloza line into the oligarchy.

A somewhat different case is García Márquez's *One Hundred Years of Solitude* which recounts the history of the small town of Macondo, not so much as it actually happened, but as its inhabitants experienced and interpreted it and as it was transmitted by popular oral tradition. Thus, when Remedios the Beauty disappears, the narrative records the fact that outsiders were of the opinion that she had run off with a man and that the story of her ascent into heaven was an invention of her family to cover up the scandal. But it is the family's version which the texts privileges and recounts in full detail, for this view of events is entirely consistent with the cultural assumptions of an isolated rural people and, indeed, is regarded as more credible than wonders of modern technology, such as the cinema. This type of so-called magic realism assumes major importance in the fiction of Asturias, Carpentier and Arguedas, where it serves to give expression to the magical-religious thought and mythical world-view of the Indian and Negro peoples of Latin America.

Another way in which the new narrative extends the range of traditional realism is by re-creating modes of spoken speech, not for reasons of costumbrism or authenticity, but to portray a society through the way in which it expresses itself orally. Bryce Echenique's *A World for Julius*, for example, captures the peculiarly honeyed speech of Lima's upper classes to mirror the pampered, insulated existence of the Peruvian oligarchy. Similarly, in Cabrera Infante's *Three Trapped Tigers*, a picture of pre-revolutionary Cuban society is conveyed on a linguistic level, through the reproduction of the type of language spoken in Havana at the time, the country's dependent status and cultural inferiority complex being reflected in self-consciousness about speaking Cuban, in the aping of cultured Spanish and in the widespread use of Spanglish. Likewise, Manuel Puig's *Betrayed by Rita Hayworth* and *Heartbreak Tango* are based on interior monologues, long dialogues and extracts from diaries and letters, through which Argentina's provincial lower middle classes reveal their lack of a sense of identity of their own in their assumption of a borrowed identity derived from pop culture in the shape of Holywood films, radio soap operas, popular songs, etc. Orality is also a feature of the fiction of Juan Rulfo, whose *Pedro Páramo* re-creates the world of rural Mexico through a narrative which initially appears to be a conventionally written text but turns out to be constituted orally, with one of the characters, Juan Preciado, emerging as the internal author as he recounts his own story and hears and transmits those of the other characters. Rulfo's oral style – which manifests itself in this novel and in the stories of *The Burning Plain*, in the frequent repetition of words and phrases, in a manner typical of the backtracking of oral narrative – is, of course, much more than a formal device, for its function is to take us inside the world of a rural peasantry whose cultural tradition is non-literate. Another writer who seeks to give expression to a popular oral culture is José María Arguedas, whose fiction portrays the world of the Indian peasantry of the Peruvian Andes. Arguedas, however, was faced with the thorny problem of translating into the alien medium of Spanish the sensibility of a people which expresses itself in Quechua, and his great achievement has been to evolve a style which captures the rhythm and flavour of Quechua to convey the spiritual world of the Andean Indians.

While the new narrative is based in part on a broader concept of realism, it also seeks to increase the expressiveness of prose by representing reality in a non-mimetic manner, encapsulating it in the way that poetry has traditionally done. In García Márquez's *One Hundred Years of Solitude*, for example, the telepathic communication, which confounds the laws of nature to reunite José Arcadio and Ursula in spirit at the moment of his murder, is conveyed symbolically in physical terms: the son's blood goes in search of the source from which it sprang, climbing kerbs, doing right-angled turns and running along the walls to avoid staining the carpets, and, as the mother follows the trail back to his body, it becomes a kind of monstrous umbilical cord re-establishing the pre-natal bond between them. In Rulfo's *Pedro Páramo*, likewise, the frustration that embitters the eponymous protagonist's life and the dashing of illusions that is the pattern of existence as depicted in the novel, are symbolized by an episode in which young Pedro and his lover climb a hill and fly a kite in the shape of a bird, only to see the string break and the kite fall back to earth, and the novel as a whole is punctuated by recurrent images of rising and falling which reiterate the central theme of the thwarting of human hopes and aspirations. Some novels, indeed, do not operate primarily on the level of plot, but develop an internal theme through the use of recurrent motifs. Such is the case of Miguel Angel Asturias's *The President*, whose underlying theme is the breakdown of all normal human relationships in a society ruled by an oppressive dictatorship. Thus, the protagonists' encounter with a postman who is too drunk to articulate properly or to deliver his letters, which he keeps dropping in the street, is one of a series of symbolic episodes expressing the generalized breakdown of communication in a country that has lost all sense of social cohesion.

One of the main forms of figurative expression employed by the new narrative is myth, many novels being structured on a mythical framework. Asturias's *The President*, which recounts the story of the dictator's henchman who falls out of favour when, under the influence of love, he repents of his misdeeds and changes his ways, re-creates in inverted terms the myth of Lucifer's rebellion against God. Ruling over an infernal world, the President is cast in the role of Satan, while his favourite, Angel Face, is identified with Lucifer, but his rebellion takes the form of forsaking evil for good, a crime of treason for which he is banished to the bowels of the earth in the President's deepest dungeon. This mythical treatment of dictatorship not only gives the novel a more universal dimension, but communicates the fundamental struggle between human decency and selfishness that lies behind the political struggle. Similarly, Rulfo's *Pedro Páramo* centres on Juan Preciado's pilgrimage to his birthplace, the town of Comala, to seek out his father, an archetypal journey representing the Mexican's quest for identity and, more generally, the human search for happiness. The journey, however, proves to be a descent into hell, for Comala turns out to be a ghost town which has been devastated by the oppression of his father, the tyrannical landowner Pedro Páramo, and whose few remaining inhabitants live in despair, convinced that they have been banished forever from the grace of God. Moreover, the narrative, based on Mexican myths about life after death, is narrated from the grave, where Comala's former inhabitants, far from finding release in the afterlife, are condemned to relive eternally the frustrations and torments of their earthly existence.

Implicit in the new narrative's challenging of the assumptions of realism and in its privileging of subjective reality and of figurative forms of expression, is a questioning of the rationalist, cultural tradition of the West. Many of the new novelists, in fact, portray the alienation of Western man. Larsen, the protagonist of Juan Carlos Onetti's *The Shipyard*, for example, caricatures the thrusting, social-climbing heroes of nineteenth-century fiction by assuming charge of a shipyard and paying court to the owner's daughter, but the world in which he operates grotesquely parodies the industrial age's spirit of optimism and progress, for the owner is bankrupt, his daughter is mad, the decaying yard is no longer operational and the two remaining employees spend their time reading out-of-date files. Larsen, in fact, represents the alienated hero who seeks to come to terms with an absurd world by entering into the game, by playing out a meaningless life as if it were meaningful. More generally, Onetti's disenchantment with Western civilization expresses itself through protagonists who are at odds with society and seek to create their own alternative reality. However, the writer who most explicitly questions the Western cultural tradition and proclaims the need for an alternative way of relating to reality is Julio Cortázar. The central theme of *Hopscotch* is the quest for the authenticity which Western man has lost, stifled by a distorting rationalism and by the conventions of the bourgeois social order. The protagonist Oliveira refuses to submit to the accepted norms and, instead, surrenders himself to the irrational, seeking to live on a more authentic and vital dimension which appears absurd by conventional standards. As the title indicates, life is presented as being like a game of hopscotch, the object being to find a way to the square of ultimate reality. In a whole variety of ways, the novel shows conventional Western modes of thought and behaviour to be absurd and an obstacle to that goal. In particular, it does not have a fixed structure and, instead, we are offered two alternative ways of reading it. It may be read in the conventional order, with or without the final section of 'dispensable' chapters, or in a shuffled order, interpolating the 'dispensable' chapters according to the author's directives so as to have fresh perspectives on the events described. The order of the book as laid out is thus merely a façade, disguising a deeper, underlying order, and, in effect, what Cortázar is inviting us to do is to throw off our habitual passiveness, to reject the given and to join him and Oliveira in their quest for a different, more authentic order. The result is that, whereas, for the passive reader, the novel effectively ends with Oliveira seemingly about to commit suicide by throwing himself out of a window, the active reader goes beyond this to the understanding that Oliveira's jump into the void is a metaphorical leap into a metaphysical state, where conventional categories are abolished and dualistic contradictions reconciled.

It could be said, however, that this type of critique of Western rationalism itself belongs to a tradition within Western culture. More fundamentally, the new Spanish-American narrative challenges Euro-centrism by expressing a Third-World experience and by drawing on its own local cultural tradition. It is true that the Spanish-American novel has entered the mainstream of world literature in that it is informed by the major intellectual currents of our age, in that its exponents share the artistic and philosophical preoccupations of modern writers in general, and in that it has consciously sought and attained a universality that earlier Spanish-American fiction sometimes lacked. That universality, indeed, is one of its main strengths. Part of the richness of Rulfo's *Pedro Páramo*, for example, is that Juan Preciado's archetypal journey creates universal resonances by evoking parallels with Greek myths, such as those of Telemachus and Orpheus. Yet to impose a purely 'universal' reading on a novel such as *Pedro Páramo* is to impoverish it, for it also – and more immediately – conjures up associations with the ancient Mexican myth of Quetzalcoatl's journey to Mictlan, the kingdom of the dead, and the world into which we are introduced is one where the indigenous cultural tradition constitutes a living presence. Likewise, the dictator of Asturias's *The President* is identified not only with Satan but with Tohil, the Maya Quiché deity who demanded human sacrifice, the effect of that association being to present the Central-American political despot as a modern incarnation of an ancestral tradition. As William Rowe (1984) has argued, a universalist approach to Spanish-American fiction incurs the risk of domesticating and falsifying texts whose subversiveness derives, in large part, precisely from their specificity.

In many works, in fact, the Latin-American people's struggle against social, political and economic domination expresses itself in cultural terms, in resistance to the dominant culture imposed by Western imperialism. This conflictive relationship between popular culture and official culture manifests itself in Augusto Roa Bastos's *Son of Man*, in the life-sized figure of Christ carved by a leper, which, despite the disapproval of the ecclesiastical authorities, is venerated by the townsfolk of Itapé in preference to the stylized crucifix in the local church. For, as a representation of the Paraguayan people's suffering and of a hoped-for redeemer who is one of their own, it articulates popular sentiments and aspirations in a way that institutionalized religion has failed to do in its subservience to an oppressive social system. Likewise, in Alejo Carpentier's *The Kingdom of This World*, an account of slave revolts in Haiti at the end of the eighteenth century, the Negroes' struggle for liberty opposes their magical world of voodoo to the rational, cerebral world of their French masters. And in Asturias's *Men of Maize*, which deals with the expropriation of Indian communal lands for the commercial exploitation of maize, the Guatemalan Indians' resistance to the destruction of their way of life is waged not only with arms, but also through the myths by which they preserve their concept of the world. For his part, Arguedas shows in his fiction that, despite centuries of oppression, the Indian peasants of the Peruvian Andes have retained their sense of identity by clinging to their traditional culture. In *The Fox Above and the Fox Below*, a greater threat to that identity is seen to be the capitalist, industrial development of recent decades, which has attracted a massive flow of migrants from the countryside to the cities and brought with it an erosion of traditional values and ways of life. But the pervasive and insidious presence throughout the novel of manifestations of Quechua culture suggests the ability of that culture not only to survive in an alien environment, but also, as it itself is modified, to exercise an 'Indianizing' influence on the country as a whole. However, such works do not merely show the dominant culture being resisted and subverted by popular culture; in their form, they themselves have been influenced by the culture which they depict. *The Fox Above and the Fox Below*, for example, is structured on Andean organizing principles and develops a style of 'oral writing' that transposes popular Quechua art forms to the printed page, and Rowe notes 'the compositional impact of popular oral culture in García Márquez, that of Guaraní culture in Roa Bastos, and of middle-American culture in Asturias' (Rowe 1984: 85). In much Spanish-American fiction, in effect, the élitist, Western medium of the novel is being subverted by popular culture.

Behind this privileging of popular culture lies not only an identification with the oppressed masses, but also a sense that Latin-American reality is radically different from that of the developed, industrial West, as well as a search for an identity whose roots are to be found in Latin America itself. Carpentier, in particular, explores Latin America's relation to the Western world, notably in *Explosion in a Cathedral*, which portrays Caribbean society against the background of the French Revolution, and, in all of his works, implanted European systems are seen to be inappropriate to the American environment. Embodying the alienation of the Westernized Latin-American intellectual, the protagonist of *The Lost Steps*, a musician resident in New York, recovers his lost identity as a man and as an artist when he undertakes an expedition to the jungles of the Orinoco, a journey that takes him backwards in time to a prehistoric world; but his eventual return to civilization implies a recognition on Carpentier's part that, for a twentieth-century Latin American, going back to one's roots has to be compatible with the realities of the modern world. That same problem is treated in Arguedas's *Deep Rivers*, the story of a young boy, Ernesto, who identifies emotionally with the Indians among whom he was brought up and who, on moving to school to receive the education that will equip him to take his place in society, finds himself alienated in the world of the whites. What sustains him is the comfort he derives from the spiritual world of the Indian, as he escapes the alienating environment of the school to listen to Quechua music and to renew his bonds with the magical world of nature, but his experiences call into question the effectiveness of Quechua values in the white world in which he must live. However, the novel's climax, which sees the Indians successfully assert themselves, reflects Arguedas's confidence in the ability of Quechua culture to flourish beyond its traditional rural confines and to change the character of national society.

In conclusion, the vitality of Spanish-American fiction in recent decades indicates that, despite an ironic awareness of the limitations of literature, writers have retained the ambition and confidence to tackle major themes. Its quality is a measure of the craftsmanship which they have brought to their writing. For, above and beyond the 'theory' underpinning the new narrative, the most significant development is that Spanish-American writers have become accomplished practitioners of their trade.

Part Two:
The Critical Agenda

6 Discourse, Power, Ideology: Humanism and Postmodernism

Linda Hutcheon

1

Figurations, usually of an ideological origin whether acknowledged or no, will be found in history as well as in the history-like. (Frank Kermode)

In the postmodern 'history-like' – be it in architecture, the visual arts, or literature – the ideological and the aesthetic are turning out to be inseparable. The overt and self-implicating paradox of self-reflexivity meeting historical grounding in the postmodern fiction of, for example, Rushdie, Fowles, Eco or Doctorow resists any temptation to see ideology as that which only others fall prey to. What postmodern theory and practice have taught is less that 'truth' is illusory than that it is institutional, for we always act and use language in the context of politico-discursive conditions (Eagleton 1986: 168). Ideology both constructs and is constructed by the way in which we live our role in the social totality (Coward and Ellis 1977: 67), and by the way we represent that process in art. Its fate, however, is to appear as natural, ordinary, commonsensical. Our consciousness of ourselves is usually, therefore, uncriticized because it is familiar, obvious, transparent (Althusser 1969: 144).

When these practical norms move from asserting how things are to claiming how they ought to be, we can begin to see the connections between ideology and existing relations of power. From the earlier Marxist notion of ideology as false consciousness or an illusory belief system, we have moved, in current critical discourse, to a different notion of ideology as a general process of production of meaning (Williams 1977: 55). In other words, all social practice (including art) exists by and in ideology (Coward and Ellis 1977: 72), and as such, ideology comes to mean 'the ways in which what we say and believe connects with the power-structure and power-relations of the society we live in' (Eagleton 1983: 14). Much of the impetus to this redefining of ideology and to its newly important position in recent discussions of art has come from a reaction against the liberal humanist suppression of the historical, political, material and social in the definition of art as eternal and universal. Postmodern theory and practice have worked to contest this suppression, but in such a way that their implication in the underlying humanist value system cannot be ignored.

Postmodern fiction – that is, what I would like to call 'historiographic metafiction' – foregrounds the problematic and complex relationship that has always existed between the formal concept of the text and the socio-political one of ideology. It also demands a concept of ideology that is concerned equally with dominant and with oppositional strategies (Kress 1985: 29), for it incarnates the contradictions of their interaction. The romantic and modernist heritage of non-engagement insists that art is art and that ideological discourse has no place in the literary (see Graff 1983). Added to this historical separation is a suspicion of the artistic that is general in much of the Anglo-American world, a view that sees art as trivial, insignificant, imaginative and therefore cut off from the social and historical realities of life. This is a view implicitly shared by commentators from both ends of the political spectrum, from the neoconservative to the Marxist.

Nevertheless, postmodernist art and theory have self-consciously acknowledged their ideological positioning in the world, and they have been caused to do so not only in reaction to that provocative assertion of triviality, but also by those previously silenced 'ex-centrics', both outside and inside the supposedly monolithic culture of the West. These are the 'different', those whose marginalization has taught them that artists should indeed have 'inherent political status because they are perceived as dealing with belief' (Sukenick 1985: 82). I am reminded of that scene in Salman Rushdie's *Shame* in which the narrator attends a production of Georg Büchner's play, *Danton's Death*, in a largely empty theatre: 'Politics empties theatres in Old London town' (Rushdie 1983: 240). However, his three guests, visitors from Pakistan, love just being in a country where such plays can even be performed. They tell the story of the military censors at home, preventing a production of *Julius Caesar* because it depicted the assassination of a head of state – until a British diplomat was persuaded to play Caesar, and Shakespeare's play could become a patriotic call for the overthrowing of imperialism. The narrator adds, forestalling our response, 'I insist: I have not made this up'.

What is at stake in this debate about the relation of the ideological to the aesthetic is the status and definition of art as an institution. With postmodern examples like Rushdie's it is hard to avoid seeing literature as part of 'the apparatus of officialdom that maintains the social and cultural status quo' (Sosnoski 1985: 93). The dominant liberal humanist tradition, in which many of us were trained and in which we still, largely, teach and write, has usually insisted on art's apolitical un-contamination by such overtly ideological agencies. But, as many an oppositional critic has insisted lately, what our official literature curricula are intended to teach (the 'great tradition') is not all they impart. Teaching and writing are forms of institutional politics (see Widdowson 1982). As a category, Tony Bennett has argued, literature 'refers not to the concept of a privileged set of texts which exemplify a universal and eternal aesthetic form of cognition but to a *specific practice of writing*, bound, circumscribed and conditioned by the historical, material and ideological conditions of its production' (Bennett 1979: 15). Postmodernist thought would add, 'and of its reception too'. Such a view recognizes the literary, not as separate (and therefore either privileged or trivialized), but rather as one practice of writing among others, all equally institutionalized: history; biography; philosophy; criticism; theory. This too is the overt lesson of post-modernism's rethinking of the boundaries of these same discourses.

It is the novel genre in particular that has become the battleground for much of this asserting – and contesting – of liberal humanist beliefs about the status and identity of art. Ian Watt's (already ideological) analysis of the rise of the English novel, for instance, has been further politicized lately by those readings of the genre in the light of class and, of course, gender. Lennard Davis has shown that the prevailing *theory* of the novel at its beginnings (as moral, conservative) must be contrasted with the reality of the *form* itself (as morally ambiguous and ambivalently both radical and conservative) (Davis 1980: 113). This would suggest that those postmodern paradoxes of historiographic metafiction are perhaps inherent in the novel as a genre – as defined by Davis as a doubled discourse which ambiguously embodies opposing political and moral functions. That is to say, the novel is potentially dangerous not just because it is a reaction against social repression, but because it also works to authorize that very power of repression at the same time (117). What postmodern fiction does, however, is to reverse that doubled process: it installs the power, but also contests it. Nevertheless, the contradictory doubleness remains.

The literary history of the novel has been inseparable from that of realism. Today, many want to claim that realism has failed as a method of novelistic representation because life now is just too horrific or too absurd. But, surely, Dickens saw nineteenth-century London as both horrific and absurd, yet he used realism as his mode of ordering and understanding what he saw, and thus of creating what we read. It is perhaps this function of realism that we have come to question today, in our self-consciousness about (and awareness of the limits of) our structuring impulses and their relation to the social order. Gerald Graff once tied Eliot's declaration of the obsolescence of fictional realism (in a review of Joyce's *Ulysses*) to the end of the 'world-view of liberal bourgeois individualism, with its optimistic belief in progress and the rational intelligibility of experience' (Graff 1975: 306). Life has not changed, then; but our faith in our ability to make sense of it might have. So too might our belief that any sense we might make could confidently lay claim to universality or 'truth'. Postmodernism suggests that the language in which realism – or any other mode of representa-tion – operates cannot escape ideological 'contamination'. However, it also reminds us, by its very paradoxes, that awareness of ideology is as much an ideological stand as commonsensical unawareness of it. The link between realism and liberal humanism is a historically verifiable one (see Belsey 1980; Waugh 1984), but the postmodern contesting of both is just as ideologically inspired, and considerably more ambivalent.

The postmodern novel, in other words, does not (as Bakhtin claimed of the genre as a whole) begin 'by presuming a verbal and semantic decentring of the ideological world' (Bakhtin 1981: 367). It begins by creating and centring a world – Saleem Sinai's India (*Midnight's Children*) or Tom Crick's fen country (*Waterland*) – and then contesting it. Historiographic metafictions are not 'ideological novels' in Susan Suleiman's sense of the word: they do not 'seek, through the vehicle of fiction, to persuade their readers to the "correctness" of a particular way of interpreting the world' (Suleiman 1983: 1). Instead, they make their readers *question* their own (and by implication, others') interpretations. They are more 'romans à hypothèse' than 'romans à thèse'.

Art and ideology have a long history of mutual interaction – and recuperation – that undercuts the humanist and the more recent formalist separation of the two. Verdi's Israelite chorus, singing of its desire for a homeland (in *Nabucco*), was greeted by its first northern Italian audiences as singing *their* song, in an allegory of their desire to free themselves from Austro-Hungarian rule; it remains the unofficial national anthem of Italy today. In John Berger's postmodern novel, *G.*, the revolutionary crowds gather in northern Italian cities around statues of Verdi, whose very name has come to stand for freedom (but only for some – it means oppression for others): V(ictor) E(mmanuele) R(e) D' I(talia). Berger's text has its own overtly ideological focus which calls our attention to this changing, but real, history of art's implication in the political.

In this novel, there is also a Livornese statue which plays an important allegorical role in the conjoining of the political and the aesthetic. It is a seventeenth-century representation of Ferdinand I, complete with naked and chained slaves adorning each of the four corners. These slaves, we are told, were modelled after local prisoners. This statue comes to be connected to the Risorgimento and then to the revolt of the new slaves – the workers – who have cast off their chains and come to life, in an ironic echoing (ironic because of the class inversion) of the Commendatore's statue in Mozart's *Don Giovanni*. But there are several levels of irony here. First of all, the 'slaves' who come to life are not just workers. Berger makes the connection between the ethnically oppressed of northern Italy – the Slavs (or *sc'iavi*) – and these slaves (or *schiavi*). The hero (known only by the initial G.), though he may die for his political activities, is no resurrected Garibaldi, despite his nickname and his partly Italian blood. He is, if anything, a Don Giovanni, so his death makes intertextual, if ironic, sense. Yet the historical Garibaldi's absent presence haunts the novel, from its early claim that its 'principal protagonist was conceived four years after Garibaldi's death' (Berger 1972: 20). This statement is followed by a long section on the importance of Garibaldi's particular blend of innocence and patriotism to Italian identity and politics. The novel's G. is neither innocent nor patriotic, however, so the link is again a deliberately ironic one.

Postmodern fiction – like Brecht's drama – often tends to use its political commitment in conjunction with distancing irony like this and technical innovation, in order to both illustrate and incarnate its teachings. Cortázar's *A Manual for Manuel* becomes a didactic manual for the revolutionaries' son, Manuel, and the reader, both of whom 'come of age' in the reading of this text. The 'aura' of the original, genuine, single work of genius is replaced, as Benjamin foresaw, by the mechanical reproduction of fragments of history – here, of newspaper clippings embedded in the text we read. But what is gained is an ideological awareness both of the political, social, and linguistic repression in Latin America and also of the modes of possible resistance (see D'Haen 1983: 70–1). The social and historical contexts are made part of the physical text we read, thereby shifting, in Charles Russell's terms (about the work of those other postmodern writers, Robert Coover and Thomas Pynchon), 'the previous social context of rebellion to the social text of ideology' (Russell 1985: 253).

2

Criticism and interpretation, the arts of explanation and
understanding, have a deep and complex relation with politics, the
structures of power and social value that organize human life.
(W. J. T. Mitchell)

Just as metafictional self-consciousness is nothing new (think of *Tristram Shandy*, not to mention *Don Quixote*), so this merging of the ideological and the self-reflexively literary in a historical context is not radically innovative in itself: witness Shakespeare's history plays' self-consciously critical involvement of their audience in the questioning of social action and authority, past and present (Belsey 1980: 95–102). But the particular concentration of these concerns in the theory and practice of today suggests that, here, there may be something we could call part of a poetics of postmodernism. Of all current forms, it is postmodern fiction that, for me, best illustrates the paradoxes of this cultural enterprise. Its self-consciousness about its form prevents any occultation of the literary and linguistic, but its problematizing of historical knowledge and ideology works to foreground the implication of the narrative and the representational in our strategies of making meaning in our culture.

One caution is in order, however. I am not saying that self-consciousness is, by definition, revolutionary or even progressive. Metafiction does not necessarily lead to cultural relevance (cf. Waugh 1984: 18) any more than self-demystifying theory is inherently radical (witness Newman 1985). It is perhaps liberal to believe that any subversion or undermining of a system of thought is healthy and good, but it would also be naive to ignore that art can just as easily *confirm* as *trouble* received codes, no matter how radical its surface transgressions. Texts could, conceivably, work to dismantle meaning and the unified humanist subject in the name of right-wing irrationalism, as easily as left-wing defamiliarizing critique: think of the works of Céline, Pound, and others. Nevertheless, it has become almost a truism of postmodern *criticism* today that the deconstruction effected by metafictional self-consciousness is indeed revolutionary 'in the deepest sense' (Scholes 1980: 212). But the *art* of postmodernism itself suggests a somewhat less sure sense of the inherently revolutionary value of self-reflexivity. The humanist faith in the power of language can be turned in on itself, for historiographic metafiction often teaches that language can have many uses – and abuses.

Language can also be presented as limited in its powers of representation and expression. The self-conscious narrator of Berger's *G.* offers a verbal description of an event and then tells us: 'The description so far as it goes is accurate. But my power to select (both the facts and the words describing them) impregnates the text with a notion of choice which encourages the reader to infer a false range and type of choice . . . Descriptions distort' (Berger 1972: 80). The important things, we learn, are beyond words, 'like an undescribed natural event'. These things are intensely real, however; indeed, more real because they are not articulated or named (159). Yet, paradoxically, the narrating writer has only language to work with and knows he is unavoidably 'a prisoner of the nominal, believing that things are what I name them' (137). Other historiographic metafictions – by writers as diverse as John Banville and Graham Swift – also frequently foreground the practical and theoretical consequences of that humanist faith in language, through their thematization and formal working-out of the ideological issues implicit in the novel genre's representational and narrative identity.

One of the most extreme examples of metafictional self-theorizing about this and other humanist certainties is to be found in Ian Watson's novel, *The Embedding*, in which the linguistic theories of Chomsky, the anthropological structuralism of Lévi-Strauss, and the political perspective of Marx meet to explicate and theorize the narrative's enactment of their implications regarding human mental processes, cultural action, and social organization. All of these theories are shown to be human constructs which can be made to operate in the interests of political power, as well as disinterested knowledge (though the two are inseparable here): they are all – potentially – discourses of manipulation. The constant intertextual presence of the intensely self-reflexive work of Raymond Roussel suggests the further contamination of both ideology with art and art with scientific knowledge, past and future. The real power of both self-referring language and knowledge turns out to be their shared ability to distance us from that brute reality with which no one in the novel seems able to cope. For one of the characters, the moment of panic is this one: 'The world was about to be embedded in his mind in its totality as direct sensory apprehension, and not as something safely symbolized and distanced by words and abstract thought' (Watson 1973: 251). The subjective and the cosmic, the personal and the public cannot be separated in this novel; nor can the aesthetic and the political.

Fiction like this is postmodern because in it language is inextricably bound to the social and the ideological (Kress and Hodge 1979: 15). Some kinds of contemporary criticism have been arguing on a theoretical level what postmodern fiction has meanwhile been busy illustrating as practice: that we need to examine critically the social and ideological implications operative in the institutions of our disciplines – historical, literary, philosophical, linguistic, and so on. The implication is that all theory is political theory, whether it is aware of it or not. In Terry Eagleton's terms:

> Discourses, sign-systems and signifying practices of all kinds, from film and television to fiction and the languages of natural science, produce effects, shape forms of consciousness and unconsciousness, which are closely related to the maintenance or transformation of our existing systems of power. (Eagleton 1983: 210)

For example, current literary theories, especially deconstruction, have been linked to both authoritarian politics (Graff 1979) and revolutionary pedagogy (Ulmer 1985). They have been blamed for the decline of the humanities and exalted as the salvation of the intellectual credibility of the academy. As many have pointed out, deconstruction is certainly compatible with conservative politics (Ruegg 1979) and with a liberal humanist preservation of the canon (Leitch 1980), but there has also been a move to make it into the companion or completion of the Marxist project (Ryan 1982; Spivak 1980). While its oppositional image has made it attractive to leftists, deconstruction (as it is practised in North America) has tended to be apolitical in its exclusive focus on textuality (see Holub 1984: 86–7). We would be wise to heed Edward Said's warning about equating the radical and oppositional in a literary context with the same in a political one (Said 1983: 158–77). It is perhaps telling, too, that deconstructive critics have, by and large, concentrated on canonical texts and avoided postmodern ones which contest, within their own very form, the same notions of unity, originality, coherence, subjectivity, and rationality as does the criticism. The self-consciously theoretical nature of historiographic metafictions like *The Name of the Rose*, *The Book of Daniel*, or *Midnight's Children* might to some extent pre-empt the deconstructive critic's demystifying: their contradictions, or aporias, are overt – and functional.

3

> *Fabrication is surrounded by and in constant contact with the*
> *world: action and speech are surrounded by and in constant contact*
> *with the web of the acts and words of other men.* (Hannah Arendt)

What postmodernism's focus on its own context of enunciation has done is to foreground the way we talk and write within certain social, historical, and institutional (and thus, political and economic) frameworks. In other words, it has made us aware of 'discourse'. As Colin MacCabe has pointed out, the use of that word has become a kind of ideological flag in film (and other) criticism, signifying that the critic does not accept to analyse the formal articulation of a genre independently of its political and ideological address (MacCabe 1978–79: 41). As such, then, 'discourse' becomes an important and unavoidable term in discussions of postmodernism, of the art and theory that will not let us ignore social practices, the historical conditions of meaning, and the positions from which texts are both produced and received (see MacDonell 1986: 12). The diverse theoretical perspectives usually grouped together under the label of 'discourse analysis' share a mode of study which looks at authority and knowledge in their relation to power, and also at the consequences of the moment in history when 'truth moved over from the ritualized act . . . of enunciation to settle on what was enunciated itself: its meaning, its form, its object and its relation to what it referred to' (Foucault 1972: 218).

This suppression of the enunciative act (and its responsibility) has led to the humanist separation of discourse from the exercise of power. Both postmodern art and theory work to reveal the complicity of discourse and power by re-emphasizing the enunciation: the *act* of saying is an inherently political act, at least when it is not seen only as a formal entity or in terms of what was said. In Foucault's words, this is a move to 'restore to discourse its character as an event' (Foucault 1972: 229), and thus to enable analysis of the controls and procedures by which discourse operates (216), both interpersonally and institutionally (Fowler 1981: 7). Art, theory, criticism are not really separable from the institutions (publishing houses, galleries, libraries, universities, etc.) which disseminate them and which make possible the very existence of a field of discourse and its specific discursive formations (the system of norms or rules that govern a certain way of thinking and writing at a certain time and place). So, when we speak of discourse, there is a concrete, material context involved.

Discourse, then, is both an instrument and an effect of power. This paradox is why it is so important to postmodernism. What Doctorow's Daniel learns by writing *The Book of Daniel* is that discourse is, in Foucault's terms, 'a hindrance, a stumbling-block, a point of resistance and a starting point for an opposing strategy' (Foucault 1980: 101). Discourse is not a stable, continuous entity that can be discussed like a fixed formal text; because it is the site of conjunction of power and knowledge, it will alter its form and significance depending on who is speaking, his/her position of power, and the institutional context in which the speaker happens to be situated (Foucault 1980: 100). Historiographic metafiction is always careful to 'situate' itself in its discursive context, and then uses that situating to problematize the very notion of knowledge – historical, social, ideological. Its use of history is not a modernist look to the 'authorizing past' (Conroy 1985) for legitimation; it is a questioning of any such authority as the basis of knowledge – and power. The narrator of *G.* is not content to explain the fact that G.'s mother wanted to be with her child all the time, in terms of general (or 'universal') categories, such as motherly love. He contextualizes it in its time and place and class, telling us that, in upper and middle-class Europe her desire 'would have been treated as hysterical. An infant, like everything else in the nineteenth century, had its own place – which was unshareable' (Berger 1972: 27).

It was Michel Foucault who was most responsible for problematizing the relation of discourse to power. Power, he argued, is omnipresent, not because it embraces all human action, but because it is constantly *being produced*: 'it is the moving substrate of force relations which, by virtue of their inequality, constantly engender states of power' (Foucault 1980: 93). Power is not a structure or an institution. It is a process, not a product. But postmodern thought inverts the power arrangements described by Foucault. He claims there is a doubled discourse: a disavowal and then reinscription of control or power. In postmodern art, there is, instead, an initial avowal or inscription, followed by a challenge to that. It too is doubled discourse but the terms differ, perhaps because it never sees itself as outside power relations – the necessary position from which to be able to disavow. We can speak of power *in* art but also of the power *of* art (Selzer 1984: 87).

Power is also, of course, a dominant theme in historiographic metafiction's investigations of the relation of art to ideology. In William Kennedy's *Legs*, Jack Diamond's desire for money and power over people is matched by Kiki's sexual power and is shared by those in his employ: 'Wasn't it funny how fast Fogarty [Jack's man] could turn somebody's head around? Power in the word. In any word from Fogarty' (Kennedy 1975: 224). The power in the word (or the law) will not save Diamond, however, from the power of politics. Similarly, in *G.*, the passivity of G.'s Uncle Jocelyn is explained in terms of the power of his economic class (the upper class) in Britain at the end of the last century: 'Their power was in no way threatened, but their own chosen image of themselves was threatened' (Berger 1972: 31).

So power is not just a general novelistic theme in this kind of postmodern fiction. It also takes on powerful critical force in the incorporated and overt discourse of protest, especially that of class, gender and racial protest. Toni Morrison's *Tar Baby*, in fact, studies all three – class, racial, sexual power – in their wide range of manifestations and consequences, both present and historical. Language is once again shown to be a social practice, an instrument as much for manipulation and control as for humanist self-expression (see Fowler 1985: 61). There is no way that power here can be abstracted from material circumstances (cf. Kroker and Cook 1986: 73–113), for it is incarnate in the very bodies of the protagonists.

Postmodernism aims to interrogate and demystify totalizing systems that unify with an eye to power. Historiographic metafictions like Banville's *Doctor Copernicus* or *Kepler* challenge science, in particular, as a dominant, totalizing system, as the positivist adjunct to humanism, and they do so through an investigation of the role language plays in both knowledge and power. Of course, theory – from Vattimo's 'pensiero debole' to the neo-Neitzscheans' apocalyptic lamentations – has been doing the same thing. While the visual arts, music, dance and architecture contest received ideological notions as well, metafiction and what we might call metatheory do it specifically in terms of language, and in such a way as to link language to politics in a manner which humanistic and positivistic thought have both resisted. In Salman Rushdie's *Shame*, that link is established in these terms:

> . . . Islam might well have proved an effective unifying force in post-Bangladesh Pakistan, if people hadn't tried to make it into such an almighty big deal . . . Few mythologies survive close examination, however . . . So-called Islamic 'fundamentalism' does not spring, in Pakistan, from the people. It is imposed on them from above. Autocratic regimes find it useful to espouse the rhetoric of faith, because people respect that language, are reluctant to oppose it. This is how religions shore up dictators; by encircling them with words of power, words which the people are reluctant to see discredited, disenfranchised, mocked. (Rushdie 1983: 251)

The linguistic and the political, the rhetorical and the repressive – these are the connections postmodernism places in confrontation with that humanist faith in language and its ability to represent 'truth', past or present, historical or fictional. For instance, in Coover's *The Public Burning*, the novel's 'Richard Nixon' is neither excused nor derided. Instead, the novel focuses on the ideology that formed 'Nixon' (and Nixon) and does so 'in a context which foregrounds the problematic (and rhetorical) nature of historical interpretation' (Mazurek 1982: 33). The relations between language and fiction, language and history, language and criticism were once accepted as relatively unproblematic ones. Postmodernism attempts to change that.

4

Each class which puts itself in the place of the one ruling before it, is compelled, merely in order to carry through its aim, to represent its interests as the common interests of all members of society, that is, expressed in an ideal form: it has to give its ideas the form of universality and represent them as the only rational, universally valid ones. (Marx and Engels)

For many today, it is the 'rational, universally valid' ideas of our liberal humanist tradition that are being called into question. And postmodern art and theory are both playing a role in that questioning, while still acknowledging that they are inevitably, if unwillingly, part of that tradition. In other words, they have not yet seen themselves as being in the 'position of the one ruling before' them, and so have not needed to 'idealize' their position, but rather have contented themselves with a challenge from within, though from the margins. And they have contested these humanist values in full knowledge that they have also been under attack from many other directions. As postmodern novels like *Star Turn* and *Gravity's Rainbow* show, there is considerable anti-humanism to be found in mechanized, technocratic bureaucracies and in most regimes of power, be they capitalist, totalitarian, or socialist.

In that much-quoted essay, 'Marxism and Humanism', Althusser outlines how Marx, in 1845, broke with his earlier theories that based history and politics on an essence of 'Man', in order to argue that this bourgeois humanism – the view that each individual carries the whole of a timeless human essence within him/herself – was an ideology; that what had seemed transparent and unquestionable was neither. But what is of particular interest, from a postmodern perspective, is that, while Marx rejected the humanist pretensions to both (individual) empirical subjectivity and (universal) idealist essence, he also understood the practical function of both as ideology (Althusser 1969: 229). What historiographic metafiction also often does, is to show how these humanist notions are unavoidably connected to direct political and aesthetic issues as well.

The narrator of *Shame* considers trying the liberal humanist line that art is universal and timeless, in his defence of the book he could have written, one that would have included more 'real-life material' (Rushdie 1983: 69). However, he realizes the secret incompatibility of humanism and realism at a political level: 'By now, if I had written a book of this nature, it would have done me no good to protest that I was writing universally, not only about Pakistan. The book would have been banned' (70). He ironically tells the reading authorities (including us) that what he has written is only fiction, 'a sort of modern fairy-tale' and so '[n]o drastic action need be taken' (70). At the end, he returns to this ironic and protective frame and makes clear the political grounds upon which humanist assumptions are being contested: 'Well, well, I mustn't forget I'm only telling a fairy-story. My dictator will be toppled by goblinish, faery means. "Makes it pretty easy for you," is the obvious criticism; and I agree, I agree. But add, even if it does sound a little peevish: "*You* try and get rid of a dictator some time" (257). On one level, this is clearly not what Mas'ud Zavarzadeh calls a 'liberal-humanist novel' that claims to totalize, to offer an integrated view of existing realities (Zavarzadeh 1976: 4). Yet, on another level it is. It does offer *a* view of existing realities, though it is one that is revealed to be deliberately contingent. It does order the chaos of experience, though it also then challenges that shaping process and the product of it, in very self-conscious ways.

Postmodern theory today has also challenged humanism's assumptions, and by 'postmodern theory' here I do not mean just the obvious: deconstruction, feminism, Marxism, and post-structuralism. The metatheoretical contesting of the assumption of timeless universality behind both art and much writing about art has also become frequent in semiotics, in art history, in psychoanalytic, sociological, and other fields, often organized around the concept of representation and its relation to subjectivity. How does culture represent the subject? How does it form part of the social processes of 'differentiation, exclusion, incorporation and rule' (Owens 1982: 10) that make representation the 'founding act' of culture?

Theory like this, along with novels like *The White Hotel* or *The French Lieutenant's Woman*, works to define the subject in terms rather different, in the end, from those of liberal humanist individualism and human essence. There is no transcending of the particularities of the historical and social system. The subject, in a novel like *Midnight's Children*, is constituted in a way that the theory would define as 'the individual in sociality as a language-using, social and historical entity' (Coward and Ellis 1977: 1). Such a definition almost has to, if not preclude, then at least challenge, the humanist faith in the individual as free, unified, coherent and consistent. The work of Benveniste, Lacan, and Kristeva has been important in changing how we can think about the subject. And such a change affects how we consider both literature and history, as the representations and recordings of subjectivity in language. Both become unstable processes in meaning-making, no longer final products of past and fixed meaning. In historiographic metafictions, all the various critically sanctioned modes of talking about subjectivity (character, narrator, writer, textual voice) fail to offer any stable anchor. They are used, inscribed, established, yes, but they are then abused, subverted, undermined. These novels are perhaps upsetting to many readers for exactly this reason.

None of these contradictions, however, invalidates the actual critique of liberal humanism. They do condition the degree of radicality of those contestations, perhaps, as does the fact that such critique can, in fact, be recuperated in the name of liberal humanist openness to all that is human. Notice this interpretation of the metafictional contesting of unified, coherent subjectivity by Charles Newman: 'To agree that art alone cannot give a complete image of man's self is potentially to reaffirm both the richness of our humanity and the possibilities of artistic enterprise' (Newman 1985: 96). Implied in this view of the artistic enterprise is a humanist valuing of complexity and universality, and also of authenticity and originality. And, as Rosalind Krauss has noted, in art, these values have served much wider ideological interests and are thus fuelled by more diverse institutions than just the restricted circles of 'professional art-making' (Krauss 1985: 162). The museum, the historian, the maker of art (and we might add, the publisher, the library, the university) – all have shared in this humanist 'discourse of authenticity' that has certified the original and repressed the notion of repetition and copy (that gives it its force). The postmodern question-ing of authority has been amusingly described by William Gass as a decline in 'theological power, as if Zeus were stripped of his thunder-bolts and swans, perhaps residing on Olympus still, but now living in a camper and cooking with propane. He *is*, but, he is no longer a god' (Gass 1985: 265).

To stress the unavoidably textual and intertextual nature of both literature and history is not to obliterate the producer; it does change his/her status, though. In historiographic metafiction, the novelist and the historian are shown to write in tandem with others – and with each other. In *G.*, the narrator overlaps his own narration with a text of Collingwood's: 'the condition of [events] being historically known is that they should vibrate in the historian's mind' (Berger 1972: 55). The novel is not just plagiarizing Collingwood's text (in fact, some of the sources or intertexts, including this one, are provided in an introduc-tory acknowledgement, as is the case in Banville's *Doctor Copernicus* as well). The novel shares the historian's view of historiography as both a contemporary event and related to self-knowledge. Just as the novel mixes historical and fictive events and personages, so its textual fabric mixes the historiographic and the novelistic.

Sometimes, however, postmodern fiction even more obviously uses the specific values of humanism in order to let them subvert themselves: the stubborn assertion and equally insistent undermining of both individuality and universality in Saleem Sinai's narrative in *Midnight's Children*, is perhaps the most blatant example. I am not at all sure that the result of this process is the 'revitalizing' of these particular parts of the humanist tradition because they 'deserve' to last (Wilde 1985: 347); I think the end result of the demystifying paradoxes is to ask us to question, but not to resolve. Like all parody, such subversion also inscribes what it undercuts, however, and so it may ironically work towards the enshrining of those values it exists to contest. But just as the postmodern is not automatically radical, despite its often leftist rhetoric of oppositionality, it does not automatically revitalize the tradition. It sits on the fence; it literally becomes a point of interro-gation. Its ironies implicate and yet critique. It falls into (or chooses) neither compromise nor dialectic. As I see it, postmodernism remains questioning, and, for many, is unsatisfactory for that reason. This judgment is itself, perhaps, a comment on the strength of our liberal humanist heritage.

5

> *Postmodernism is about art's dispersal, its plurality, by which I*
> *certainly do not mean pluralism. Pluralism is, as we know, that*
> *fantasy that art is free, free of other discourses, institutions, free,*
> *above all, of history. And this fantasy of freedom can be*
> *maintained because every work of art is held to be absolutely*
> *unique and original. Against this pluralism of originals, I want to*
> *speak of the plurality of copies.* (Douglas Crimp)

Copies, intertexts, parodies – these are among the concepts which
have challenged humanist notions of originality and universality.
Together with positivistic science, humanism has also tended to mask
what current theory wants to unmask: the idea that language has the
power to constitute (and not only to describe) that which it represents.
According to this perspective, there can be no value-neutral discourses
– not even science or history, and certainly not literary criticism and
theory. These are the kind of issues that postmodern theory and
practice bring to our attention. The art's interrogation of the values
underlying our cultural practices, however, is always overt, always on
the surface, not hidden in the depths to be unearthed by the discerning
(deconstructing) critic. Indeed, the art often acts as a contesting of the
criticism or theory. The disciplines of history and literary studies have
been challenged by historiographic metafiction's problematizing of
both historical knowledge and literary representation, by its foregrounding of the process of the production of facts out of events
through definite ideological and literary practices (see Adler 1980:
250).

But, if postmodernism no longer privileges continuities nor values
humanist essences, this does not mean that it is not more than willing to
exploit the power of both. It is part of the paradox of both the fiction
and the theory I have been calling postmodern that they are willing to
acknowledge, even as they contest, the relation of their writing to
legitimacy and authority. For Hayden White, even to narrativize the
events of the past is already to moralize, to impose closure on a story
which did not end and whose constructed end suggests that there is a
moral meaning inherent in those events (rather than in the narrative
structuring of the historian) (White 1980: 18, 24, 27). Though
challenged by Louis Mink (1981: 778) on the grounds that every story
permits, but does not demand, a moral interpretation, White's point
holds for the ideological, if not the specifically moral, as he himself
argued earlier: 'there is no value-neutral mode of emplotment,
explanation, or even description in any field of events, whether
imaginary or real' (White 1976: 34). The shift from the humanist
concern for the moral to a postmodern concern for the ideological is
visible in White's work – as it is in much recent theory in other fields as
well. Even the use of language itself is seen by White to entail less a
moral than a particular political positioning of the user in relation to the

world: 'all language is politically contaminated' (35). What Catherine Belsey challenges in the humanist reading of literature, could apply to the reading of history: 'What we do when we read, however "natural" it seems, presupposes a whole theoretical discourse, even if unspoken, about language and about meaning, about the relationships between meaning and the world, meaning and people, and finally about people themselves and their place in the world' (Belsey 1980: 4). But the perspective here is ideological, rather than moral. Despite obvious similarities, the contexts differ considerably. One difference is that race, gender, ethnicity, sexual preferences have all become part of the domain of the ideological and political, as the various manifestations of centralizing and centralized authority are challenged. While some French poststructuralist theory has argued that the margin is the ultimate place of subversion and transgression (e.g. Kristeva 1980: 92), another branch has shown how the margin is both created by and part of the centre (Foucault 1973: 10), that the 'different' can be made into the 'other'. Postmodernism tends to combat this by asserting the plurality of the 'different' and rejecting the binary opposition of the 'other'.

Postmodern metafictions have looked to both the historiographic and fictional accounts of the past in order to study the ideological inscriptions of 'difference' as 'inequality'. In Fowles's *A Maggot*, the twentieth-century narrator fills in the background of the eighteenth century's sexism and classism, as it is needed, in order to explain his characters' actions – such as the 'crudely chauvinistic contempt' (Fowles 1985: 227) of the middle-class English lawyer, Ayscough, for his poor Welsh witness, Jones. We are told that the roots of such contempt lie in the real religion of the century, the 'worship, if not idolatry' of property (227): 'this united all society but the lowest, and dictated much of its behaviour, its opinions, its thinking' (228), including its notion of justice. Like many other postmodern fictions, this one is not content to say something about the past and stop at that. This novel forges a link with the present: 'Jones is a liar, a man who lives from hand to mouth . . . [yet] he is the future and Ayscough the past; and both are like most of us, still today, equal victims in the debtors' prison of History, and equally unable to leave it' (231).

There are also links between the centre and the margin. The position of black Americans has worked to make them especially aware of the possible political and social consequences of art, but these writers know that they are still part of American society. Maxine Hong Kingston's articulation of this same paradoxical positioning is in terms of Chinese-Americans. When these ex-centrics visit China, she claims, 'their whole lives suddenly made sense . . . They realize their Americanness, they say, and "You find out what a China Man you are"' (Kingston 1980: 295). This is the contradictory position too of Wiebe's Métis, Rushdie's Indian, Kogawa's Japanese-Canadian and of the many women, gays, hispanics, native peoples, and members of the working class, whose inscription into history in the sixties and since has forced a recognition of the untenable nature of any humanist concept of 'human essence', or of universal values that are not culturally and historically dependent. The social result of this is not necessarily 'the all-embracing and enervating cultural pluralism that dominates contemporary society' (Russell 1985: 241). Another result is the postmodern attempt to negotiate the space between centres and margins in ways that acknowledge 'difference' and its challenge to our supposedly monolithic culture, as defined by liberal humanism.

Feminist theory has clearly been one of the most potent decentring forces in contemporary thought, and its rhetoric has been largely oppositional (gender's binary oppositions are perhaps not that easily surmounted). Witness the opening of Judith Fetterley's *The Resisting Reader*: 'Literature is political. It is painful to have to insist on this fact, but the necessity of such insistence indicates the dimensions of the problem' (Fetterley 1978: xi). Feminism has, in fact, almost replaced the more traditionally political concerns (such as nationalism) in places like Quebec, where women artists and theorists are rearticulating power relations in terms of gender and language (but less as French versus English this time).

Historiographic metafiction has participated in this politicizing of sexuality in typically postmodern ways, insisting on both the history of the ideological issues and their continuing relation to art and society. The heroine of Susan Daitch's *L.C.* (1986) receives her political education through the aesthetic and the personal. The novel is set in Paris in 1848, so the public dimension is overt. But it is the personal relations which the fictive Lucienne Crozier has with various artists, including the historical Delacroix, that teach her both about the role of art in politics and about the marginalized role of women in both domains: they are muses, models, observers, diversions. The novel's complex framing relates Berkeley 1968 to Paris 1848 (they are equally markers of revolutionary contexts). But the conclusions of both story and frame – outside those marked contexts – question the patriarchal values underlying (male) revolutions, but offer no positive substitute: Lucienne's journal manuscript is used and abused by those whose political and economic interests it can serve.

In Christa Wolf's *No Place on Earth*, two historical personages, the poets Kleist and Günderrode, are made to meet in fictional space. Their initial perception of the gender roles they must fulfil differ. Kleist looks at the woman poet and sees only her security:

> She is provided for, whatever that may mean; she is not compelled
> to concentrate her thoughts on the most trivial demands of
> everyday life. It seems to him a kind of advantage that she has no
> choice in the matter. As a woman she is not placed under the law
> of having to achieve everything or to regard everything as nothing.
> (Wolf 1982: 107)

Günderrode's version of her fate as a woman is different: 'By the age of seventeen we must have accepted our fate, which is a man, and must learn to accept the penalty should we behave so improbably as to resist. How often I have wanted to be a man, longed for the real wounds, to which you men expose yourselves' (112). In fact, as the two poets realize, 'man and woman have a hostile relationship' within each of them: 'Woman. Man. Untenable words. We two, each imprisoned in his sex' (108). The postmodern answer to gendered oppositions is not androgyny, or at least not here; it is rather an interrogation of the very opposition upon which inequality is founded.

In historiographic metafiction, such interrogation is often directly connected to that of other similarly unequal oppositions, such as race and class. In Coetzee's novel, *Foe*, the enabling conceit of the text is that Defoe's *Robinson Crusoe* was indeed a real tale told to its author, but the teller was a woman, Susan Barton, and the tale somewhat different from the one we have come to know. In this novel, however, her awareness of the inequalities of gender do not save Susan from other ideological blind spots: she berates Cruso [*sic*] for not teaching Friday how to speak: 'you might have brought home to him some of the blessings of civilization and made him a better man' (Coetzee 1986: 22). The narrative's exploration of these 'blessings' and of Friday's status in their regard makes it another of the challenges to the liberal humanist –and imperialist – heritage that lives on in Coetzee's own nation, South Africa. Like Susan, Friday cannot tell his own story, but it is not because he has been silenced by a controlling male writer: here it is the white slave traders who literally (and symbolically) have removed his tongue. Susan shares the assumptions of her age, but her gender helps her see a little at least of her own ideological motivations: 'I tell myself I talk to Friday to educate him out of darkness and silence. But is that the truth? There are times when benevolence deserts me and I use words only as the shortest way to subject him to my will' (60). Language paradoxically both expresses and oppresses, educates and manipulates. Though Foe denies her charge, she asserts that his ignoring of her 'true' castaway story of Cruso is comparable to the slavers robbing Friday of his tongue (150). What she learns is to question the humanist assumptions underlying her own ironic claim that she is 'a free woman who asserts her freedom by telling her story according to her own desire' (131): her sex, like Friday's race and Foe's class, condition her freedom.

In theory, the work of feminists, Marxists and black critics, among others, has argued this kind of interaction of the discourses of the marginalized. They have done so in such a powerful way that many feel today that they have created a new cultural hegemony, in the Gramscian sense of a new set of values and attitudes which validates what is now a dominant class in its power. But within each group there is little sense of unity or power: some claim that feminism is the discourse of the white, middle-class woman. Alice Walker calls her fiction 'womanist' to set it apart from this discourse (see Bradley 1984:

35). But there is a black feminist discourse, a Marxist feminist discourse, and, of course, a humanist feminist discourse. From a metatheoretical point of view, it is this plurality of feminism*s* that makes the postmodern valuing of 'difference' possible.

No acceptable non-totalizing alternatives may be available, but the questioning of the existing order should not stop for that reason. The interrogations of the 'different' form their own discourse, one that attempts to avoid the unconscious traps of humanist thought, while still working within its power-field. Like feminists, postcolonial theorists and artists are initiating their own discourse, with its own set of questions and strategies (see Bhaba 1983: 198). Black and gay critics now have quite a long discursive history. And all of these marginalized ex-centrics have contributed to the definition of the postmodern heterogeneous 'different' and to its inherently ideological nature. The new ideology of postmodernism may be that everything is ideological. But this does not lead to an intellectual or practical impasse. What it does is underline the need for self-awareness, on the one hand, and on the other, for an acknowledgement of that relationship – suppressed by humanism – of the aesthetic and the political. In E. L. Doctorow's words: 'a book can affect consciousness – affect the way people think and therefore the way they act. Books create constituencies that have their own effect on history' (in Trenner 1983: 43).

7 Postmodern Culture(s)

Hans Bertens

After the tentative beginnings of the critical discussion in the late 1950s (Charles Olson and Irving Howe) and the 1960s (Harry Levin, Susan Sontag, Leslie Fiedler, Ihab Hassan and others), 'postmodernism' became an explosive academic growth industry in the early and mid-1970s, when the discussion, which had – with the exception of Sontag's contributions – originally restricted itself to literature, began to draw into its orbit more and more developments in contemporary culture: developments in architecture, painting, film, and the performing arts. Almost inevitably, 'postmodernism' lost the typological connotations it had had for many of the early contributors to the debate and became a periodization instrument, the key concept for an understanding of our era. Thus, Hassan postulated a postmodern episteme: 'Religion and science, myth and technology, intuition and reason, popular and high culture, female and male archetypes . . . begin to modify and inform one another . . . lineaments of a new consciousness begin to emerge' (Hassan 1980: 110). And Fredric Jameson and Hal Foster argued, a good deal less exuberantly, that postmodernism is an inescapable and schizophrenic condition imposed on us by late-capitalist society (Jameson 1983; Foster 1984).

It is not accidental that the critical discussion of postmodernism was for a long time an almost exclusively American affair. Postmodernism meant a good deal more in America than elsewhere in the Western world, more particularly Europe, where the debate did not really get under way until the late 1970s, when the whole issue of postmodernism was more or less co-opted by poststructuralist criticism, and when the notion of a postmodern society or episteme began to gain wider currency. But even then, Europe was slow to follow the American interest in postmodern art, as is illustrated by the first prominent result of the internationalization of the discussion: Jean-François Lyotard's *La condition postmoderne* (1979) and the ensuing debate with Jürgen Habermas. Instead, European interest in postmodernism tended to restrict itself initially to the political and philosophical (poststructuralist) issues involved. That this state of affairs does not necessarily reflect American critical prowess and European lassitude has been convincingly argued by, for instance, Andreas Huyssen who sees postmodernism as, at least in part, a continuation of the avant-garde of the early twentieth century. (In fact, Huyssen sees the early phase of postmodernism as the specifically American 'endgame' of the historical avant-garde (Huyssen 1984).) If there is such a continuity between postmodernism and the avant-garde, then the overwhelming American interest in postmodernism is not surprising. After all, the original avant-garde did not have much impact in America, so that an American avant-gardist movement was bound to draw wide critical attention – and resistance.

It reflects no bias on my part that I will devote a seemingly disproportionate part of this chapter to American attempts to come to grips with postmodernism, firstly in the field of literature, then in the much broader field of postmodern culture. My procedure will firstly be to offer a necessarily selective account of postmodernism's twisted genealogy. Much of the current confusion surrounding the term has its origin in the initial stages of the critical debate, more specifically in the fact that a number of similar, yet different postmodernisms were proposed almost simultaneously by different critics. An examination of the original issues involved will bring to light both the affinities and the differences between these various critical constructs (not all of them called postmodernism at the time, although clearly recognizable as postmodern from our vantage point), and may suggest a way out of the conceptual labyrinth that one has come to associate with post-modernism. But let me first give some examples that illustrate postmodernism's elusive character.

Michel Benamou saw 'performance' as 'the unifying mode of the postmodern' (Benamou 1977: 3), and distinguished 'two visions' in his postmodern performance, 'one shamanistic, the other futuristic' (5). Christopher Butler noted a dialectic between two major modes:

> the dialectic between the huge over-organization of *Finnegans Wake* and the deliberate lack of it in the *Cantos* conditions the whole of the postmodern period; and what mediates between these at all points is the phenomenological concentration upon the mental processes of the artist. (Butler 1980: 5)

Hal Foster distinguishes a 'neoconservative postmodernism', which privileges style and resorts to pastiche, and a poststructuralist post-modernism which is 'profoundly anti-humanist' (Foster 1984: 67). Andreas Huyssen makes a distinction between an earlier post-modernism, which has strong affinities with the historical avant-garde, a postmodernism of the 'anything goes' variety (echoing Lyotard's dissatisfaction with a purely eclectic postmodernism, as expressed in the latter's 'Answering the Question: What is Postmodernism?' (Lyotard 1983)), and a current postmodernism which is characterized by the changes brought about by the women's movement, a new ecological sensibility, a new attitude towards non-European, non-Western cultures, and a new political awareness (Huyssen 1984). Fredric Jameson sees pastiche and (Lacanian) schizophrenia as key elements in his variety of postmodernism and offers a very interesting catalogue of what constitutes postmodern culture:

. . . the poetry of John Ashbery . . . but also the much simpler talk poetry that came out of the reaction against complex, ironic, academic modernist poetry in the 1960s; the reaction against modern architecture and in particular against the monumental buildings of the International Style; the pop buildings and decorated sheds celebrated by Robert Venturi in his manifesto, *Learning from Las Vegas*; Andy Warhol and Pop art, but also the more recent Photorealism; in music, the moment of John Cage but also the later synthesis of classical and 'popular' styles found in composers like Philip Glass and Terry Riley, and also punk and new-wave rock with such groups as the Clash, the Talking Heads and the Gang of Four; in film, everything that comes out of Godard – contemporary vanguard film and video – but also a whole new style of commercial or fiction films [such as *American Graffiti*, *Star Wars* and *Raiders of the Lost Ark*], which has its equivalent in the contemporary novel as well, where the works of William Burroughs, Thomas Pynchon and Ishmael Reed on the one hand, and the French new novel on the other, are also to be numbered among the varieties of what can be called postmodernism. (Jameson 1983: 111)

This is an awe-inspiring list. On closer examination, however, almost everything that Jameson mentions may be brought within the frame-work of three distinct postmodern cultures: an avant-gardist post-modernism (the talk poetry, pop art, John Cage, early Godard, William Burroughs); a poststructuralist postmodernism (Ashbery, the later Godard, Pynchon, the new novel) and what I will call a sensuous, aesthetic postmodernism (Venturi's 'decorated sheds', later pop art, Photorealism). These three postmodernisms, similar yet distinct, have their origins in the critical discussion as it took shape in the 1960s in the USA, and much confusion might have been avoided if they had been kept scrupulously apart.

1 Early sightings

The earliest still relevant use of the term postmodernism must be attributed to the American poet-critic Charles Olson, who used it repeatedly in the 1950s, without ever offering a proper definition. However, Donald Allen and George Butterick cannot be far from the mark both in defining Olson's postmodernism as 'ultimately, an instant-by-instant engagement with reality' (Allen and Butterick 1982: 11) and in their argument that the Black Mountain poets, the Beats and the poets of the New York School essentially took their example from Olson's poetics, sometimes with mystical purposes, sometimes not. For Allen and Butterick, this postmodern poetic practice is 'marked by an acceptance of the primordial, of spiritual and sexual necessities, of myth, of the latest understandings of science, chance and change, wit and dream' (12); in short, by an all-embracing acceptance of the here-and-now, an acceptance that is often characterized by a certain reverence, an awe which induces in some of these postmodern poets a 'preliterate, prerational' state.

This poetic postmodernism clearly extends the line of William Carlos Williams in its existential preferences, in its reluctance to separate art and life, in its anti-formalism and in its refusal to intellectualize or ignore certain areas of experience. The enemy is a certain form of modernism (seen as dominant in England and America) which aestheticizes experience with its formalism, denies the integrity of the object world by drawing it into the subject's orbit, exhibits essentialistic tendencies and is shamelessly élitist in its contempt for mass society and its cultural products. That this 'high modernism' may well be a rather narrow critical construct that does scant justice to the diversity, even within English and American modernism, is not relevant here; it is the modernism of the American New Critical establishment of the 1950s, the modernism of autonomous, institutionalized art.

The attack on this very American image of high modernism was intensified in the mid-1960s by Leslie Fiedler and Susan Sontag. For Fiedler, postmodernism signifies a total break with the élitist modernist past; it looks ahead, is oriented toward the future and celebrates a new spontaneity that he also finds in the American counter-culture of the 1960s (see Fiedler 1965). In subsequent publications, Fiedler further explored his own postmodernism, which tended heavily towards pop art. The new postmodern novel would draw upon the Western, upon science fiction, upon pornography and would close the gap between élite and mass culture (Fiedler 1975). This pop postmodernism would be 'anti-artistic' and 'anti-serious'; it would create new myths –although not the authoritative modernist myths – it would create 'a certain rude magic in its authentic context', it would contribute to a magical tribalization in an age dominated by machines and make 'a thousand little Wests in the interstices of a machine civilization' (Fiedler 1975: 365).

Sontag shares Fiedler's aversion to 'meaning'. As she puts it: 'It doesn't matter whether artists intend, or don't intend, for their works to be interpreted . . . the merit of these works lies elsewhere than in their "meanings" ' (Sontag 1966: 19). For Sontag, the new art she describes is characterized by 'a flight from interpretation', and that flight gives rise to parodic, abstract, or decorative forms, all defying interpretation. Postmodern art may even become 'non-art' in order to escape being interpreted. (The connection with the modern avant-garde is obvious here.) Whereas modernist art claimed depth beneath its surface and begged to be interpreted in its insistence on layering and codes, postmodern art presents itself as surface. What we have in Sontag is a plea for sensuousness – 'In place of a hermeneutics of art we need an erotics of art' (23) – and an interest in form.

Looking back, we can see that Fiedler's postmodernism, in particular, with its iconoclastic spirit, its interest in pop, in happenings, in an immediacy of experience, has strong affinities with the anarchistic, vitalist stream in the historical avant-garde. Its implicit ideology is reflected in the contemporary writings of Norman O. Brown, Herbert Marcuse (especially their revisions of Freudian psychoanalysis and their attacks on Freud's acceptance of the present reality system as final), Marshall McLuhan, Buckminster Fuller and others. Yet, although, like the avant-garde, it is oriented towards the future, what is conspicuously lacking is a political programme. True enough, there is an undeniable expectation that the millennium is near and that the bourgeois establishment and its preferred form of art (high modernism) have run their course, but such Utopian hopes do not quite constitute a programme.

In comparison, the 'new sensibility' that Sontag defines is far more intellectual but less political, that is, less directly engaged with the social world, although it is aesthetically political in its avant-gardist revolt against modernist poetics. Sontag places form against Fiedler's formlessness. Whereas Fiedler urges an immediacy of (formless) experience in a vulgarization of Olson's poetics, Sontag pleads for an immediacy in our experience of art. Her immediacy is an immediacy of form, a form that does in fact rule out experience because of its anti-representational stance. That does not mean that she does not share Fiedler's eclecticism: 'From the vantage point of this new sensibility, the beauty of a machine or of the solution to a mathematical problem, of a painting by Jasper Johns, of a film by Jean-Luc Godard, and the personalities and music of the Beatles is equally accessible' (quoted in Wasson 1974: 1190). In fact, Sontag does not only see a peaceful coexistence between the new art and Fiedler's 'machine civilization', she even sees a deep complicity. As Richard Wasson has noted, Sontag's 'new art extends its medium and means into the world of science and technology, into the popular, and does away with old distinctions' (Wasson 1974: 1190). There is no doubt that Sontag's new art is political in the sense that it rejects modernist aesthetic categories and the modernist concern with epistemology (as does Fiedler's counter-cultural postmodernism). However, if it is stripped of this political edge, what is left is a preoccupation with sensuousness – an erotics of art – and an absolutely eclectic form. In other words, a postmodernism that is currently under heavy attack, a post-modernism that recognizes no 'old distinctions', uses the most sophisti-cated techniques and technology in its dazzling display of form and is resolutely apolitical and ahistorical: the postmodernism of visually brilliant thrillers such as Jean-Jacques Beineix's *Diva* (1982) or the high-tech rock videos of recent years (a recent video promoting a song by The Squeeze referred brilliantly to Dali, Magritte, and Escher, merely for the sake of visual effects); the postmodernism of the 'decorated shed' and the equally eclectic 'historicism' in the visual arts.

What has emerged so far is a new art that, first of all, rebels against a modernism that is seen as élitist, authoritarian, obsessive in its imposition of subjective meaning upon the unsuspecting object world, as essentialist and aestheticizing. The new art (postmodernism) proposes an anti-essentialist attitude, either in a desire for a non-intellectual immediacy of experience (Olson, Fiedler), or in a rebellion against modernist epistemology (Sontag). It insists on contingency, on the personal and provisional character of 'meaning' (Olson, Fiedler) – or even its absence (Sontag) – and on the erasure of traditional boundaries between high and low art, between art and science, between art and life, in an all-encompassing embracing of experience. The affinities of Fiedler's postmodernism with the modern avant-garde are obvious. In fact, one might also speak of a revival of that avant-garde, but almost wholly depoliticized and infused with a *laissez-faire* existentialism.

In the late 1960s and early 1970s the critical debate on post-modernism widened its scope. In 1969 Richard Wasson identified a postmodernism (although he did not use the term) that shares in the revolt against modernism, but is far more intellectual than the postmodernisms of the 1960s. Wasson traces this type of post-modernism in four exemplary writers: Iris Murdoch, Alain Robbe-Grillet, John Barth and Thomas Pynchon. According to Wasson, these writers 'are sceptical of modernist notions of metaphor as a species of suprarational truth that unifies paradoxical opposites and modernist conceptions of myth which make it a principle of order for art and of discipline for the subjective self' (Wasson 1969: 460). Rejecting modernist aesthetics (that is, the aesthetics of Wasson's new critical modernism), they set out to subvert metaphor and myth as subjective attempts at transcendent ordering and seek to restore the world outside the subject, in all its object-ness and total inaccessibility. The difference and distance between subject and object world must be accepted, not denied through aesthetic strategies. As a result, the work of these writers is characterized by a radical ontological doubt, the end of epistemology.

Whereas, in the earlier postmodernisms, the revolt against modernism is largely unreasoned – a necessary liberation from, on the one hand, the constraints of high modernism and its insistence on significant meaning and, on the other hand, the repressive intellectual, social and sexual climate of the 1950s – in Wasson's concept that revolt is primarily intellectual. The epistemological basis of modernist aesthetics is seen as radically unsound, in fact as non-existent. Wasson quite rightly points out that this anti-modernism builds upon high modernism itself: 'It would not be difficult to make a case that the work of these writers really constitutes another manifestation of the modernist rejection of romantic notions of personality and history' (Wasson 1969: 476). To be more precise, what we find in this postmodernism is a radicalization of the epistemological thrust of high modernist writing (see Brian McHale 1986, 1987). In fact, the modernist obsession with epistemology (significant meaning), rejected out of hand by the postmodernisms of the 1960s, is here radicalized to the point at which it turns against itself and the end of epistemology comes into sight, to be replaced by the creation of ontologies (used in the sense of Thomas Pavel and McHale) that have no epistemological pretensions. It is this anti-epistemological postmodernism that would, in the late 1970s, be co-opted by a poststructuralism that could also legitimately be seen as a radicalization of modernist preoccupations (see Huyssen 1986).

This postmodernism and the postmodernism(s) of the 1960s (often erroneously seen as identical) form the basis for all distinctions that have since been made in literary postmodernism. Gerald Graff, for instance, distinguishes between an anti-intellectual and hedonistic postmodernism, which reflects 'a less soberly rationalistic mode of consciousness, one that is more congenial to myth, tribal ritual, and visionary experience' (Graff 1979: 31–2), and a postmodernism, exemplified for instance by Borges, that presents 'solipsistic distortion as the only possible perspective' but is nevertheless able 'to suggest the historical and social causes for this loss of objective reality' (56) – in other words, an intellectually responsible postmodernism. Ihab Hassan, who contributed more than any other critic to post-modernism's current popularity, also distinguishes an avant-gardist counter-cultural postmodernism and a poststructuralist postmodern-ism that is characterized by decentring and indeterminacy. Whereas, in his early writings, Hassan sees two different modes within post-modernism which both echo the avant-garde – an 'autodestructive, demonic, nihilistic' mode and a 'self-transcendental, sacramental' one – he later tends to oppose these two modes to another postmodernism that is poststructural and characterized by a 'new immanence of language' (Hassan 1980: 97). Graff, Hassan, and many others distinguish two postmodernisms which are both in revolt against the assumptions and aesthetic strategies of high modernism. Whereas the one can be described as epistemologically neutral, the other signals the end of epistemology and adopts a defiantly anti-epistemological attitude. However, as I have suggested, we need a third post-modernism, post-epistemological and characterized by its interest in form and art's 'erotic' power.

There is, of course, a 'fourth' postmodernism which gained currency in the early 1970s, the Heideggerian postmodernism of William Spanos and the critics associated with *boundary 2*. But, although Spanos's postmodernism is interesting enough in its own right, it is too exclusive in its rejection of, for instance, Roland Barthes, Marshall McLuhan, Charles Olson, and Leslie Fiedler, of concrete poetry, the *nouveau roman* and pop art. Spanos has his reasons to see all this as ahistorical and apolitical, but his interest in 'the recovery of the authentic historicity of modern man' (Spanos 1972: 158) surely leads him too far away from what is generally accepted as postmodernism (see Bertens 1986).

Poststructuralist postmodernism has by now certainly come to dominate the critical debate in literary criticism, as have such recent studies as Allen Thiher's *Words in Reflection* (1983) and Brian McHale's *Postmodernist Fiction* (1987). In such studies, the emphasis upon a postmodern world view, in which reality is constituted by linguistic signs and in which what is represented is the impossibility of representation, is pre-eminent. But that does not mean that the other postmodernisms have disappeared. Aesthetic, 'erotic' postmodernism, especially, is still very much with us in the other arts.

2 Three cultures

The discussion of postmodernism in those other arts follows the pattern I have described. Most critics see either an avant-gardist postmodern culture, a poststructuralist postmodern culture, or both, and juxtapose these postmodernisms with an idealist, autonomous modernism that privileged art in its aesthetic withdrawl from the world – where it still claimed a unique authenticity – or in its élitist social aspirations, and which was, as Jameson puts it, 'linked to the conception of a unique self and private identity, a unique personality and individuality, which can be expected to generate its own unique vision of the world and to forge its own unique, unmistakable style' (Jameson 1983: 114). That brand of modernism is represented by the rationalist, Utopian Bauhaus ideology with its teleological view of progress in architecture (Mies van der Rohe, Gropius, Le Corbusier) and by Clement Greenberg's formalist high modernism in the visual arts. Rosalind Krauss, for instance, contrasts a modernist sculpture which 'had become pure negativity . . . the combination of exclusions' (Krauss 1985: 282) – in other words, Greenberg's formalism seen in a starkly negative way – with the 'expanded field' of postmodernism, in which 'practice is not defined in relation to a given medium – sculpture – but rather in relation to the logical operations on a set of cultural terms, for which any medium – photography, books, lines on walls, mirrors, or sculpture itself – might be used' (288). Krauss, incidentally, exemplifies the poststructuralist view of postmodern culture, seeing postmodern art as 'an art of a fully problematized view of representation, in which to name (represent) an object may not necessarily be to call it forth, for there may be no (original) object' (38). Not surprisingly, she finds postmodern antecedents not in the modern avant-garde, but in an anti-representational strain within modernism, in modernist collage, for example (a strategy that for her sets up 'discourse in place of presence'). In her argument for continuity between an alternative – in her case anti-representational – modernism and postmodernism, Krauss is representative of those critics of postmodern culture who have, on the whole, been far more alive to that continuity than have their literary counterparts. J. G. Merquior, for instance, sees in his 'two programmes in postmodern aesthetics', the one 'structuralist' and the other 'neo-dadaist' (Merquior 1986: 16), nothing but perverse continuations of modernist vices. Andreas Huyssen makes a brilliant case for continuity between the modern avant-garde and what he calls the first phase of postmodernism, its counter-cultural phase of the American 1960s (see Huyssen 1986). Michael Newman argues in an equally brilliant article with respect to poststructuralist postmodernism that:

> Many of the arguments which assume Greenberg's theory of modernism and assert a postmodernism using post-structuralist categories may in effect be retheorizing a pre-Greenbergian modernism. This is an attempt to maintain a reflexive radicality, a questioning of the institution of art, and an emancipatory ethic – art as a contribution to knowledge and self-awareness; but without a utopian conception of historical development and, in most but not all cases, without any commitment to a specific political project. Looked at critically, this might be seen as an attempt to maintain the stance of a modernist avant-garde in conditions where this is no longer possible or appropriate, and to do so through critical discourse. (Newman 1986: 32)

Even more clearly than in the purely literary-critical debate, every postmodernism creates its own modernist antecedents.

But let me offer an inventory of what, up to this point, have emerged as the characteristic features of a general postmodern culture, a postmodern culture not yet subdivided into poststructuralist, neo-avant-gardist, neoconservative and other postmodern cultures. All critics agree that the effacement of the distinction between high and mass culture is absolutely central. Postmodern culture incorporates pop culture, but borrows also, as Huyssen and others have pointed out, from pre-modern and non-modern cultures in its anti-modernist refusal to privilege Euro-American attitudes.

The distinction between high and mass culture is not the only one that is given up. All traditional barriers are under attack in postmodern culture. Rothenberg finds 'an unquestionable and far-reaching breakdown of boundaries and genres: between "art and life" (Cage, Kaprow), between various conventionally defined arts (intermedia and performance art, concrete poetry) and between arts and non-arts (*musique concrète*, found art, etc.)', a breakdown that leads to the situation where there is 'no hierarchy of media in the visual arts, no hierarchy of instrumentation in music' (Rothenberg 1977: 13). He argues that postmodern art is characterized by an ever-changing interaction with its environment: 'the value of a work isn't inherent in its formal or aesthetic characteristics . . . but in what it does, or what the artist or his surrogate does with it, how he performs it in a given context' (14). Huyssen notes a similar abandonment of traditional boundaries in postmodern theatre, which 'attempt[s] to bridge the gap between stage and audience and experiment[s] with new forms of immediacy and spontaneity in performance' (Huyssen 1986: 164), and links this with social spin-offs such as the teach-ins and the sit-ins of the 1960s.

Fredric Jameson sees pastiche (a 'bland' parody of all available styles) and schizophrenia ('the fragmentation of time into a series of perpetual presents' (Jameson 1983: 125)) as two important hallmarks of postmodernism, both, of course, characterized by a refusal to respect traditional hierarchies. Referring to the hierarchy of high and mass culture, Jameson notes that:

> The newer artists no longer 'quote' the materials, the fragments and motifs, of a mass or popular culture, as Joyce (and Flaubert) began to do, or Mahler; they somehow incorporate them to the point where our older critical and evaluative categories . . . no longer seem functional'. (Jameson 1984b: 65)

Michael Newman argues that, 'Parody is so widespread in contemporary art that it is tempting to regard it, together with appropriation, allegory and bricolage, as one of the characteristic strategies by which we might define a postmodernist art' (Newman 1986: 47–8). (This parody, incidentally, is not Jameson's neutral, bland parody, but a poststructuralist parody, 'which *begins* with the assumption of the impossibility of authority, origin, full presence and so on'.) In painting, Bonita Oliva's 'trans-avant-garde' ranges eclectically through all historical periods and cultures, borrowing what it sees fit to borrow, and in postmodern architecture, we find the same eclecticism that is the result of an underlying refusal to accept the authority of former hierarchies and traditional distinctions. The four 'preoccupations' of postmodern architecture that Demetri Porphyrios distinguishes in his admirably succinct survey all point in this direction: the 'emphasis on fragmentation . . . on the disintegration of the compositional and stylistic systems that lived on from earlier years'; the 'use of ironic commentary and parody'; the 'emphasis on phantasmagoria at the expense of material quality or significant meaning' and, finally, 'the demise of the public realm', the undermining of 'tradition, of history, of culture and of practical reasons' – all these signify a farewell to tradition and the value system of high modernism (Porphyrios 1986: 30).

There is, then, a general postmodern culture which is characterized by a rejection of hierarchies, an effacement of distinctions, an eclectic mixing of materials and codes. Within this general culture we may distinguish three postmodern cultures which correspond to the three cultures discussed in the earlier section of this chapter.

There is, first of all, a postmodern culture that has strong affinities with the modern avant-garde. It is (often playfully) iconoclastic, embraces popular culture in its reaction against high modernism and has a feebly political programme, in that it aims at a liberation from a repressive bourgeois ideology. It seeks to reintegrate art and life and is suspicious of intellectualizing, in its emphasis on an immediacy of experience and in its anti-formalism. This is the postmodern culture of the 1960s: the pop art of Warhol and Lichtenstein (and all the other arts – Op art, etc. – that followed in its wake); the zany novels of Richard Brautigan and Kurt Vonnegut; the music of John Cage and other experiments with aleatory art; theatrical 'happenings' and 'performances'; the subversive use of modernist montage and collage on record covers and posters; the plea for a rapprochement between 'consumer' architecture and 'serious' architecture in Robert Venturi's *Complexity and Contradiction in Architecture* (1966) and his later *Learning from Las Vegas* (1972); even TV productions such as Monty Python with its mixing of media, its playing with gender, its parodies, its eclectic use of historical material, its playful use of poststructuralist techniques such as meta-commentary and self-cancellation.

The revolutionary tone of this postmodernism, its adversary ethos, and its heady self-assurance align it unmistakably with the modern avant-garde; even its naive faith in, and often reliance on, technology echoes such avant-gardist movements as Futurism and Constructivism, as Huyssen has pointed out. Undoubtedly, this avant-gardist postmodern culture saw its heyday in the 1960s, but that does not imply that it has disappeared. What is true, though, is that its target has shifted. For this type of postmodernism, the real enemy is poststructuralist postmodernism – a poststructuralism that has seemingly intellectualized both world and unique subject into virtual non-existence and is, from an avant-gardist point of view, even more life-denying than modernism ever was.

This poststructuralist postmodern culture has dominated critical discussion since the late 1970s, but it too has its roots in the 1960s. As Michael Newman points out, 'The idea of the "death of the author" quickly entered the discourse of conceptual art . . . and was subsequently taken up by postmodernism to construct a critical space for works using appropriated imagery and stereotypes' (Newman 1986: 39). Conceptual art, which as an articulated programme dates from 1966, epistemologically problematized both art and the role of the artist. Newman, revealing a poststructuralist bias in the process, in fact locates the beginning of the discourse of postmodernism in conceptual art, presumably because of its anti-essentialist stance. Placing the heritage of conceptual art even more firmly within a poststructuralist framework, he notes that 'post-conceptual art takes on board Lacan, Althusser, Foucault and later Derrida in order to formulate a critique of the bourgeois subject' (Newman 1986: 38). As I have already noted, parody, too, is for Newman a poststructuralist strategy, as is bricolage, which 'might be seen as a possible paradigm for the constitution of the "decentred" subject and its products' (46).

This 'decentring' of the subject and the infinite deferment of meaning are central to poststructural postmodernism. Hal Foster states that poststructuralist postmodernism 'assumes "the death of man" not only as original creator of unique artifacts but also as the centred subject of representation and history'. It 'launches a critique in which representation is shown to be more constitutive of reality than transparent to us' (Foster 1984: 67). In architecture, Porphyrios notes the postmodern preoccupation with fragmentation and disintegration: 'Buildings are de-composed, exploded or attacked by foreign bodies until they disintegrate. There is an emphasis, therefore, on fastidious syntax that *decentralizes* both composition and iconography' (Porphyrios 1986: 30; my italics). Finally, for Craig Owens, postmodern culture and poststructuralism are inseparable. Seeing allegory as the key to postmodern art, Owens argues that postmodern allegoric strategies are designed to reveal absence, the absence of origins – (inter)textuality is all (Owens 1980). Postmodern art deconstructs itself and signals its insufficiency.

This is a neat division: an avant-gardist postmodernism versus a poststructural one. However, there is no room here for a good many cultural expressions which are clearly postmodern in appearance – anti-hierarchic, eclectic, fragmentary, interested in pop culture, and so on – but which cannot be categorized in either culture. There is, therefore, another category of postmodernism which is often called neoconservative, that is, accused of schizophrenia, of a perverse historicism, of a return to 'painting' (that is, representation) and other unspeakable crimes. As Hal Foster has commented:

> In art and architecture neoconservative postmodernism is marked by an eclectic historicism, in which old and new modes and styles . . . are retooled and recycled. In architecture this practice tends to the use of a campy pop-classical order to decorate the usual shed (e.g., Charles Moore, Robert Stern), and in art to the use of kitschy historicist references to commodify the usual painting (Julian Schabel is the inflated signifier here); indeed, the classical often returns as pop, the art-historical as kitsch. In what way is such a work *post*modernist? It does not argue with modernism in any serious way; to a great degree its postmodernism seems a front for a rapprochement with the market and the public – an embrace that, far from populist (as is so commonly claimed), is alternatively elitist in its allusions and manipulative in its clichés. (Foster 1984: 67–8)

Like a good many other critics, Foster argues that this postmodernism proclaims a return to history but is in fact deeply ahistorical. The last point is certainly correct, the earlier highly doubtful. Huyssen saw this postmodernism as being embodied in the *Documenta 7* exhibition in Kassel:

> [It] rests on an all but total confusion of codes: it is anti-modern and highly eclectic, but dresses up as a return to the modernist tradition; it is anti-avantgarde in that it simply chooses to drop the avantgarde's crucial concern for a new art in an alternative society, but it pretends to be avantgarde in its presentation of current trends; and, in a certain sense, it is even anti-postmodern in that it

abandons any reflection of the problems which the exhaustion of high modernism originally brought about, problems which postmodern art, in its better moments, has attempted to address aesthetically and sometimes even politically. (Huyssen 1984: 7–8)

This is a highly illuminating summary because it shows, even more clearly than Foster's criticisms, how this postmodernism fails for its detractors. Put crudely, it lacks the political commitment of the avant-garde (which, in a weak form, is retained by avant-gardist post-modernism), and it lacks the epistemological commitment of poststructuralist postmodernism (even if that epistemological commitment results in a poststructuralist end of epistemology).

We can now bring these postmodernisms together in a single model with, as its crucial features, socio-political commitment, attitude towards the modernist aesthetic, interest in form and epistemological commitment. Such a model would look as follows:

	Socio-political commitment	*Attitude towards modernist aesthetic*	*Interest in form*	*Commitment to epistemology*
Avant-gardist postmodernism	Direct, but weak (critique of socio-political status quo)	Rebellious	Low	Weak
Poststructuralist postmodernism	Indirect, but strong (critique of bourgeois subject)	Intellectual rejection	Strong	Very strong
Aesthetic, erotic (neoconservative) postmodernism	None	Indifferent	Strong	None

Needless to say, this is a simplification that will not necessarily allow an easy classification of all postmodern works of art. Two, or even all three, postmodernisms may coexist peacefully within, for instance, one and the same novel. One might well argue that the failure to recognize this coexistence has vexed much recent criticism, especially literary criticism. It is virtually impossible to keep up with the flood of publications that attempt to place Pynchon, Coover, Brautigan, Barthelme, and other American postmodern writers in the poststructuralist camp. One can only do so, however, at the expense of other important elements in their work, elements that are clearly avant-gardist in nature (Pynchon's eschatological interests in *Gravity's Rainbow*, Coover's political stance in *The Public Burning*) or even purely aesthetic. There is, in fact, not much purely poststructuralist postmodernism to be found in American or, for that matter, British fiction.

What we are witnessing in these exclusively poststructuralist readings of much postmodern art is a highly interesting falsification of history. Just as the 1950s created their high modernism – the most élitist, intellectual, academic of all modernist manifestations – so the late 1970s and 1980s have created their 'high postmodernism'. Once again, the vanguard of the academic establishment has focused on the most élitist, most intellectual mode within a broad cultural movement, and is proclaiming that mode as the movement's only true representative, its only authentic voice – even if that voice can only tell us about the inescapable inauthenticity of everything and all. It is tempting to think that this overwhelming interest in high postmodernism has its source in the contemporary critic's deep desire to be 'professional', to move with grace from criticism to philosophy – and back again. And that, too, is not new: it is a next stage in the professionalization of criticism in this century, a professionalization that gave us, earlier, high modernism.

But let me go back to the model that I have just presented and point out how it clarifies the critical discussion. If Huyssen tells us that Warhol 'simply reproduces mass reproduced reality like Coca Cola bottles, Brillo boxes' and that, unlike Duchamp in his polemic against the distinction between art and non-art, he 'is no longer even interested in such a polemic' (Huyssen 1986: 148), he refuses to admit Warhol into the avant-gardist camp and places him in the neoconservative, uncommitted camp. If Newman argues that 'Pop Artists . . . turned their images into high art emblems in a way which blocked any insight they might have afforded into the social relations of consumerism and ideological reproduction' (Newman 1986: 35), he accuses them of epistemological indifference. If Jameson speaks of postmodernism's pastiche, its strategy of 'bland' parody, he has in mind its political and epistemological indifference. From the point of view of avant-gardist postmodernism, both poststructuralist postmodernism (although it may legitimately be said to be political in its critique of the subject and of representation) and neoconservative postmodernism are under attack; from the poststructuralist point of view, both avant-gardist postmodernism (for its naive indifference to epistemology and its equally naive refusal to really question representation) and neoconservative postmodernism are also under fire.

As usual, prescriptive norms (art should be political, epistemological, or both) are being applied as evaluative criteria. One might, in fact, argue that these norms are essentially modernist in character, going back to the modern avant-garde and to modernism's epistemological interest, respectively. There is simply a postmodernism, with a wide variety of manifestations, that privileges form over content. It does not involve a return to history and representation. Arguably, this aesthetic, sensuous postmodernism that appeals to an erotics of art has been with us right from the start, in some of the new art that Susan Sontag described in the 1960s. Aesthetic postmodernism is Sontag's anti-interpretative art become indifferent to interpretation, while retaining its sharp interest in form and in art's erotic possibilities. It prefers 'surface wit over deeper investigation', as Charles Jencks puts it in a reference to Phillip Johnson's architecture (Jencks 1981: 86), and is usually ironic about itself, while still appealing to the senses. It is that new anti-modernist art which is no longer interested in the modernist aesthetic: it starts from the assumption that modernism is dead and buried and goes on to plunder its grave for techniques and ideas.

There is no denying that this aesthetic, politically and epistemologically indifferent, postmodernism is often close to what Newman calls 'the cynical nihilism of fashion and the mass-culture industry' (Newman 1986: 48). But that does not deny its status as art. Moreover, such an indictment – which, to be fair to Newman, would be endorsed by most, if not all, important critics in the field – again repeats high modernist obsessions: the distaste for the masses (even if it is masked in phrases like 'mass-culture industry', which suggest that the masses cannot help being manipulated – but then they never could) and the authenticity of art, an art that offers a superior discourse in a fallen world.

We must accept architectural 'historicism' – the 'decorated shed' – pastiche, phantasmagoria, the deceptive return to narrative and painting, the use of high technology as in rock videos, a finally committed eclecticism, in their own right. Aesthetic postmodernism and its erotic, often high-tech off-shoots are there, as important as avant-gardist and poststructural postmodernism. Perhaps its combination of technical sophistication and lack of commitment is a sign of the times, as Jameson argues. If that is the case, there is even more reason to monitor it closely, and even less reason to do so from an essentially modernist point of view.

8 Narratives of Postmodernism

John Mepham

There are four kinds of answer to the question, What is postmodern about postmodernist fiction? The first is historical and takes the form of a narrative. It defines the postmodern in terms of its movement away from, or rejection of, some aspects of modernism. The second is philosophical and sees postmodernist fiction as arising on a site cleared by philosophy (or 'poststructuralism'). All sorts of conceptual slums have been demolished, it is said, by the realization that 'meaning is undecidable' and that 'reality is constructed in and through language'. What is postmodern about postmodernist fiction is its allegiance to these philosophical positions (Thiher, 1984). The third can be called ideological (or pedagogic). It defines postmodernist fiction in terms of its intended effects, which are that it should 'problematise reality', 'unsettle the reader's sense of "reality"' (Waugh 1984: 22, 52) or unmask or lay bare 'the process of world-construction' (McHale 1987: 101). What is postmodern about postmodernist fiction is its aim to teach us a lesson in how worlds are made. The fourth definition is in terms of the textual strategies which it employs. These strategies are designed to foreground the textuality of the fiction ('metafictional' strategies), to force constant reinterpretation by 'reframing', or to generate multiple ontologies, a plurality of worlds. Such strategies and their variants have a long history in both literary and philosophical fictions, and it is difficult to sustain the idea that they are characteristically 'post-modern'.

Let us consider first the historical approach to postmodernism and its fiction, which sees these cultural phenomena as part of the general story of our age. One version of the story is this. There was initiated in the Enlightenment period the project of modernity, the building of a world based on reason, truth and justice. This project was sustained through the enormous changes of the nineteenth century, but eventually began to fall apart. Its basis, the legitimation of knowledge and of social justice by certain 'grand narratives', lost credibility as a result of developments within both the sciences and society (Lyotard 1984). After a transitional period of crisis, of mourning and nostalgia for the defunct forms of legitimation, we have now entered the postmodern age. There has now been completed a decisive historical break with the Enlightenment project and with its politics (both liberalism and socialism). The break is registered in many way: 'postindustrial' society, 'postsocialist' politics, 'postmodernist' culture, and so on. This view, that there has occurred or is occurring a deeply significant rupture or discontinuity with the forms of society, politics and thought of the last 200 years, is very widespread. Connections are plotted between the development of fiction and changes in every aspect of social life (see Rorty 1985, on the debate between Lyotard and Habermas).

Symptoms of this decisive seismic event are discerned everywhere. It is as if we were breaking loose from forms of culture, experience and identity which have characterized a whole epoch (the 'modern') and a great cultural labour, attempting to diagnose our new condition, is under way in many different intellectual and aesthetic fields. Concepts sprout up everywhere – 'the post-modern predicament' (Lawson 1985), 'post-philosophy' (Rorty 1982), as well as the more familiar 'poststructuralism' and 'postmodernism'.

That is the story into which discourses on postmodern fiction are woven. Developments in fiction are narrated as developments within culture, and cultural postmodernism is seen everywhere and in everything. A recent inventory of cultural items which have been described as 'postmodern' includes the following:

> The décor of a room, the design of a building, the diagesis of a film, the construction of a record, or a scratch video, a television commercial, or an arts documentary, or the intertextual relations between them, the layout of a page in a fashion magazine or critical journal, an anti-teleological tendency within epistemology, the attack on the metaphysics of presence, a general attenuation of feeling, the collective chagrin and morbid projections of a post-war generation of baby boomers confronting disillusioned middle age, the 'predicament' of reflexivity, a group of rhetorical tropes, a proliferation of surfaces, a new phase in commodity fetishism, a fascination for images, codes and styles, a process of cultural, political or existential fragmentation and/or crisis, the 'decentring' of the subject, an 'incredulity towards metanarratives', the replacement of unitary power axes by a plurality of power/discourse formations, the 'implosion of meaning', the collapse of cultural hierarchies, the dread engendered by the threat of nuclear self-destruction, the decline of the University, the functioning and effects of the new miniaturised technologies, broad societal and economic shifts into a 'media', 'consumer' or 'multinational' phase, a sense (depending on who you read) of placelessness . . . or the abandonment of placelessness . . . or (even) a generalised substitution of spatial for temporal coordinates . . . (Hebdige 1986)

The one thing missing from this list, however, is postmodernist fiction. What were 'modernism' and 'modernist fiction'? The problem, of course, is that these too are conceptual constructs which come in many versions. There were many 'modernisms' and they differed from each other aesthetically, ethically and politically (see Berman 1982; Anderson 1984).

It is easier to find a coherent narrative of the postmodern if we look not at literature, but at architecture, and it is perhaps no surprise that the history of architecture has been such a crucial frame of reference in the development of the idea of the postmodern (Jencks 1986). Architectural modernism was still firmly rooted in the Enlightenment project. It is an aesthetic equivalent to positivism in philosophy, and is conceived in terms of the social project of emancipation by technology and science. Its most visible form in architecture was the International Style; its ideology was the rational analysis of function, the enthusiasm for modern materials, the dislike of decoration. Among its famous concepts was that of the house as a machine for living in (Le Corbusier). This 'positivist modernism' was the publicly most visible form of modernism as a more general aesthetic movement. It was dramatically repudiated by the demolition of tower blocks of flats which had been found uninhabitable. Not only were the unlamented modernist buildings themselves reduced to rubble, but also the aspirations which they embodied, to social harmony and beauty to be achieved by the control of the physical and social environment by professional intellectuals.

As David Edgar has argued, 'postmodernism' in this context sometimes signifies a rejection of the élitism of the avant-garde, and a critique of the modernist project as monolithic and soulless.

> From abstract painting to atonal music, from expressionist drama
> to free verse, from (as Tom Wolfe put it) 'Bauhaus to Our House',
> the modern movement is seen as being part of the 20th century
> socialist project of imposing on society a preconceived rationalism
> that neither could nor attempted to accommodate the infinite
> variety of actual human experience and aspiration and desire in
> the real world. (Edgar 1987)

But in both architecture and, even more, literature, there is disagreement as to where to draw the line. Is the Pompidou Centre in Paris postmodernist, as many writers assume, or is it late modernist? How particular works sort into the two classes depends on the tale you tell. For example, according to David Edgar's story, the radical suppression of coherent narrative form, the refusal to construct a coherent fictional world are among those late modernist forms of narrative art now repudiated for their hermeticism and lack of popular appeal. Postmodernism, for him, includes a return to coherent fictional worlds, perhaps interwoven in complex ways, as in Dennis Potter's *The Singing Detective*, and combined with elements of music hall or vaudeville entertainment forms. This is the repudiation of 'realism' without falling into the trap of producing unintelligibly 'conceptual' art.

The equivalent in literature to these ways of defining the postmodern in architecture and television is provided by John Barth, who also gives high priority to the project of breaking with late modernist forms:

> My ideal postmodernist author . . . aspires to a fiction more
> democratic in its appeal than such late modernist marvels (by my
> definition and in my judgement) as Beckett's *Stories and Texts for
> Nothing* or Nabokov's *Pale Fire*. He may not hope to reach and
> move the devotees of James Michener and Irving Wallace – not to
> mention the lobotomized mass-media illiterates. But he *should*
> hope to reach and delight, at least part of the time, beyond the
> circle of what Mann used to call the Early Christians: professional
> devotees of high art! (Barth 1980b)

So the 'postmodern' is a variable historical category, constructed by
diverse historical narratives. The narrative which one chooses to tell is
itself an expression of aesthetic and value positions. Those who give
high priority to the erasure of the boundary between 'high art' and
'popular culture' would define the postmodern differently from those
who place greater emphasis on more radical experiments in form.

Let us now examine that version of the grand narrative of modernism
and its repudiation on which discourses on postmodernist fiction are
more usually founded. In this story, modernist literature is taken to
represent a culture which was a half-way stage in the itinerary away
from the Enlightenment. Modernism was an incomplete break with the
great, confident art forms of the nineteenth century. Richard Rorty
(1982) has represented positivism as 'a half-way stage on the way to
doing without God' and towards 'the end of philosophy'. Similarly,
modernist art has been seen as a half-way stage between 'realism' and
the postmodernist refusal of representation. Modernist fiction, according to this view, was based on a realist representation of subjectivity, on
the world as constructed in and by consciousness. Its emphasis was on
the stream of consciousness, the lived experience of time and memory,
and the effects of the unconscious on conscious experience. Its main
practitioners were Proust, Joyce and Woolf. Another emphasis which
these three have in common is what we might call the representation of
epiphany (in Joyce's term) – it took the vocation of art to be the
representation of the overwhelming importance and quasi-religious
significance of 'moments of vision', or of 'being' (Woolf), of involun-
tary memory (Proust), or of 'epiphanic' moments of insight (Joyce).
According to this story, with the shift to postmodernism, there is a
move away from conceiving the world as constructed in subjectivity
towards a conception of the world as constructed through language
(Waugh 1984).

Not only was modernism, thus defined, an incomplete break with the
past, it was also an art of nostalgia for lost traditions. Just as the atheist
is incompletely emancipated as long as he/she spends long hours
furiously shaking his/her fist at the non-existent God, so the modernist
was still trapped in an obsession with the world he/she had lost. 'Oh
word, thou word that I lack!' says Shoenberg's Moses, an exemplary
gesture of modernist nostalgia for traditional authority of expression.
The modernist hero is alienated (see Lionel Trilling 1965 on modernism

as an art of alienation), that is, separated from those traditions which used to sanction the voice of the artist as prophet, as miraculous authority, as prince. T. S. Eliot's Prufrock finds with regret that he cannot adopt the voices of John The Baptist, Lazarus or Hamlet.

Postmodernism, in this story, is a movement which is released from such a deadening regret for lost social roles of authority and prophecy. It is free to enjoy itself, to have fun. 'A mourning process has now been completed', says Lyotard. 'Most people have lost the nostalgia for the lost narrative' (Lyotard 1984: 41). Postmodernist literature, freed from those ancient responsibilities, can therefore use low art forms (thriller, detective story, fantasy, and so on), can imitate or make fun of past traditions (pastiche, parody) and can invent ever more radically innovative and subversive forms. From modernism to postmodernism is from *The Castle* to the carnival, from agonized silence to inconsequential babble.

Confirmation of this story is provided by evidence of just how much modernism did still employ the vocabulary of the Enlightenment project, the vocabulary of rational consensus, of universals of reason and value, of totality and synthesis (the aim of producing in both thought and institutions, unified wholes in which the interests and needs of all are non-conflictually combined in a beautiful, rational harmony). Raymond Williams (1986), for example, finds that we have passed 'beyond the modern', both because of the crucial significance of new technologies (cinema, television, recorded music, and so on), but also because we are now distanced from the aesthetic, intellectual and psychological universals of the modernist period. Similarly, the contest between Lyotard and his great opponent in philosophy, Jürgen Habermas, seems to rest on the question of universals (see Rorty 1985). Habermas is seen as a modernist philosopher, still in pursuit of the idea of universals of reason, of rational agreement, of consensus based on unobstructed communication. Lyotard, the philosopher of the postmodern, champions not consensus, but dissent and paralogy (innovation by argumentation which breaks the established rules of reasoning).

As for modernist literature, a key witness to the fact that similar values and priorities could be discovered there is Erich Auerbach. His version of 'modernism' can be found in the last chapters of his *Mimesis* (1953), and it is again a modernist realism of consciousness, found in Proust, Joyce and Woolf. Auerbach's theme might be called *the recontextualization of fragments*. Subjective experience is, he argues, discontinuous and fragmentary. Writing can provide a double context in which an episode can appear both within the fiction, as fragmentary, and simultaneously within the written text, as located by what Proust called 'analogy', as part of a meaningful whole. The narrative is a context within which the discontinuous fragments of experience are composed into a unity. Everyday life and forms of comprehension do not afford positions from which a synthesis of the fragments into a unity can be realized. The ambiguously located 'voice' of free, indirect discourse (perhaps modernist fiction's most characteristic textual strategy) brings 'the severed parts' together (in the words of Virginia Woolf). In this textual context, their full significance can be revealed. Proust's narrator's taste of madeleine, Clarissa Dalloway's vision of tranquillity on a sea shore in *Mrs Dalloway*, Gabriel Conroy's view of the snow falling outside his hotel window ('The Dead' in *Dubliners*) are each verbally contextualized by the narrative in such a way as to reveal (and 'relevation' does not seem too strong a word) what Auerbach calls 'the omnitemporality of events'.

Postmodernism repudiates this 'omnitemporality' and puts in its place its notion of 'the presence of the past'. This does not mean authentic memory or living tradition, but the ironic use of old forms, in parody or pastiche (as in Fowles's *The French Lieutenant's Woman*), or the quotation of old material for decorative embellishment or stylistic wit (see Hutcheon 1988). In Auerbach's construction of modern fiction, the presence of the past is seen as the discovery of ways of writing about moments of experience which make of them something so analogically powerful that they connect up with and inform the totality of life through an act of 'symbolic snythesis'.

These modernist authors failed to find any possibility of symbolic or narrative synthesis in the domains of society or history. In this, they were out of step with other varieties of modernism, which were based on narrativized social history and social project (as in Le Corbusier's writings, in Futurism or Russian Constructivism, or, in literature, in the ironic histories of Thomas Mann). Proust's Marcel learns of the banality of the history that had once enchanted him when Madame Verdurin becomes the Duchesse de Guermantes. In *Ulysses*, historical unity of meaning is a matter of '*metem pike hoses*', a comic and incredible version of the transubstantiation of souls and the repetition of life stories. For Virginia Woolf, nature and history are nonsense; the indifference of war and of natural process is narrated in the 'Time Passes' section of *To the Lighthouse*. These writers had no belief in the grand narratives of social and historical process. But, in contrast with their postmodernist successors, this incredulity was incomplete. They turned inwards and there discovered a domain in which the great Enlightenment aspirations of intelligibility, order, synthesis and totality were found, according to Auerbach, to be still operable.

> The great exterior turning points and blows of fate are granted less importance; they are credited with less power of yielding decisive information concerning the subject; on the other hand there is confidence that in any random fragment plucked from the course of a life at any time the *totality* of its fate is contained and can be portrayed. There is greater confidence in *synthesis* gained through full exploitation of an everyday occurrence than in a chronologically well-ordered *total* treatment which accompanies the subject from beginning to end, attempts not to omit anything

externally important, and emphasises the great turning points of destiny. (Auerbach 1953: 484; my italics.)

In this account, the recontextualization of fragments replaces chronological narrative of the subject's itinerary through life as the dominant formal strategy of fiction. Not only do modern aspirations to completeness and intelligibility survive here, the essential presupposition is that axiom of the modern age, the unity, changeable but ultimately coherent, of the self and of a life.

> For there is always going on within us a process of formulation and interpretation whose subject matter is our own self. We are constantly endeavoring to give meaning and order to our lives in the past, the present, and the future, to our surroundings, the world in which we live; with the result that our lives appear in our own conception as *total entities* . . . These are the forms of order and interpretation which the modern writers here under discussion attempt to grasp in the random moment – not one order and one interpretation, but many, which may either be those of different persons or of the same person at different times; so that overlapping, complementing, and contradiction yield something that we might call a *synthesised cosmic view* or at least a challenge to *the reader's will to interpretive synthesis*. (Auerbach 1953: 485; my italics.)

Nothing could be better calculated to raise a postmodernist snigger than this culminating flourish, the 'cosmic view', in which we move from humanism to something even more all-embracingly universal.

One could argue that Auerbach's story is not accurate, even in respect of those authors on whom he concentrates. We might want to point out more 'postmodern' elements in the work of these authors, such as the famous 'orts and fragments' of Woolf's *Between the Acts* or the pastiche sections of *Ulysses*. Moreover, this view of things leaves out many other important modernist works from the same period which could not convincingly be described in these terms (surrealism, Kafka, Roussel, Thomas Mann). Nevertheless, this discourse on modernism is adopted by the critics of postmodernist fiction as a useful way of drawing lines, of demarcating between the two.

For example, McHale argues along these lines, drawing on the vocabulary of Mikhail Bakhtin. The novel, including the modernist novel, is characterized by heteroglossia, the representation of different languages, the pluralism of voices. But beneath the polyphony there is a master voice or master language. Just as Auerbach saw modern fiction as representing different interpretations which are synthesized into a totality, so too in McHale's story, modernist fiction contains many voices, but they are orchestrated and controlled by one master voice which imposes its privileged interpretation on all the others. The text is, therefore, in spite of appearances, monological. The reader's will to interpretative synthesis is engaged and encouraged to give credence to this implicit monological discourse; the many interpretations are contextualized by it into total and coherent meaning. Of *Ulysses*, for example, McHale says: 'The world is stable and reconstructible, forming an ontologically unproblematic backdrop against which the movements of the characters' minds may be displayed. Modernist fiction is short!' (McHale 1987: 234). Whereas modernist works, he argues, display heteroglossia within a unifying monological perspective ('Modernist texts integrate the multiple worlds of discourse into a single ontological plane, a unified projected world' (165)), postmodernist fiction prefers polyphony as a positive principle; it is a pluralization of worlds of discourse.

Is this narrative of modernist and postmodernist fiction convincing? Do not both *To the Lighthouse*, and even more obviously *The Waves*, project different worlds, without privileging any one of the discourses? Kafka, often a thorn in the flesh for literary narratives and taxonomists, reappears in McHale's story as one of the founding fathers of postmodernist fiction. Each way of telling the story of the move from modernist to postmodernist fiction reshuffles the pack and increases one's incredulity or lack of confidence in such narratives. McHale's discourse is both a chronological account and a conceptual demarcation; postmodernism is what comes after modernism but it is also a particular 'poetics' of plurality. When, as in Kafka's case, the post-modernist phenomenon appears not after, but at the founding moment of modernism, the whole chronological aspect of the discourse becomes incoherent. This is the point at which Lyotard is driven to make his famously fatuous remark, that the postmodern 'is undoubtedly a part of the modern . . . A work can become modern only if it is first postmodern. Postmodernism thus understood is not modernism at its end but in the nascent state, and this state is constant'. (Lyotard 1984: 79)

Though Lyotard's remark signals the definitive breakdown of the discourse on postmodernist fiction as historical narrative, one can say that the terms of Auerbach's discourse and their rejection do serve, if we are careful to curb our will to interpretative synthesis, our desire for *system*, to identify some of the notable features of post-Second World War fiction which discourses on postmodernist fiction attempt to understand. This fiction has often emphasized the decentring or disintegration of the subject, the effort of fiction to defeat rather than to endorse the reader's will to interpretative synthesis, the reality of contradictions, not to be worked out or resolved in a monological discourse, the plurality of discourses and of worlds. Instead of the fragment from which we draw forth all human life, postmodernist fiction postulates a plurality of discursive contexts or frames, within which even the seemingly most reliable and stable unities take on a shifting, disturbingly plural aspect. Even the commonplace unity of the US mail system bifurcates, and is seen to contain within it, or in parallel to it, a centuries-old disruptive conspiratorial sect (in Thomas Pynchon's *The Crying of Lot 49* (1967)).

Modernist fiction endorsed the reader's will to read the fragment into a totality, so that the reader is like Cuvier, the paleontologist, who could, on the basis of some fragment of jaw bone or skull, reconstruct an entire mastodon. In postmodernist fiction, this move to reconstruction breaks down, for both the reader and the fictional characters. In *The French Lieutenant's Woman*, the hero Charles Smithson, an amateur of the scientific study of fossils, which unmistakably signifies the modernity of his thinking, reaches the limits of his understanding when confronted by the uninterpretable Sarah Woodruff who, at least in some of the several versions of the story which the reader is invited to choose between, is a figure signifying the postmodern future and the defeat of systematic thought.

Modernist fiction, in the story we have been reporting, found no way of unifying social and historical events within a meaningful narrative, and therefore shifted attention to the inner world. Some post-Second World War fiction has turned its attention back again to the representation of society and history, and manages through its fictional narrators to found coherent visions and grand narratives. What marks such fiction off, however, is that it is utterly incredible. The narratives of *The Tin Drum* or *One Hundred Years of Solitude*, of *Midnight's Children* or *Slaughterhouse-Five* are like do-it-yourself grand narratives, as if, since the culture provides nothing credible by way of history, the narrators have no option but to provide their own, however bizarre. It is as if life is impossible without them, as if the history of our century cannot be told except by inventing 'outlandish', even extra-terrestrial points of view. The history of India is too crazy to be told except as a secret magic conspiracy of midnight's children. The bombing of Dresden is unnarratable except from the Trafalmadorian point of view adopted by Billy Pilgrim (in *Slaughterhouse-Five*), which is the only resource he has available to him to keep going after his experience of that air raid. Crises make life meaningless, so the character's try

> to re-invent themselves and their universe. Science fiction was a big help! Rosewater said an interesting thing to Billy one time about a book that wasn't science fiction. He said that everything there was to know about life was in *The Brothers Karamazov*, by Feodor Dostoevsky. But that isn't *enough* anymore, said Rosewater. (Vonnegut 1979: 70–1).

Whereas, 'modernist fiction' still put its trust in the synthesized order of beginnings and endings (the achieved 'vision' which ends *Dubliners* or *To the Lighthouse*), 'postmodern fiction' feels free to dispense with these arbitrary conventions. A fiction may have no ending at all, but circle back to its own beginning (*Finnegans Wake*, or Gabriel Josipovici's 'Mobius the Stripper').

In the face of such a proliferation of themes, textual strategies and effects, the (paradoxical) temptation to produce a unifying narrative or concept is, it seems, overwhelming. Hence the premodern narratives about postmodernist fiction, in which the whole plurality of phenomena is seen as the unfolding of one coherent story, that of cleansing fiction of all its remaining vestiges of Enlightenment ideology, of universals, totality and closure. Postmodernism is militant and vigilant: 'We have paid a high enough price for the nostalgia of the whole and the one . . . Let us wage a war on totality' (Lyotard 1984: 82). The postmodern philosopher, ludicrously adopting this military posture, tells a simple tale about the naivity of tale-telling, grandly narrativizes his incredulity towards grand narratives.

This is the story of the passage from modernist to postmodernist fictions told in terms of the narrative of the modern as half-way stage out of the Enlightenment. Let us move on to one of the two main philosophical characterizations of the postmodern, which stands in contrast to Auerbach's vision of the modern as *the recontextualization of the fragments*. We might call it the 'postmodern' as *undecidability of meaning* arising from *the fragmentation of pluralization of contexts*. What we are talking about here is the philosophical discourse of 'poststructuralism' and its relations with discourses on postmodernist fiction.

If Auerbach's modernism takes the recontextualization of the fragment as a general metaphor for the pursuit of a timeless humanity and the will to interpretative synthesis, poststructuralist philosophy, here represented by Jacques Derrida's *Spurs: Nietzsche's Styles* (1979b), has taken the possibility for endlessly reconstructing context as a general metaphor for the openness of all texts.

Among the papers found at Nietzsche's death there was one on which was written, in inverted commas, 'I have forgotton my umbrella'. No sentence is intelligible without a context. The meaning of a sentence is not made up from some reference to a series of meanings achieved by its words, but is its usage, within a language game, in a specific, practical context which provides the anchoring to life that makes meanings possible. The context of utterance includes the speaker or writer, tone of voice and gesture, purposes and intentions, as well as the surrounding scene of the utterance. These kinds of information may allow the reader/hearer to assign a particular meaning to the utterance. So the spoken word 'Fire!', for example, might be interpreted in different contexts, as an order to pull a trigger and kill somebody, a warning that a building is going up in flames, part of an explanation of the basic categories of material being in classical Greek philosophy, a foreigner's request for a match, and so on.

Nietzsche's written remark, Derrida argues, is open to many possible interpretations. It may be a citation, a memorandum, an example he intended to use in an argument, a joke, or it may have been a demented verbal flourish devoid of meaning altogether. It may not even be Nietzsche's at all. Or perhaps it is a metaphor ('I am out, unprotected, in the storm . . .'). Perhaps it shoud be read as an expression of a disguised, unconscious castration anxiety to be interpreted within a Freudian framework (note the use of umbrellas in D. M. Thomas's *The White Hotel*). We do not know. It may never be possible to disambiguate the sentence. We may never know what the context of the utterance was. The meaning of the remark will therefore remain forever undecidable. It is a text.

> Because it is structurally liberated from any living meaning, it is
> always possible that it means nothing at all or that it has no
> meaning. There is no end to its parodying play with meaning,
> grafted here and there, beyond any contextual body or finite code.
> (Derrida 1979b)

It is the absence of a contextual body, the source of living meaning, which produces the undecidability.

Or perhaps Wittgenstein's (1953) metaphor of language being on holiday, being disconnected from any particular language games, is relevant here. The fragment can be grafted by the reader in imagination into many games. We could even imagine that what Nietzsche meant by this note was to say: 'The will to meaning has its limits. It is possible to produce a text which, though perfectly grammatical, is infinitely open in its play'. Furthermore, Derrida goes on to argue, perhaps not only this little text, but the totality of Nietzsche's text, his writings, are of the same sort. Indeed, perhaps all texts are of the same sort, since none are so unambiguously contexted, or caught up in life, that we can decide with certainty what their singular meaning is. Any text will be open to the reinterpretation that will result from taking it as figurative rather than literal, as a joke rather than as 'serious', as irony rather than as straightforward assertion, and these are reinterpretations that are never entirely closed off. So, everything which is textual is undecidable.

What is at issue here is once again the notion of 'totality'. John Austin (1962) recognized, but without seeing the full implications of it, that to understand speech acts, to know which acts are being performed with which effects, would require 'a mastery of the total context' (Culler 1983): 'the total speech act in the total speech situation is the only actual phenomenon which, in the last resort, we are engaged in elucidating' (Austin 1962; Derrida 1979b). So, rather than Nietzsche's fragment providing us with a challenge to our will to interpretative synthesis, with a metaphor for the revelation of meaning by recontextualization, quite the opposite is involved. The fragment can itself be taken as a metaphor for the undecidability of all texts, since our will to meaning will always be defeated by the plurality of possible reinterpretations of context. 'Meaning is context-bound, but context is boundless' (Culler 1983).

We are in the same situation when it comes to understanding anything at all, since everything is textual – a past event, a life, a society – all present themselves to us, for our will to meaning to get to work on, in the form of words, utterances, texts. Often, perhaps too often, the item that gives rise to crisis by simultaneously inviting and defying understanding is represented as a woman: Mary Crick in Graham Swift's *Waterland*; Sarah Woodruff in John Fowles's *The French Lieutenant's Woman*; A . . . in Alain Robbe-Grillet's *La Jalousie*, and so on. I myself prefer the idea that the unmastered 'truth' is a greasy pig:

> How do we seize the past? Can we ever do so? When I was a
> medical student some pranksters at an end-of-term dance released
> into the hall a piglet which had been smeared with grease. It
> squirmed between legs, evaded capture, squealed a lot. People fell
> over things to grasp it, and were made to look ridiculous in the
> process. The past often seems to behave like that piglet! (Barnes
> 1985: 14)

We have various defences, which to some extent protect us against radical undecidability in practice. When we are dealing not with a text but with a voice, the contextual body provides us with that living meaning which, as Derrida points out, is absent in the case of Nietzsche's fragments. We (sometimes) trust our ability to read the body of an interlocutor and to ground our interpretations of a conversation on our imaginative understanding of another's bodily plight. When to invoke undecidability and when to invoke norms which lead to decisions, to closure of meaning, is a practical-ethical question (Butler 1984). Consider, for example, the moving, fragmentary notes written by Kafka in order to communicate with his friends as he lay dying, unable to speak. Even though they are in some cases even more fragmentary than Nietzsche's note, their meaning can be retrieved by our grasp of the situation of their 'utterance'.

The presence of the body and the 'speaker' sometimes, even in such difficult circumstances as these, gives us some reliable basis for understanding and trust that enables us to 'read' what is being written. Of course, it is always *possible* to speculate playfully on alternative interpretations of what is going on. For example, if we came across somebody apparently injured and in great pain, we could ask whether this is a stunt, a film, a joke, or a robot. But to invoke undecidability here would be ethically unacceptable. It would be like saying that unless meaning presented itself with a certain perfect but impossible clarity, one would not be prepared to give any credence to any meanings whatsoever.

This is not to propose, as a solution to problems of interpretation, a simple dichotomy (decidable, embodied speech as against undecidable, disembodied text). For one thing, as countless broken hearts can testify, embodied speech is not necessarily reliable. As Barthes disarmingly points out in *A Lover's Discourse* (1978), under the heading 'The Uncertainty of Signs': 'whether he seeks to prove his love, or to discover if the other loves him, the amorous subject has no system of sure signs at his disposal'. In both life and literature, there are some contexts in which it is appropriate to invoke undecidability, and others in which it is appropriate to invoke trust. Systematic undermining of trust, of a sense of reliable interpretation, can be achieved by a systematic ambiguity, or plurality of context, for each utterance. This is the textual strategic rule of postmodernist fiction, to produce systematic uncertainty of signs by locating each one of them within more than one interpretative framework, thereby frustrating the reader's will to interpretative synthesis.

There are many ways in which fiction can exploit the possibilities for producing undecidable elements, or elements which hover unstably between two or more interpretations, as a result of being inserted within different frames or contexts. Textual strategies of foregrounding and reframing and so on are calculated to engage the reader in a play of plural interpretations, so that the reader's sense of a stable, reliable (fictional) world is disturbed. The world or worlds projected by the fiction are 'problematized', or shown to be liable to erasure. The reader, operating with different possible worlds in mind at the same time, finds that they 'flicker', or show 'iridescence' (McHale 1987: 99). So, why choose textual strategies which promote postmodernist undecidability?

In the first kind of fiction, which we can call *mimetic relativism* (and which some classify as postmodernist while others do not), the text projects a possible world. The world, however, is projected as open to radically different interpretations which neither characters nor readers are in a good position to choose between. In the absence of a traditionally authoritative narrator, the reader's will to interpretative synthesis is engaged, but within different and incompatible frameworks between which the fiction itself proposes no resolution. For example, in *The Crying of Lot 49*, the heroine Oedipa Maas is suspended between various possible interpretations of a whole series of strange events: are they coincidence, conspiracy or paranoia, and if conspiracy then by whom? In *Slaughterhouse-Five*, the terrestrial and the Tralfamadorian interpretations of the history of Earthling societies are each presented and there is no adjudication between them. Even if the reader is not convinced by the story of Billy Pilgrim's sojourn in a Tralfamadorian zoo, he/she is still left with the possibility that an interpretation of Earth's history from a non-terrestrial perspective may be required if one is to make any sense of it. Other celebrated examples are Salman Rushdie's *Midnight's Children*, Mario Vargas Llosa's *The War at the End of the World*, and Umberto Eco's *The Name of the Rose*. In this last novel, it is as if the world is suspended between two epochs (as it is in our own time, according to the proponents of the postmodern) and that it is this fact of being in a transitional phase which produces the phenomenon of co-existing frames of interpretation, and hence of undecidability. In this case, and in all the other novels mentioned here, undecidability is presented as a *historical* phenomenon. There is a historical and cultural motivation for the choice of 'postmodern' textual strategies, if that is what they are. Problems of 'textuality' and incredulity towards 'official' grand narratives are represented as arising in particular kinds of conditions – circumstances of historical catas-trophe, crisis or outrage (*The Tin Drum, Slaughterhouse-Five*) or contexts associated with transitional periods of modernization or nation building (*War at the End of the World, Midnight's Children* and *Shame*).

The second kind of textual strategy for producing undecidability depends on what we call *abortive mimesis*. In this case, the problems arise from inconsistent or interrupted mimesis. Possible worlds are projected at different and incompatible ontological levels, so that when items appear within two different worlds they are 'unreadable'. Mimesis stops and starts and the reader is forced to reframe but can never arrive at a coherent and stable solution. An analogy commonly invoked here is that of the drawings of impossible worlds or objects by Max Escher. Examples in fiction abound, and Brian McHale (1978) gives a detailed and thorough examination of the textual strategies involved. The term 'metafiction' is also used for this kind of text (Waugh 1984; Martin 1986). The most celebrated example is Robbe-Grillet's *Dans le labyrinthe* in which, for example, a scene of two soldiers sitting in a café changes back and forth between being an event in the fictional world and an event depicted in a painting in the fictional world. Other examples involve the breaking into the frame of the fictional world by the (fictional) author or reader. In *The French Lieutenant's Woman*, the author joins a character on a train journey, even though he lives in another century and exists on a different ontological level. Calvino's *If on a Winter's Night a Traveller* opens with 'the reader' sitting down to start to read this very book. 'Vertigo' is a word commonly used to describe the effects of such textual strategies, for the reader is confronted not only with an undecidable situation, but with a logically impossible one. Paradoxes abound. Words are shown to be liable to erasure.

The third kind of textual strategy we can call *non-mimetic*. Instead of interrupted mimesis as before, there is now an absence of mimesis altogether. McHale describes this as fiction in which there is a

> confrontation between worlds of discourse outside of any
> motivating context, in a representational void; where the only
> worlds we are able to reconstruct are the worlds of discourses, and
> not any fictional world that might plausibly contain them. (McHale
> 1987: 169)

In this case, undecidability is generated not by recontextualizing verbal segments within a variety of possible fictional contexts, but by radically decontextualizing them altogether. The writing does not construct a fictional world at all. Mimesis, or reference, is defeated. The only contexts the verbal segments have are each other. The text is a verbal collage which invites local interpretations as puns, hints, connotations. The most famous example is *Finnegans Wake*.

The purpose of strategies of abortive and absent mimesis is usually said to be to undermine the reader's naive realism. Seeing how it is possible, by means of verbal deviance and play, to prevent a coherent fictional world from coming into (fictional) being, the reader is made aware of the fact that the world is constructed in and through language. These methods also allow verbal arts other than those of reference and narrative to flourish and to become the focus of the reader's attention (puns and other word play, lists, metrical effects, and so on). This way of setting out the different reframing strategies, different ways of reversing or obstructing the movement from the fragment to the totality by an insistent pluralization of contexts, allows us to present and contrast two quite different ways of thinking about and classifying postmodernist fictions, that is, two quite different ways of drawing the line between the modern and the postmodern.

Brian McHale's criterion for the demarcation is that postmodernist fictions involve 'many worlds', whereas modernist fiction involves only one world but many interpretations of it. On this criterion, the first kind of textual strategy above would be modernist, the others postmodernist. He does in fact manage to draw together under the one heading ('the ontological dominant', 'alternative worlds' and so on) an extremely heterogeneous collection of novels. Over and above those which involve the textual strategies of abortive mimesis and defeated mimesis, he also includes novels which seem more accurately thought of as profusely mimetic. He manages to do this by classifying together novels which involve 'multiple worlds *of discourse*' and those which involve *reference* to more than one (fictionally) existing world (or 'zone'): he conflates an *aesthetic of hyper-realization* with an *aesthetic of derealization*. Thus, on his postmodernist shelf we will find not only the experimentalist avant-garde (Donald Barthelme, Borges) but also a whole collection of 'popular' works of fantasy and science fiction. I find it more accurate to say that textual strategies of the second and third kind do not involve 'multiple worlds', indeed, that in the end they involve no worlds at all, since mimesis is either not initiated or is systematically obstructed.

The grand narrative of the development from modernist to post-modernist forms that is involved here is as follows. Works using the first kind of textual strategy are based on a nostalgia for 'unproblematic' or 'naive mimesis', for 'direct access to extra-linguistic and extra-textual reality' (McHale 1987: 164). Postmodernist fiction repudiates this impossible dream and does all that it can to advertise 'textuality'. It point towards the future because it is part of the grand narrative of emancipation from past illusions (realism, mimesis) and is based on a more sophisticated philosophical grasp of the relations between language and reality. In a way, postmodernist fictions are said to 'participate in that very general tendency in the intellectual life of our time toward viewing reality as *constructed* in and through our languages, discourses, and semiotic systems'. Their vocation is the 'project of unmasking the constructed nature of reality' (164).

Others, however, have a completely different story to tell. For them, novels of the first kind, mimetically relativistic texts, are postmodernist, whereas novels of the other two kinds are located in branch lines of modernism. For example, novels which involve mimesis which is interrupted by the foregrounding of its own construction ('metafictions') might be seen as in a line of descent from the modernist aesthetic of fabrication (Josipovici 1977). Those which involve an anti-mimetic strategy could be classified as something like hermetic or decadent late modernist, based on an aesthetic of derealization which goes back through Sollers to Mallarmé. Postmodernism is then seen as a healthy return to ironic mimesis after a time of avant-garde experiments in minimalist non-mimetic art. We have already referred to John Barth and Charles Jencks who argue in this vein. It may be, though it is far from clear, that Linda Hutcheon (1987: 12) is one of this same camp. Her definition of postmodernist fictions as 'historiographic metafictions', which are 'intensely self-reflexive and yet lay claim to historical events and personages' suggests that she might be. The heavyweight of this team, however, is Umberto Eco. In his 'Postmodernism, Irony and Enjoyment' in *Reflections on the Name of the Rose* (1985), he argues that postmodernism is a term 'bon à tout faire'. The postmodern is forever being unearthed in surprising places and will no doubt soon be discovered in Homer (in fact, *The Odyssey* would surely be a postmodernist fiction on McHale's criteria!). According to Eco, each historical period develops a cycle of 'modernist' art, and this, as it evolves, generates an avant-garde ('mannerism') which demolishes the past and occupies itself in producing a metalanguage of impossible texts. Avant-gardism leads to silence. There then arises, in reaction to this, a 'postmodernist' aesthetic. Writers look for a way back to writing which is enjoyable without being escapist, of reviving a relation to past styles which avoids both total rejection and simple repetition. Postmodernism is an ironic rethinking of the past. In our time, postmodernist fiction is not the anti-mimetic experimentalism of the obscurantists, but the pleasurably ironic return to fictional forms of coherent story telling.

> I think of the postmodern attitude as that of a man who loves a very cultivated woman and knows he cannot say to her, 'I love you madly', because he knows that she knows (and that she knows that he knows) that these words have already been written by Barbara Cartland. Still, there is a solution. He can say, 'As Barbara Cartland would put it, I love you madly'. At this point, having avoided false innocence, having said clearly that it is no longer possible to speak innocently, he will nevertheless have said what he wanted to say to the woman: that he loves her, but he loves her *in an age of lost innocence*. If the woman goes along with this, she will have received a declaration of love all the same. Neither of the two speakers will feel innocent, both will have accepted the challenge of the past, of the already said, which cannot be

eliminated, both will consciously and with pleasure play the game of irony . . . But both will have succeeded, once again, in speaking of love. (Eco 1985: 67)

Fiction which is based on these same principles can avoid both the naive philistinism of commercial realism and the sophisticated vacuity of meaning of the anti-mimetic schools.

This way of thinking about postmodernist fiction has the following advantages. It is not blind to the break in forms that we have noted as textual strategies; but it recognizes that, just as with the break in forms which came to be called modernist, they cannot all be drawn together usefully into one category. They are used to widely different aesthetic, ethical and cultural effects. Secondly, this position helps us to resist that teleological tendency of thinking which assumes that those works which are formally the most radical and experimental in their break with the past are also the most sophisticated philosophically and represent an 'advance', a pointer to the direction of literary development. Instead they are accorded a certain respect as minor branches of the modernist tradition, but denied the accolade of being the 'Post'. Rather than the category of 'postmodernist fiction' marking a single, well-defined rupture with tradition, it instead signposts a combination of formal innovation and continuity of concern. Though mood and technique have changed, we can recognize a tradition of ironic fiction which operates with double frames ('I love you' taken both as a quotation from the discourse of romantic fiction and as a declaration of feeling); which cultivates a certain undecidability (unanswerable questions); which is self-reflexively aware of the second-hand meanings which fly up as one uses what is inevitably an 'old' language; but which has not lost touch with the cognitive and ethical vocations of literature.

'Postmodernist' might not be the best label for the novels in the later stages of this line, which we would see as running, in the present century, from Kafka's *The Trial* (was K guilty?), Thomas Mann's *Doctor Faustus* (who are we to believe, Serenus Zeitblom or Adrian Leverkuhn?), through early Alain Robbe-Grillet (has the husband in *La Jalousie* any grounds for jealousy?) to Kurt Vonnegut, Graham Swift and Milan Kundera. To promote these more recent works to the rank of 'postmodernist', and to demote such as Robbe-Grillet's *Projet pour une révolution à New York* or Calvino's *If on a Winter's Night a Traveller* to the late modern, would at least be a way of focusing attention on the limitations of a fiction of reiterated stereotypes of sexual violence and fictions which enjoy the paradoxes of self-reference. It would be a way of making a case, at least, for the view that fiction should not abandon the *ethical* in a retreat to the *aesthetic*. In an age of lost innocence, of incredulity, of indecidability, it is more, not less, important for fiction to return to the investigation of the contours of freedom and necessity, of integrity and betrayal, of commitment and recklessness, of trust and complacency. To say 'I love you' ironically is easy. What is it to work, marry, have children, go to war, ironically, with no grand narratives in support?

This is the terrain of such novels as Kundera's *The Unbearable Lightness of Being*. It is 'postmodernist' and 'antirealist' in having a fictional author who self-reflexively muses on how he comes to create his characters, and who intervenes with commentary on the action in ironic mood. Unlike *The French Lieutenant's Woman*, however, with which it shares these features, it proceeds to construct a coherent fictional world and narrative (no jokey meetings between 'author' and characters) and uses them as a means of exploring the possibilities of fidelity in an age of lost innocence. A formally different work, Christa Wolf's *Cassandra: A Novel and Four Essays* (1984), is 'postmodernist' in its self-reflexive presentation of the conditions of its own production, and its opening move from the voice of an 'author' to the voice of the character Cassandra. But far from it adopting what in postmodernist culture are fashionable positions (disbelief in the possibility of distinguishing between fantasy and reality, the autonomy of art), it positively argues that its myths and fantasies are presented as routes back to the real. It is a repudiation of the aesthetic, a return to the political, to a literature of resistance, of witness, of inquiry.

9 Postmodernism and Feminisms

Dina Sherzer

To this date, postmodernism in literature has been associated with texts written by men, and texts written by feminist writers have been classified under feminism. Chronologically, feminist writers irrupted almost simultaneously on the postmodern scene in several countries in the 1970s as the postmodernist male production was dwindling after years of remarkable activity. Is postmodernism replaced by feminism? Is postmodernism present in feminism? Is feminist postmodernism different from the men's postmodernism? Such questions have begun to be discussed (Owens 1983; Sherzer 1987) and what follows is a contribution to the relationship between postmodernism and feminism in several countries where both movements have played and are playing crucial roles in shaping the literary and intellectual climate. After an assessment of several aspects of the *nouveau roman* and feminist writing practices in France, I will discuss the feminist writings of a selection of authors in relation to postmodernism in several South American countries, in Spain, Germany, and the USA.

Feminism is an essential part of postmodernism. For, indeed, as Ihab Hassan puts it, one of the traits of postmodernism is decanonization of all master codes, all conventions, institutions, authorities: 'We deconstruct, displace, demystify the logocentric, ethnocentric, phallocentric order of things' (Hassan 1987b: 445). This general decanonization is what feminism is all about, for feminist texts deconstruct women's oppression and displace the centre of attention away from men in favour of women's culture and possibilities. In this sense, then, a feminist text, but also any ethnic, minority, or Third World text, can be nothing but postmodern. But this is an epistemological and cultural consideration. Another distinctive facet of postmodernism has to do with specific literary representational practices. These have been studied in texts written by men, while studies on feminist texts have tended to focus mainly on feminist content. Hence the need to confront the representational practices of feminists and postmodernists.

In *Contemporary French Fiction* (1986), I analyzed one text written by each of the following new novelists – Samuel Beckett, Michel Butor, Roger Laporte, Robert Pinget, Jean Ricardou, Alain Robbe-Grillet, Maurice Roche, Claude Simon and Philippe Sollers, and one text by each of the following feminist writers – Hélène Cixous, Marguerite Duras and Monique Wittig. Some women writers and critics argue that texts written by women have specific characteristics which make them different from texts written by men. Xavière Gauthier explains that in the published version of *Les Parleuses* (1974), the interviews and discussions she had with Marguerite Duras, nothing has been deleted or corrected because

> . . . we both are women. It is not impossible that if full and well-seated words from time immemorial have been utilized, lined up, piled up by men, the feminine could appear as this slightly wild grass . . . It is perhaps one of the reasons why these discussions run the risk of appearing to nostalgics of beet fields (or of the ordered battlefield) like an inextricable tangle of liana and ivy, an entanglement of climbing or subterranean plants. (Duras and Gauthier 1974: 67–8)

Gauthier advocates, and therefore valorizes, disorder and looseness instead of order and tightness which are, according to her, men's modes of writing. Claudine Herrmann, in *Les Voleuses de langue* (1976: 139–41), suggests that in women's writing there is an interest and a search for incoherence and a lesser tendency to subordinate and coordinate elements and to order them hierarchically. Cixous speaks of the femininity of a text which manifests itself in its immediate flux: 'Nonsens, chantson, sangson' (Cixous 1977: 62).

My examination of texts written by women and by men, however, reveals that the differences between them are not so clear and categorical as these theorists, in their feminist enthusiasm, would want them to be. Like the men's works I have analyzed, Cixous's, Duras's and Wittig's are open texts characterized by fragmentation and discontinuity. Abandoning plot and causality, dislocating narrative organization, disrupting syntax, exploiting word play and intertextuality, displaying lexical, narrative, and typographical manipulations, favouring repetition, looseness and lack of hierarchy, these texts are clearly in the same postmodern epistemology as those of Beckett, Butor, Laporte, Ricardou, Roche and Sollers. Cixous, Duras and Wittig are postmodern feminists. Furthermore, postmodern feminism is displayed at its best in the blurred genre of the feminist essay-manifesto that flourished in the 1970s: Catherine Clément and Hélène Cixous's *La jeune née* (1975); Luce Irigaray's *Ce sexe qui n'en est pas un* (1977) and Annie Leclerc's *Parole de femme* (1974). These texts are witty montage, parodic, deconstructive, intertextual minglings of philosophy, literature, personal experiences, lyricism and word play. Poststructuralist critics Roland Barthes, Jacques Derrida and Jacques Lacan have been praised for their writerly critical practices. The women are up to them, but their slant is feminist and irreverential.

Still along the line of reasoning which insists that there are clear-cut, sharp differences between the ways men and women writers inscribe representation, Annie Pratt, commenting on American and British fiction from the last two centuries, arrives at the following conclusions:

> Women's fiction manifests alienation from normal concepts of
> time and space precisely because the presentation of time by
> persons on the margins of day-to-day life inevitably deviates from
> the ordinary chronology and because those excluded from the
> agora are likely to perceive normal settings from phobic
> perspectives. Since women are alienated from time and space,
> their plots are cyclical, rather than linear, and their houses and
> landscapes have surreal properties. (Pratt 1981: 11)

While there might be such tendencies in the texts Pratt describes, they
cannot be taken as clear markings, absolute distinguishing features
separating and differentiating men's and women's writings. Cixous's,
Duras's and Wittig's texts deviate from chronology, manipulate it, and
contain surreal and uncanny landscapes; but such characteristics
cannot be a reflection of their biography, or a reflection of their
alienation. Otherwise the conclusion which imposes itself is that, since
the works of the men writers I have examined also manipulate
temporality and chronology, their authors are marginal and alienated.
In contemporary French texts, men and women writers alike avoid
linearity and chronology, not because of particular details in their
personal or psychological histories, but because they are postmodern
manipulators, exploiters, and explorers of the possibilities and limits of
representation.

Is it a question of content then which makes texts written by women
different from texts written by men? Freud argued that creativity is the
result of unsatisfied wishes which vary according to the sex of the
creator: 'Either they are ambitious wishes, serving to exalt the person
creating them, or they are erotic. In young women erotic wishes
dominate the fantasies almost exclusively . . . in young men egoistic
and ambitious wishes assert themselves plainly enough alongside their
erotic desires' (Freud 1908: 47–8). What about the texts which have
been my focus here? The texts written by women might well be shaped
by erotic desires; but erotic daydreamings are certainly blatant in
Ricardou's, Robbe-Grillet's and Simon's morphological, erotic,
voyeuristic writing; in Roche's word play where sexual innuendo is
constantly lurking; and in Sollers's 'screwing ledgers' as his narrator
puts it. Cixous, Chawaf and Irigaray are feminists who have advocated
writing which focuses on the female body and on woman's feelings and
emotions, and they have emphasized the necessity of so doing in order
to capture feminity and to write authentic feminine texts. Ironically,
what was to be feminine, feminist and revolutionary is now considered
by critics such as Toril Moi (1987) and Domna Stanton (1987) as a
pitfall, a trap into which feminists put themselves and which places
women back where the patriarchal order had them in the first place, on
the side of the body and of sensitivity, close to the senses and nature.

Sometimes texts are labelled as either feminine or masculine. Lisa
Appignanesi shows that a feminine imagination informs the works of
Henri James, Robert Musil and Marcel Proust. She notes that George

Eliot and George Sand are said to have a strong masculine side in their writing. Appignanesi's idea of femininity and masculinity in the creative imagination corresponds to Freud's characterization of woman as passive and emotional, uninvolved in everyday life activities, and of man as active, rational and participating in them. She defines feminine art as an art

> which is distinctly separate, wholly alienated from common daily reality; art which may see life from a depersonalized position as a static object to be described, not as a complex process in which the artist is a participant; art which gives evidence of that social irresponsability which is akin to Freud's description of the feminine as lacking conscience and a higher moral sense.
> (Appignanesi 1973: 14–15)

Are Cixous's, Duras's, and Wittig's works feminine in this sense? And what about the men's works discussed here? According to the Freudian definition, Wittig's *Les Guérillères* (1959) is definitely masculine; it presents female characters aware of their marginal situation and energetically involved in changing it. Rationality, involvement and action aimed at having an influence on the surroundings and at changing existing conditions are the animating principles of the text. Duras's *L'Amour* (1971) defies classification. It is neither feminine nor masculine in the sense discussed here. It is neutral because the characters have opted for outsiderhood or anomie; they refuse involvement with anything, in order to protect themselves. Cixous's *Souffles* (1975) is both masculine and feminine, masculine because it contains awareness of and takes stands on a contemporary issue which is widely discussed and debated, the domination of patriarchal society, but also feminine because it describes interiority and irrational feelings and states outside reality and movements toward the hedonic enjoyment of one's own body. What about the men's texts; how do they align along this feminine/masculine dichotomy? One would have to say that Ricardou's *L'Observatoire de Cannes* (1965), Robbe-Grillet's *La Maison de rendez-vous* (1965) and Simon's *Triptyque* (1973) are feminine texts. They are written by narrators who are completely involved in their apolitical, asociological, self-centred representation. Beckett's *L'Innommable* (1953), Pinget's *Quelqu'un* (1955) and Laporte's *Fugue* (1970) are also feminine, in that they portray narrators turning inward on themselves, in their solipsistic examination of themselves as writers in the very moment of and as part of what they write. Butor's *Mobile* (1962), Roche's *Circus* (1972), and Sollers's *H* (1973) could be characterized as displaying masculine traits because they implictly present political and sociological issues through their montage of discourses.

My remarks are not designated to pit the men and the women against each other, nor to say that feminine writing is better than masculine writing or vice versa. The morphological writings of Ricardou,

Robbe-Grillet and Simon, and the solipsistic stance of Beckett's, Laporte's and Pinget's narrators are not instances of passivity; rather they are intellectual explorations of representation and reflections on the act of writing. And what these comparisons show is that in contemporary French writing, active and passive, introspection, inwardness, sensitivity, goal orientation, involvement, or outwardness are independent of the gender of the writer.

That women tend to be more politically oriented and to write masculine texts is understandable given the intellectual climate of our time. By writing about absence, difference, the body, eroticism and sexuality, Cixous, Duras and Wittig legitimize them. Through their discourse they propose alternatives to male representation and expression. As Lyotard points out in *La condition postmoderne* (1979), scientists legitimize their research and their discoveries by writing narratives about them. Women achieve a similar effect in writing about such topics as sexuality, dynamism, vitality, independence and awareness of themselves as women; they confer legitimacy to them and to themselves. Furthermore, the message of these women writers concerns not only women; it addresses itself to individuals in general and teaches them to deconstruct their mentality, their ways of thinking and of being, that is, it teaches them to question what they have always accepted, to look for the underpinnings and assumptions they live by. These women are not highly strung, excited or biased, as might be suggested. They are lucid, learned and concerned. However, if pragmatic readers expect to find characters they can identify with, they might be disappointed. For, each in her own way, these women at the cutting edge of feminism and postmodernism propose characters who escape from reality, either because they live in Utopia, as in *Les Guérillères*, because they live on a semi-mystic, mental and physical high, as in *Souffles*, or because they are immobile and prostrated, as in *L'Amour*.

In order to give a correct and fuller account of feminist postmodern production in France, one should mention the works of Chantal Chawaf such as *Rétable, La Rêverie* (1974) and *Le Soleil et la terre* (1977). For Chawaf, writing is to bring back into literature the paganism of the Middle Ages which has been suppressed by rationalism. With a sensual, verbal exuberance, she writes about the body of woman as a subject for love, eroticism, maternity and for bringing life and joy in harmony with nature, while the world of culture associated with men, warriors and destroyers, is synonymous with war, killing and pollution. She is best characterized by the terms post-modern, feminist, ecologist and pacifist.

It is commonly said that women writers tend to rely on their own biography. Is biography a source of inspiration only for women? It is a fact that certain women writers have used aspects of their lives in their texts. Duras discusses the influence on her of scenes of her childhood in Indo-China, and she explains that these elements are part of a primeval scene about which she keeps writing. Cixous, in her theoretical and creative works, quite often refers to herself as someone born in Algeria and therefore considered as a *pied noir*, and as someone coming from a Jewish family and speaking German with her mother; all this contributing to make her feel eccentric and not completely French, explaining her awareness of oppression and her sensitivity to difference. But women's fiction is not necessarily more autobiographical than men's. Pinget's sketches of provincial life, Simon's description of village life, Ricardou's Cannes and Robbe-Grillet's Hong Kong are certainly in some ways derived from their personal experiences. Sollers, in *Vision à New York*, an interview with David Hayman (1974), talks about his past, his childhood and his upbringing, and provides details which are found in *H*. That Beckett studied Dante and philosophy at Trinity College certainly accounts for references to the *Divine Comedy*, to Descartes and to Bruno in his works. Similarly, it would be erroneous to say that only women inscribe their unconscious and their drives, for, as Kristeva has shown in *La Révolution du langage poétique* (1974), from the end of the nineteenth century to the present, texts have continually freed themselves from the constraints of normative syntax, causality and reason, and have let the unconscious surface, or as she puts it, we witness an irruption of the semiotic and a disruption of the symbolic.

Another question which comes to mind is that of influences. Is it possible to say that men writers are indebted to past or contemporary authors or philosophers and that women writers are not, or vice versa? Again, concrete examples prove that there is no difference. Cixous is influenced by Joyce, Freud and Lacan. Wittig acknowledged her debt to Robbe-Grillet, Pinget and the films of Godard. Roche points to Rabelais and Joyce; Sollers to Joyce, Lacan and Derrida; and Laporte to Blanchot and Derrida. An interesting constellation and intersection indeed, which again point to the same postmodern set of characteristics – fragmentation, manipulation, play, openness. Even the refusal to emulate anyone, the adamant desire to keep one's own independence, is not specific to one gender. Duras and Beckett share this very attitude.

Thus, interest for experimentation in representation and in language, eroticism, femininity, masculinity, presence of autobiographical details and influences from other writers are components which cut across sexual differences. Can we conclude, then, that there are no differences between the ways men and women write? Despite similarities, it is undeniable that women bring a distinct perspective to the panorama of contemporary French writing. I am not claiming here that only women can write like Cixous, Duras and Wittig or that only women can write about certain topics. I am pointing out that women have written about certain topics and men have not. While some men's texts flirt with social and political issues, they are not committed and do not overtly denounce evil and exploitation, and while other men's texts do not refer to any social or political problems, the women's texts adopt much clearer and more precise stances. Cixous's and Wittig's texts aim directly at subverting phallocentric stereotypes, and Duras takes a stance by writing about outsiderhood and refusal of any involvement, which she considers a political move. Like Ricardou, Robbe-Grillet, Roche, Simon and Sollers, Cixous, Duras and Wittig write about the body, eroticism and sexuality. But, unlike these men writers who adopt an ambiguous attitude at best, or treat the woman's body as an object, these women deliberately attack such phallocentric and patriarchal attitudes, and propose a healthier and more harmonious sexuality.

The presence of certain archetypes in the texts of Cixous, Duras and Wittig is a distinctive feature which does not exist in men's writings. The affirmation of woman's strength, the possibility of her rebelling and becoming independent and the enjoyment of her body, which manifest themselves in *Souffles* and *Les Guérillères*, can be identified as belonging to the Demeter/Kore archetypal system, Demeter representing feminine power and determination because she dared oppose herself to Pluto in preventing him from raping her daughter. The cult of Isis and Dyonisos, which was permitted to women throughout Greek and Roman history, provided them with an outlet for celebrating their eroticism, pride and joy. *Souffles* and *Les Guérillères* are also reminiscent of such rituals. The woman of *L'Amour* is like Daphné who transforms herself into a willow to escape the amorous enterprises of Zeus. Withdrawing into herself, in absence, is for the woman a means to protect herself and to have nothing to do with the rest of the world. The presence of these archetypal patterns and ritual-like behaviour is a form of intertextuality linking Cixous's, Duras's and Wittig's texts to the past.

Having presented the French postmodern feminists in relation to the new male novelists, I now propose an overview of the feminist literary production in several other countries. Among the contemporary women writers in Latin America, several of them emerge as postmodern feminist writers. Following a long tradition in Latin America, some of them turned to Europe, and more specifically to France, for models and for intertextual effects which were perhaps intended consciously or unconsciously to legitimize their own efforts. Julieta Campos from Mexico is represented by Juan Bruce-Novoa (1984) as being among the avant-garde of innovative writing in Latin America. He points out that her first novel, *Muerte por Agua* (1965), is a synthesis of Virginia Woolf and Nathalie Sarraute and explores the psychological process of a woman caught in the banal and boring activities of daily life. Robbe-Grillet-like descriptions of objects are a feature of this text. *Tiene los cabellos rojizos y se llama Sabina* (1974) also follows in the wake of Robbe-Grillet and Sarraute, but it privileges women as active agents, narrators, creators and recreators. A montage of units and fragments, it contains a complex intertextual texture, polyvalent and dialogic, which is a feminist deconstruction of masculine logocentrism. The postmodern writer Julio Cortázar is mentioned in relation to Julieta Campos.

In *Las andariegas* (1984), Albalucia Angel from Colombia writes a text which, according to Malva E. Filer (1985), is at the same time essay, poetry and fiction, and which consciously recalls Wittig's *Les Guérillères*. Angel brings to the fore feminine experience which has been undervalued. Like Wittig, she reads critically other texts and stages a battle of texts. The mythology of the Kogi, Indians living in Colombia, the conquest of America and the destruction of the natives shape this Colombian/French intertextual work. Still in this French context, it is appropriate to discuss Clarice Lispector; not because this Brazilian writer, who died in 1977, was influenced by the French, but because she was translated and published in France by the women's publishing house *des femmes*, and was and still is praised by Cixous, who considers her the greatest writer of the twentieth century. There are affinities between the two writers which explain Cixous's attitude. Lispector is a writer of great sensibility who, like Cixous, describes inner states and feelings of characters, mystical and visionary experiences. Like Cixous, she also has a great feeling for language, uses repetition and manipulates grammatical norms, syntax and punctuation. Focusing on women's experiences, she writes texts in which plot is almost non-existant. Such traits can be observed in one of Lispector's principal works, *Uma Aprendizagem ou O livro dos Prazeres* (translated into English as *An Apprenticeship or The Book of Delights* (1986)).

Self-consciousness on the part of a female narrator, fragmentation, linguistic play and intertextualities with various mythologies characterize the work of the Argentinian writers Silvia Molloy and Luisa Valenzuela. Magdalena García Pinto, in her study of *En breve cárcel* (1981), shows how Molloy mingles textual fragments of memories and dreams to explore the prison/passion of love and writing, and how Molloy's text is a space where plot disappears and which articulates the organization and the reconstruction of the past around the myth of Diana. Sharon Magnarelli (1979) documents how Valenzuela, in *El gato eficaz* (1972), dramatizes basic problems of contemporary feminine life, while deploying relations and myths which link women, feline figures like cats and sphinxes, and language. This constructive destruction, as Magnarelli puts it, defies all the rules that we can attribute to a fictional narrator. This technique can be compared to that of the postmodern writer José Donoso in *El obsceno pájaro de la noche* (1970). It is interesting that an advertisement for a novel by Valenzuela, translated into English as *He who searches* (1987), contains the following statement:

> Luisa Valenzuela's novel has been compared to García Márquez's
> *One Hundred Years of Solitude*, with its now famous 'magic
> realism'. *He Who Searches* is multifaceted in structure, combining
> narrative references with old-fashioned tale-telling, realism,
> psychoanalysis, Feminism, politics, and suspense, all of them
> tinged with a patina of eroticism that reflects the feminist
> perspective that has come to be associated with Luisa Valenzuela.

Two other feminist writers ground their postmodernism in ethnicity. According to Efraín Barradas (1985), Anna Lydia Vega from Puerto Rico, in *Vírgenes y mártires* (1981) and *Encancaranublado y otros cuentos de naufragios* (1983), invents a baroque language which is a mixture of popular Puerto Rican Spanish and educated Spanish in order to achieve a new aesthetic and feminist ideology. Barradas qualifies Vega's texts, which display a formal experimentation and an identification with the Caribbean world. Elizabeth Otero-Krauthammer (1985) focuses on *Las genealogías* (1961) by Margo Glantz from Mexico. She indicates that the text is a collage of heterogeneous entities which include dialogues, multiples voices, Russian, Mexican and Yiddish proverbs and sayings, photographs, recipes, lists of art works, superstitions and religious beliefs. Through this dialogic, carnivalesque work, a female protagonist searches for her identity, for the meanings of Mexico and for the significance of her Jewish ancestry and of the old world versus the new world in her life.

Postmodernism is alive and thriving among Latin-Amican feminist writers. Their implicit or explicit relationships with Robbe-Grillet, Sarraute and Wittig, the fact that Cortázar, Donoso and Márquez are mentioned in relation to them, their fragmenting the referential contents of their texts, their establishing intertextual connections and their theatricalizing language with word play, syntactic manipulations and typography are evidence of the postmodernity of these feminists. But to what extent do these feminist writers convey the complexity of the Latin-American reality from the point of view of women? And what is the social class of these women? Are they voicing the points of view and describing the experiences of upper-class, middle-class or working-class women? And what is their ethnicity – European descent? Mestizo? Indian? Postmodernism in Latin America has offered us monumental novels, by such writers as García Márquez and Vargas Llosa, rooted in political, sociological and historical reality, as well as being fantastic, elaborate linguistic constructs. Can this also be said of Latin-American feminism?

As far as Spain is concerned, it is particularly significant that an article by Gonzalo Navajas (1987) devoted to the rhetoric of the Spanish postmodern novel discusses not only works by men writers such as Juan Goytisolo, Martin Santos and Juan Benet, but also works by the feminist writers Carmen Martin Gaite and Esther Tusquets. Clearly the writings of these women are felt to be, and placed on, a par with those of the men. But what is more, Navajas points out that a considerable number of characters in Spanish postmodern fiction, whose theme is the conflict between I and the other, are women. He adds that, within the Western cultural world, the Spaniards have given to women a position of subordination much more marked than anywhere else, and that the women protagonists of Spanish post-modern fiction try to organize their lives in opposition to that subordination. As an example, Navajas cites two novels, one by a man,

Extramuros (1978) by Jesús Fernandez Santos, and *El mismo mar de todos los veranos* (1978) by Esther Tusquets. Another theme of Spanish postmodernism, which is a logical correlate to that of women opposing themselves to the masculine mode of domination, is the questioning of the masculine mode of domination. Again, this theme is to be found in men's writing, for instance in *La cólera de Aquile* (1979) by Luis Goytisolo, as well as in such women's writings as Tusquets's *El mismo mar*. There is also another stance which is specifically feminist, the creation of women characters without reference to any masculine presence. Thus, in the texts of Carmen Martin Gaite, *Retahílas* (1976) and *El cuarto de atrás*, the feminine world is presented as valid, specific and self-sufficient. Although Navajas does not discuss the textual properties of the works he deals with, it should be noted that the women's texts display characteristics associated with postmodernism. Gaite's are hybrid texts, made up of dialogues discussing social, intellectual and philosophical issues. And Tusquets produces writerly texts in a luxurious, abundant, compelling Spanish which reflect a genuine pleasure in writing.

German feminists tend to anchor their writings in everyday reality, and they put their postmodern efforts to consciousness-transforming ends. *German Feminism: Readings in Politics and Literature*, edited by Edith Hoshino Altbach et al. (1984), is an excellent introduction and presentation, with extracts in English of texts written by feminist writers. 'Writing I encountered language', says Verena Stefan in the foreword to her text *Sheddings* (1978) (Altbach 1984: 53–4), which was an enormous success in Germany. It comprises various encounters with language, reality and textuality, with a postmodern orientation which the various passages translated in Altbach propose. The desire to change language, to use writing as an attack against patriarchy, and the creation of Utopian worlds, akin to the strategies chosen by Cixous and Wittig, are present in *Sheddings* and in *Trobadora Beatriz* (1974) by Irmtraud Morgner. *Sheddings* is described in the following manner: '[It is] composed of the stream of consciousness observations of a young woman fleeing the urban battle of the sexes for the company of women in the country, shedding successive layers of femininity until she reaches her true metamorphic form' (Altbach 1984: 15). This experience is accompanied by a search for a new language, and Stefan writes:

> I walk around for days without finding any words, or can't choose between the words I do find. They are all inadequate. It wouldn't be so bad if all I had to do was choose the words and then arrange them in a certain order, construct the phrases and arrange them in a certain pattern, and having done this, find that everything I wanted to say would be there in black and white. But I must create new words, must be selective, write differently, use concepts in a different way. (105–6)

Trobadora Beatriz is presented in Altbach as being a fantastic montage novel which draws on a wide range of literary traditions in order to create a complex and visionary picture of women's struggle to enter history (213).

Other German feminist writers have opted for a different orientation. They anchor their texts in the raw concrete reality of contemporary everyday life, while manipulating language and writing as well. *Palisades or Time Spent in a Mad House* (1971) by Helga Novak is about the treatment of women in a mental health facility. It is introduced as being a semi-documentary text, providing detailed descriptions of a woman narrator's stay in the facility, which unmask structures of oppression. It is also a text where typographical and linguistic manipulations foreground the materiality of language. In *Women as lovers* (1977), Elfriede Jelinek concentrates on contradictions between the women's dreams of love and a better future and the grim reality of the 'natural cycle' that awaits them (Altbach 1984: 126). Jelinek's style involves repetitions, clichés and plain, direct language presented in units of different lengths, with no capitals. Witty, biting, lucid, it tells it like it is for the country girl Paula: life is death, love is hatred and contempt. Margot Schroeder's *Take it as a Woman* (1975) is about the tribulations of a Hamburg housewife, mother and part-time grocery clerk. The text is a mosaic of utterances, conversations, and thoughts full of humour and irony.

Parody, a postmodern genre which involves rewritings of forms of discourse and of rhetorical novels, is the genre that is found in the novels of Jutta Schutting. In *Park Murder* (1975), she parodies journalistic writing, thus criticizing the reporting of violent crimes. This is a text about language and about mass media. Elizabeth Alexander also parodies the media and, in the extract translated in Altbach (137–9), focuses on the marketing of feminine hygiene products.

In a recent article, Elaine Showalter (1987), after referring to the French *écriture féminine*, adds that many feminists felt excluded from a stylistics that seemed to privilege the non-linear, experimental and surreal. She captures what seems to be a strong tendency in the production of American writers today. Introducing a collection of articles dealing with the writers Ann Beattie, Grace Paley, Annie Dillard, Anne Redmond, Cynthia Ozick, Anne Tyler, Alice Walker, Maxine Hong Kingston, Toni Morrison and Marge Piercy, Catherine Rainwater and William Scheick point out that the authors of the articles suggest 'essential as well as incidental connections between these women writers and their male and female American precursors' (Rainwater and Scheick 1985: 4). Anne Beattie is linked to Henry James, Sherwood Anderson and Ernest Hemingway; Anne Dillard to David Thoreau; Anne Redmond to Flannery O'Connor; Anne Tyler to Eudora Welty and Toni Morrison to William Faulkner. Only two of the writers are connected with postmodernism, Cynthia Ozick and Anne Tyler. Cynthia Ozick, according to Ellen Pifer, is a 'feminist deeply committed to the social, political, and intellectual equality of women'

(Pifer 1985: 100). Her fiction is described as deploying self-referential devices, parody, sophisticated and playful narrative techniques and intertextual constructions drawing upon the traditions and lore of Judaism. Two of Ozick's recent short stories, 'Puttermesser: Her Work History, Her Ancestry, Her Afterlife' and 'Puttermesser and Xanthippe' (*Levitation: Five Fictions* (1982)), are about Ruth Puttermesser, a New York City lawyer struggling against the forces of discrimination and corruption in this world, while dreaming of a better one to come. Pifer assesses Ozick's fiction as creating a deeply orthodox vision of reality with postmodern techniques. Anne Tyler writes family novels, but she disrupts the conventional expectations of the genre. According to Mary F. Robertson who analyses her three most recent novels, Tyler's strategy is to give the semblance of order in the overall family design of the novels, but to hollow out such an order. Robertson writes:

> while Tyler would seem to be the last candidate for the ranks of the postmodernists, who are usually perceived as stylistically radical, her assault on the notion of what is a proper family makes her close in spirit to other postmodernists who regularly engage in what might be category assassination, questioning just about every conventional distinction between one concept and another that we use to order our lives and our thoughts. (Robertson 1985: 128)

Another woman writer, not included in the above collection, distinguishes herself on the American scene. This is Kathy Acker, whose fifth novel *Great Expectations* (1982) is presented as being her most accomplished experimental work and in which there is a female voice that goes beyond feminism. While Carl Sagan, a popular American novelist and scientist, in his novel *Contact* puts women characters in the roles of president of a country and leading physicist, Kathy Acker appropriates the master's pen, taking on the patriarchal, phallocentric role of the writer of a pornographic text. What we read then is not pornographic representation produced by a man, but one produced by a woman who, in so doing, trangresses and disturbs by her very gender. This inversion is one of the postmodern moves in Acker's text. *Great Expectations* is also a dynamic, witty, roguish and full-of-frenzy montage of different types of discourse, such as dialogues, letters, self-conscious comments about the writing and the content of the book itself and graphic scenes of sexual intercourse with sado-masochistic overtones. The title, borrowed from Dickens, is the first of the many intertextual allusions found in the text, which has strong inclinations towards France, as if the narrator had been a graduate student in French at Colombia, referring to the scholarly journal *Semiotexte*, to one of its editors, to Proust's *Remembrance of Things Past*, to Madame de Lafayette's *La Princesse de Clèves* and, of course, to the divine marquis, Sade. Interestingly, her reference to New York with its multi-ethnicity and the passages emphasizing the predictable rhetoric of the discourse of violence inflicted on women treated as objects capture the sick frenzy that a woman might experience.

Apart from these few cases, postmodern writing techniques do not seem to interest American feminist writers. Being American and more pragmatic, as the stereotype has it, they probably consider such representational techniques fit for the surfictionists such as Barth, Barthelme, Coover, Federman, Sorrentino, or Sukenick, but as detracting attention from their message and preventing them from being effective by focusing too much on linguistic and textual manipulations at the expense of feminist content.

Postmodernism is an intellectual, aesthetic, Euro-American movement which involves both men and feminist writers, and as the case from Spain shows, the writer does not have to be a woman to be a feminist. Feminism is not incompatible with postmodernism; in fact, many feminists have chosen to express themselves with postmodern techniques. More and more postmodern feminists are compared to postmodern male writers. These comparisons are double-edged. It is a patronizing attitude towards women to claim that they measure up to men. But it is also a legitimizing one, in that it means that the women are not beneath or marginal to the main male production. They are in the mainstream. On the other hand, the postmodern feminists are valorizing men's postmodernism by showing the usefulness of postmodern writing techniques.

There are two pertinent questions, Why did so many women begin writing in the 1970s? And why did many of them opt for postmodern representational techniques, which after many years and many books have lost their subversive edge and are acceptable, integrated and predictable? In answer to the first question, one can say that women had been repressed and that feminism, together with the decanonization of postmodernism, gave them the impetus and the forum to express themselves. As for the second question, one could say that postmodern representational techniques are one of the ways a writer has to construct reality in a decentred world. They also offer possibilities of expression that do not rely only on the referential content, but also on language and on manipulation of modes of representation. In addition, the feminists have shaped their own postmodernism, by adding a polemical and political slant which has been lacking in men's texts.

10 Postmodern Characterization: The Ethics of Alterity

Thomas Docherty

> . . . *I do beguile*
> *The thing I am by seeming otherwise*
> (Shakespeare)

It is by now a commonplace that postmodern fiction calls into question most of the formal elements of narrative that an earlier mode took for granted. The notion of 'character' is no exception; like the political dissidents of some totalitarian regimes, 'characters' have begun to disappear. But 'disappearance' has itself become a crucial component of postmodern characterization, and is not merely the result of an 'assault upon character' (Maddox 1978). In all former understandings of the process of characterization in narrative, one simple dichotomy prevails: appearance versus reality. Reading character has always been a process whereby the reader learns to probe and bring to light the murky depths of individual essences. He/she reads the visible presentation of character as a mere 'index of implications'; the process of reading involves the revelation of those implications, the 'depths' or idiosyncracies of particular, individuated characters. It is thus that 'character', as an element distinguishable from the narrative, is produced. Under the influence of existentialist philosophy, however, the notion of an essential reality in postmodern narrative has consistently been called into question. The result, in characterological terms, is twofold: firstly, 'appearance versus reality' as a paradigm is replaced by 'appearance versus disappearance'; secondly, character never *is*, but is always *about-to-be*, endlessly deferred. This elusiveness of character, it is often suggested, makes postmodern narrative in some sense 'unreadable', and many readers find it tedious in its disappointment of their characterological expectations. Lennard J. Davis explores this view; but his response to it is not to suggest, as have many other recent critics (Bayley 1960; Harvey 1965; Swinden 1973), that the novel or narrative is somehow inherently bound up with an interest in character or 'human being' as an axiomatic given. On the contrary, Davis argues, like Zeraffa (1969), that the paradigmatic shift in postmodern characterization and the resultant 'unreadability' of narratives demonstrate that 'the very idea of character in the novel is itself ideological' (Davis 1987: 107), by which he means to suggest that character, and the interest in these 'essential individuals', is historically and culturally specific, the product of a particular ideological moment.

Two views on the history of narrative are in contention here. The first offers a historicist 'argument of periodicity' which charts various changes in the history of narrative. This argument goes that, once upon a time, there were novels with plots, ethnographic settings and recognizable individuals known as characters; this was at a moment when the individual was becoming interesting in and of him/herself for religious and political reasons (a dominance of individualistic Protestantism and a nascent capitalism). Then the Industrial Revolution took place and characters entered into a strife-ridden relation with an environment, being characters only to the extent that they circumvented the dehumanizing effects of the mechanics of plot and the determinacy of ethnographic setting (Taine 1873–1908). At a yet later moment, characters became archetypal models, as authors 'looked within', in Woolf's celebrated phrase (Woolf 1929: 189), to describe the life of the human psyche in itself and in general. Finally, in the postmodern period, they disappear altogether and narratives become boring. This is a neat history, but wrong in its theoretical orientation, for it assumes that there was indeed a time when individuals did exist as some essence which was not always already an ideological construction. A more radical view, as Jameson suggests, is

> what one might call the poststructuralist position . . . not only is
> the bourgeois individual subject a thing of the past, it is also a
> myth; it *never* really existed in the first place; there have never
> been autonomous subjects of that type. Rather, this construct is
> merely a philosophical and cultural mystification which sought to
> persuade people that they 'had' individual subjects and possessed
> this unique personal identity. (Jameson 1983)

In a West, at least, which is witnessing the resurgence of a particular earlier moment of capitalist development and its concomitant 'values', there is an obvious ideological reason for stimulating this nostalgic desire for an earlier historical moment when 'we were all individuals', and for an earlier mode of narrative which seemingly celebrated that individuality. But this latter and more radical view allows us to suggest that postmodern narrative and the types of characterization that proceed in it simply 'lay bare' the techniques and problems of character which have in fact *always* existed in narrative. Postmodern narrative, in its demystifying revelation of the technical elements of fictional characterization, allows for a radical rereading of the history of narrative, calling into question the supposed certainties of the individuated essences of characters in an earlier fiction dominated by the 'appearance versus reality' paradigm.

1 The Evasion of History: Character, Empire, Identity

Prose narrative consolidates in a specific form known as the 'novel' in the eighteenth century, an age which represented itself as one of Reason and Enlightenment, when an ideology of liberalism stressed the importance of individualism (though not of specific individuals) in the social formation. Conventionally, the novel is thought to respond to this by recognizing the importance of the individual, and hence focusing on specific individual characters. But these characters are also the site of the dramatization of 'enlightenment'; as such, they become the models of a particular manifestation of what the age and ideology considers as 'reasonable'. The novel, typically, organizes itself around a plot in which an individual character stands at a tangent to his/her society (and is thus 'interesting' or extra-ordinary), and proceeds to the reconciliation of society and individual in a movement which identifies the interests of both and which reveals those interests to be reasonable and now self-evident, because brought to light.

While operating as a critique of a social formation, the novel orientates the reader through the *point de repère* of a recognizable character; and, given the necessity of having this character stand out, it in turn usually becomes the main centre of interest. The character, as our way into the hypothesized world of the fiction, becomes its main message too. It would clearly be fallacious to suggest that 'character' did not appear in writing prior to this historical moment; however, it was only during the Enlightenment that it came to have this central, organizing dominance as the model for 'individuality' in a social formation, as a recognizable and exemplary 'type'.

This age is also, crucially, the age which saw the invention of a specific category of primary relevance to character in the novel, for it was during this century that the concept of 'human nature' was invented. Foucault has argued that 'man is only a recent invention, a figure not yet two centuries old, a new wrinkle in our knowledge [who] will disappear again as soon as that knowledge has discovered a new form' (Foucault 1974: xxiii). The delineaments of this new form are now being traced in postmodern modes of narrative and characterization.

The construction of 'human nature' in the eighteenth century went hand in hand with the supervention of antiquity: it represented the 'ancients' winning the 'battle of the books' and the battle of competing philosophies against the 'moderns', and was thus a major defeat of a 'modernity'. The ancient tradition, in the form of a continuity hypothesized from antiquity, suggested that the present, eighteenth-century state of affairs and state of understanding had always been the case. To this extent, it was supposed to be *natural*, non-secular or non-historical. The concept of Enlightenment, that very metaphor, enacts the trope which is axiomatic to the novel and its characters, for it claims simply to render visible a latent nature that was always there. The corollary of this, of course, is that there *is* an essential nature which is located in the human being which makes him/her able to be in conformity with the wider 'natural' environment, or social formation. 'Man', according to this argument, is always and everywhere the same, at the most fundamental of levels; 'man' has simply to be brought from his darkness into enlightenment. If we transpose these metaphors of light and dark, we arrive at a 'white mythology': 'the white man takes his own mythology, Indo-European mythology, his own *logos*, that is, the *mythos* of his idiom, for the universal form of that he must still wish to call Reason' (Derrida 1982: 213). If humanity is always and everywhere the same, traditional and non-secular rather than geo-graphically and historically culture-specific, a justification is provided for the excesses of imperialism: in principle, the oppressed is being 'enlightened', granted a position in the social formation of the colonialist, who of course assumes his own 'enlightenment', an enlightenment supposedly guaranteed by a rationalist epistemology and a traditionalist antiquarianism. Further, the coining of 'human nature' also allows for the construction of a cultural form whose task it is to dramatize the bringing to light of this mysterious truth of human being. In prose narrative, character accordingly becomes understood theoretically as an allegorical type: not only 'individual' but also, as in the tradition of bourgeois democracy, 'representative' (Watt 1957; Josipovici 1971).

It is here, of course, that many critics have identified a radical potential in the form of the novel (Swingewood 1975; Orwell 1962; Williams 1970; Eagleton 1976; Zeraffa 1969), for it seems to be inherent to the novel that a certain democratic importance is afforded the individual within a dominant social formation. But another way of looking at this suggests that the novel thus understood, as a bourgeois liberal-democratic form, is a primary locus of bourgeois values and of the regularization, legitimation, even normatization of certain bougeois codes, together with the assimilation of other, contrary codes and practices which remain silenced or which are shown to be 'unreasonable' by the novel and its characters.

Thus, the notion of character as locus of the revelation of an essential human nature provides a form which, while seeming to grant some measure of independence and a democratic equality to the individual, actually serves to proffer a normative role for the individual in a specific social formation: in short, the novel's characters enact certain practices as socially *normative*. Thus, for example, Defoe's Robinson Crusoe can 'express' his innermost self in his construction of life on his island; but no matter how this is done in its detail, the text works to legitimize the practices of the same economic individualism which bolsters the imperialist and colonialist expansion of trade routes (Watt 1957: 69ff). *Moll Flanders*, similarly, may perform a critique of the social codes which lead to her criminality; but the text and its central character simply reiterate the legitimization of the notion of private property. To take a later example, Jane Austen's novels, while certainly granting a huge central importance to individual women characters as the main centre of attention and interest, simply operate to legitimize the bourgeois marriage and family which marginalized women in the first place.

If the novel is a conservative art-form, then it is so primarily because of the way in which its characters have been theorized and understood, as representative examples of human nature. Reading character in this way involves a simple *anagnorisis*: characterization enacts a scene of recognition in which the reader discovers, essentially, the 'truth' of him/herself reflected in the character, or, as we say, 'identifies' with the character (Davis 1987: 124ff). The reader 'discovers' a nature or essence of character which was always already known by that reader, for he/she shares in its 'human nature'. Thus, such a theoretical notion of the 'truth of identity', in the revelation of an essential human nature through characters in narrative, circumvents cultural specificity and historical difference: since human nature is, by definition, always and everywhere the same, and since 'most great novels exist to reveal and explore character' (Harvey 1965: 23), then an eighteenth-century fiction seems to exist to reveal and explore fundamentally the same thing as a late twentieth-century fiction.

Prior theoretical understanding of character as locus of an essential identity has worked to legitimize a particular, non-secular understanding of human being, of what it is to be a human in a specific social formation. With an eighteenth-century optimism, this understanding assumes that, in the relations between individuals and the social formation which they construct and which constructs them, 'whatever IS, is RIGHT' (Pope 1975: 515), or at least that to change things would be 'unreasonable', 'unenlightened', or simply criminally 'illegitimate'. But if character is anything in narrative, it is a locus of temporal difference. While it could be argued that portraiture or photography is, in its essentials, an art of simultaneity, its product to be perceived 'at once' and in space, it is certainly the case that narrative is sequential, that its constituent elements, including characterization, come as a piecemeal process and in a fragmentary mode. Postmodern narrative makes this abundantly clear, for it insists on offering the merest fragments of character, without ever allowing for a fully coherent construction of an identifiable whole; it is, as it were, like a series of torn photographs, a photo-montage; and frequently, of course, in its narcissistic self-consciousness (Hutcheon 1980), it offers fragmentary portraits of the artist or writer. Postmodern narrative stresses the 'difference' from which an 'identity' is always recuperated or salvaged in prior theorizations of the process of characterization; that earlier notion is concerned with establishing and identifying a finished *product*, the character as named and identified individual; this postmodern mode establishes the differences which are revealed as the 'characterization' progresses as *process*, without ever managing to establish a final product.

Some modernist narratives take this 'heterogeneity' of character, the notion of character as process, into account. While a writer such as Lawrence thought that he was mining a seam of essential reality in character (Lawrence 1958: 75), Woolf was examining, often in a wilfully incoherent mode, the ambiguities offered by characters who never actually acted but were always 'between the acts'. She was interested in characterization as a process whereby the supposed essence of character always escaped, where characters were somehow never fully there, like the ghostly Mrs Ramsay in *To the Lighthouse* or the character, such as it is, of Percival in *The Waves*. Woolf's novels are largely about the process whereby the relations between characters always escape reification; they are largely about the *failure* to write a 'character' as the bearer of some essential truth of human nature, and an interest in character is replaced by an examination of the mobile and fluid inter-relations among shadowy half-articulated figures. Similar arguments could be advanced concerning, for instance, Mann's delineation of the relations between Aschenbach and Tadzio in *Death in Venice* (1912); another crucial example would be Proust's *A la recherche du temps perdu* (1913–27) in which, despite the autobiographical impetus, the text tells us little of the 'essence' of Marcel, replacing that by a series of shifting relations with Swann, Albertine, Saint-Loup and so on. In the later example, the reader reaches, at the 'close' of the novel, a hypothetical understanding of Marcel; but, as the novel ends at the point where Marcel becomes a writer and can now write the text which has just been read, the reading exercise has, logically, to be repeated, but at a different level of understanding: the 'identity' which the reader proposes for Marcel at the close of the novel is itself to undergo a differential epistemological shift in a reiteration of the reading of the character.

Even in these modernist experiments, however, it is to be stressed that character is still organized around the basic notion of anagnorisis or re-cognizability: the individual characters can, at some level, be 'known', cognized and recognized. Theorists of character have always made a distinction between characters in novels and persons in a 'life' which is supposed to be constitutively different from textual semiotics. This distinction, fundamentally, hinges on the opposition between ontology and epistemology. As Davis puts it, in a formulation which echoes Bayley:

> Personality is what living beings have. Our personalities may not
> be coherent; they may not be readily understood by us; they may
> be misinterpreted or not even accessible to others; but they are
> what we refer to when we refer to ourselves. 'Character' on the
> other hand is what people in novels have. They are characters with
> characteristics. (Davis 1987: 111)

Personality is purposeless and complex; character is purposeful and simple, a small set of definable and essentially *knowable* traits.

Personalities have a degree of existential contingency, lacking in characters who merely enact functions in organized plots and delimited locations. Where personality is an ontological category, character is an epistemological one. If character has been most frequently construed as the medium through which we gain access to the world of the social formation being elaborated in a text, then it is important that it be epistemologically comprehensible. If this medium becomes as seemingly contingent as personalities in the different ontological level of 'real life' or history, if it becomes inconsistent or fundamentally shadowy and unknowable, unrecognizable, then there enters a confusion between categories. What has been assumed by a reader to be an epistemological category begins to operate in the manner of an ontological one: the 'fictionality' of the text and its characters is called into question and there arises a confusion about the relative ontological status of characters, on the one hand, and readers or authors, on the other. It is this confusion that we see most frequently entertained in postmodern narrative.

The confusion can take either of two orientations. On the one hand, it can operate in a conservative mode, whereby 'characters' are 'raised' to the level of personalities, without the text ever casting any doubts upon that ontological category itself. This would be the case, for instance, in a text such as *Daniel Martin* by John Fowles (1977), where Fowles introduces what Hamon calls *personnages-référentiels* (Hamon 1977: 122–3) – that is, proper names from the realm of history – and where these names or *personnages* are introduced at the same level as the other fictive 'characters' in the text. In *Daniel Martin*, the critic Kenneth Tynan appears as a 'character', with the result of confusing or eradicating the ontological distinction between such a 'personality' and the 'characters' of, say, Daniel or Jenny in that text. A similar working of the same manoeuvre is to be found in cases where a character, introduced in one text, reappears, perhaps in a minor role, in another. This happens, for example, in the novels of Alison Lurie where 'Leonard Zimmern' figures in a central role in *The War Between The Tates* (1974) and reappears in a more peripheral role in *Foreign Affairs* (1985). This 'character' appears to transcend the limitations of a role in one plot, and the illusion is created that what seemed to operate at the epistemological level of character now begins to operate as if it were at the ontological level of personality.

On the other hand, the confusion of character and personality can take a more radical dimension, whereby the result is the calling into question of the ontological status of author and reader. In this case, personality becomes transfigured as nothing more or less than a nexus of semiotic signification: persons in history become equated with characters as the effects of textuality, and become signifiers devoid of a signified. This view is elaborated by Federman when he argues that:

the people of fiction, the fictitious beings, will also no longer be well-made characters who carry with them a fixed identity, a stable

set of social and psychological attributes – a name, a situation, a profession, a condition, etc. The creatures of the new fiction will be as changeable, as illusory, as nameless, as unnamable, as fraudulent, as unpredictable as the discourse that makes them. This does not mean, however, that they will be mere puppets. On the contrary their being will be more genuine, more complex, more true-to-life in fact, because they will not appear to be simply what they are; they will be what they are: word-beings . . . That creature will be, in a sense, present to his own making, present to his own absence.
(Federman 1975: 12–13)

When characters become as contingent as personalities in this way, the result is that they 'participate in the fiction only as a grammatical being' (Federman 1975: 13), and become aware of their purely linguistic or textual status, precisely to the extent that they are incoherent, self-contradictory, contingent as personality. The category of personality, then, is radically questioned, and the validity of its claims to an ontological status doubted. The most obvious examples of this would be texts such as Sorrentino's *Mulligan Stew* (1981), the 'magic realism' of Márquez's *Autumn of the Patriarch* (1978), or Ronald Sukenick's *98.6* (1975) where 'Ron' operates firstly as a seemingly coherent medium on the fiction, and then proceeds to become inconsistent, incoherent and the merest empty signifier whose 'meaning' constantly varies in a thoroughly contingent manner. In cases such as this, what was taken as an ontological category becomes an epistemological problem.

The problem raised by this category confusion in postmodern characterization can be properly articulated in Heideggerian terms as a question of 'fundamental ontology and the search for the human place'. That mode of understanding character (the 'pre-modernist' mode, so to speak) is almost entirely epistemological. It renders 'other people' fundamentally knowable, offering the reader the illusion of having a position from which his/her own identity is guaranteed through its distinction from a basically knowable and recognizable 'otherness' or alterity. The epistemological steadiness or predictability of 'character' in this older mode grants the reader a position of security in his/her own identity, an identity which is of a different ontological status from that of the character and which transcends that lower status. In short, it offers the illusion of a control over the characters, whereby the reader can place or locate them in the plot not only in relation to each other, but also in relation to the reader's own position, a position which, in transcending the hypothetical world of the characters, offers the illusion of omniscience and its corollary, omnipotence. This situation is precisely akin to a mode of imperialist control of the Other in which, by pretending to 'know' the Other fully and comprehensibly, a Self can assure itself of its own truths and status. To this extent, 'reasonable' characters in the paradigmatic plot of enlightenment share that eighteenth-century predilection for the imperialist or colonialist control not only of other places, but also of other 'positions' (cf. Davis 1987: 52ff); in novelistic terms, this translates into control of other 'points of view' or, in short, of other characters. It is this imperialism of reading character which the more radical problematization of the ontological status of the reader, such as we have it in postmodern characterization, begins to challenge. It does so by problematizing the 'human place', by converting 'position' into 'disposition' or, to put this in poststructuralist terms, by displacing the reader and deconstructing the relation which obtains between reader and character.

Robbe-Grillet is well-known for his iconoclastic attacks on the conventions of the novel, and certainly the conventional 'character' in his work begins to disappear. Yet he also vigorously asserts the primacy of subjectivity in his *chosiste* novels. These two positions, attacking character and instating human subjectivity in his texts can perhaps be reconciled when we consider the influence of cinema on his writing. The attack on character turns out to be an attack on the particular kind of imperialist epistemology which promises the possibility of full enlightenment, the hypothetical omniscience of the 'pre-modern' reader. Here, the point of view is strictly limited and localized, and Robbe-Grillet can claim to be attacking the epistemological status and tenets on which conventional character rests, and to be replacing them with something making a greater claim on ontological presence of some kind.

The assignation of a place to the reader is crucial in this approach. It would be apposite to suggest that this is merely an articulation of what happens in much modernist fiction, such as that of James, Conrad or Ford, in which the reader is deliberately denied immediate access to the omniscient perspective he/she frequently has in that mythic 'classic realist text', the Victorian or realist novel. But it is vital to note that, even in those modernist texts which are narrated from one or more local points of view or by incompetent narrators, the entire text can finally be harnessed in the brace of full epistemological satisfaction. *Nostromo* (1908), for example, offers only confusion in its opening juxtaposition of a number of points of view and temporal perspectives, but that initial fragmentation is proleptically instrumental in the establishing of a more encompassing position or place from which all the contradictions can be reconciled, forming a coherent whole. Such a *provisional* series of displacements in modernist fiction could be compared with the multiple openings of Flann O'Brien's *At Swim-Two-Birds* (1939), the fundamental shift of position in Butor's *La modification* (1957), or the series of mutually exclusive and contradictory points of view which operate throughout Robbe-Grillet's *Dans le labyrinthe* (1959), such as the opening description of the weather 'outside'. While the trajectory in the modernist experiment with point of view remains firmly within that 'imperialist', epistemological project, moving from mystification to enlightenment, in the postmodern experiment that orientation is reversed.

A novel which sits precisely on the borderline traced here between modernist and postmodern characterization is Robbe-Grillet's *La Jalousie* (1957). The central 'character' of this text, usually referred to by criticism after Morrissette as *le mari jaloux*, remains unnamed and is not described throughout the entire text. In most fiction, proper names operate as 'pegs on which to hang descriptions' (Searle 1970; but cf. Derrida 1977, Docherty 1983): they promise coherence and identity, organizing varied points of view into recognizable locations. But in texts which eschew such use of the proper name, as in Sarraute's *Portrait d'un inconnu* (1956), Wurlitzer's *Flats* (1971) or, here, Robbe-Grillet, a different set of problems arises. In *La Jalousie*, the reader is able to hang a number of descriptions around 'A . . .' and 'Franck', but remains unable to localize the character-traits which accrue to the *je-néant* (Morrissette 1975), the narratorial figure who remains anonymous. But it is precisely this narratorial figure who operates as the reader's point of access to the world of the text, including its descriptions of the other 'characters'. The result is that it is the reader who comes to inhabit this position, the position behind the blinds, from which the world and the text of *La Jalousie* are generated, and from which 'jealousy' originates. This text does not work to produce a character suffering from the character-trait of jealousy as his distinguishing mark; on the contrary, it seduces the reader into occupying the position defined by the trait, now, of course, a personality rather than a mere character trait, since it is located in the reader whose ontological place is in history. This is a fully phenomeno-logical performance, offering the reader a perceptual space in and through which he/she, as subject of the experience of *La Jalousie*, mediates the sense of the world of objects described within the text. The reader comes to 'inhabit' the place from which the text is generated. The logic of this is that the desired effect is not so much to give the reader an epistemological *understanding* of a jealous character; on the contrary, it is to produce a jealous *experience*, an experience whose historical or existential reality is not to be doubted, even if it remains not epistemologically understood or accessible. The text operates in the more radical mode of questioning the ontological validity of the reader's status, rendering the position of the reader as an effect of textuality; to this extent it is postmodern in its seduction of the reader, making the reader the primary 'character' of the text's enactment. However, as a phenomenological performance, it also allows for the stabilization of the subject-position of the reader; in other words, it grants the reader an *identity*, classifiable as 'the Subject of Jealousy', and this identity is not modified by any *temporal* displacement or difference in the position of the reading subject. The text sets up *spatial* relations between reader and character, but still is not open to history, even though the 'character' in the text operates at the level of the historical personality of the reader. Access to an ontological mode is gained; but this is an ontology without history, a being without time, so to speak.

This type of novel hovers on the edge of postmodernity, but allows for the full confusion explored by existentialist thought in, for example, the character of Antoine Roquentin in Sartre's *La Nausée*, who ponders a famous dilemma:

> Voici ce que j'ai pensé: pour que l'événement le plus banal
> devienne une aventure, il faut et il suffit qu'on se mette à le
> *raconter*. C'est ce qui dupe les gens; un homme, c'est un conteur
> d'histoires, il vit entouré de ses histoires et des histoires d'autrui, il
> voit tout ce qui lui arrive à travers elles; et il cherche à vivre sa vie
> comme s'il la racontait.
> Mais il faut choisir; vivre ou raconter. (Sartre 1938 and 1977: 61–2)

When Sartre ponders this, the very terms of the debate postulate the notion of a true or authentic 'real' Self which lies covered under a fictive one; these are the terms of the debate between ontology and epistemology, personality and character. This debate remains profoundly humanist, proposing a dichotomy of surface (appearance) and depth (reality) which has dominated the understanding of characterization and its immediacy of presentation of characters, albeit from strictly delineated positions, there is no longer any depth to character. 'Character' in these terms does indeed disappear, for everything is always already on display, is 'obscene' (Baudrillard 1976), since surface is all that there is. Beckett's Unnamable is precisely this type of fictive character:

> perhaps that's what I feel, an outside and an inside and me in the
> middle, perhaps that's what I am, the thing that divides the world
> in two, on the one side the outside, on the other the inside, that
> can be as thin as foil, I'm neither one side nor the other, I'm in the
> middle, I'm the partition, I've two surfaces and no thickness,
> perhaps that's what I feel, myself vibrating, I'm the tympanum, on
> the one hand the mind, on the other the world, I don't belong to
> either . . . (Beckett 1979: 352)

This ghostly 'medium' is the typical postmodern figure. The spatial metaphor of surface and depth is replaced, after the influence of cinema, by temporal sequence and development: a figure in one scene or 'shot' can be thoroughly transfigured by the next, thus countering the notion of a transcendent Self lying 'behind' the surface 'apparitions' and 'disappearances'. In fact, according to Eisenstein, it is precisely such a *discontinuity* between shots that is of the essence of cinematic montage, and in postmodern narrative, such a discontinuity is taken on, as a challenge to the notion of a 'real' identity or Self-sameness which underpins various mystifying or disguised 'appearances'. In postmodern narrative, 'character', such as it is, is there immediately, in all its 'obscenity'; the medium that is character is itself unmediated, and it is this that distinguishes such characterization from all prior modes.

In narratological terms, character is nothing other than the potential for story, for the releasing of temporality and sequence, or, in short, for narrative itself. This is outlined by Todorov in his suggestion that character be understood as 'homme-récit' (Todorov 1971: 81–2). *Vivre*, then, is *raconter*; or, as Foucault would have it, social formations and the very concept of identity are formed through the interplay of discourses. But the postmodern turning of this involves the multiplication of identities and the consequent fragmentation of the phenomenological subject-position which is afforded the reader in a text such as *La Jalousie* and its modernist precursors. Instead of offering the reading subject a specific or identifiable single ontological place, a 'clearing' in which a supposedly non-temporal identity can be established, postmodern narrative not only renders the reader of the status of textual discourse, making him/her the merest effect of the interplay of linguistic discourses, it also 'dis-positions' the reader, produces a *number* of conflicting positions from which the narrative is to be read.

The most basic manner in which this attack on the singularity of the human's 'place' is carried out is through the elaboration of a multiplicity of conflicting narratives, or 'hommes-récits'. In Robbe-Grillet's *Dans le labyrinthe*, for instance, each mention of the 'character' of the soldier operates as the release for another narrative beginning, often a narrative which contradicts the one which was in sequence before it. If the reader is using this character in a mode similar to the *je-néant*in *La Jalousie*, then the effect is to replace the elaboration of a particular, specifiable place for the reading subject with a non-specific, nonidentifiable sequence of changing positions, or dispositions. This is the situation described by Borges in his story, 'The Garden of Forking Paths'. Here, Stephen Albert ponders Ts'ui Pên's labyrinthine manuscripts. He imagines the way in which Ts'ui Pên might have realized the task of writing an infinite, unending book, and can come up with nothing better than the circular text (such as Proust's *A la recherche*, Gide's *Les Faux-monnayeurs* and Joyce's *Finnegans Wake*), until he lingers on a particular sentence in the manuscript:

> I lingered, naturally, on the sentence: *I leave to the various futures (not to all) my garden of forking paths*. Almost instantly, I understood: 'the garden of forking paths' was the chaotic novel; the phrase 'the various futures (not to all)' suggested to me the forking in time, not in space. A broad rereading of the work confirmed the theory. In all fictional works, each time a man is confronted with several alternatives, he chooses one and eliminates the others; in the fiction of Ts'ui Pên, he chooses – simultaneously – all of them. *He creates*, in this way, diverse futures, diverse times which themselves also proliferate and fork. Here, then, is the explanation of the novel's contradictions. Fang, let us say, has a secret; a stranger calls at his door; Fang resolves to kill him. Naturally, there are several possible outcomes: Fang can kill the intruder, the intruder can kill Fang, they both can escape, they both can die, and so forth. In the work of Ts'ui Pên,

all possible outcomes occur; each one is the point of departure for other forkings. (Borges, *Labyrinths* 1978: 51)

Some postmodern narratives are like this hypothetical fiction. While modernist and earlier modes of narrative and characterization offer the reader a set of spatial relations (a plot) in and through which he/she finds a specific identity or place from which to know the fiction and its characters, postmodern narrative offers a proliferation of such positions, denying priority to any of them. This is the case in the heavily overplotted fictions of Pynchon, where the introduction – or eruption – of a character's name is the signal for another plot or for a further disorienting turn in an already complex baroque intrigue, as in Pynchon's own self-parody, 'The Courier's Tragedy', in the midst of *The Crying of Lot 49* (1966).

The temporal disposition or dislocation of the reading subject described here is itself dramatized as the material of Calvino's *If on a Winter's Night a Traveller* (1979), where because of a series of errors at the binder's, various hypothesized 'novels' are interleaved with each other. The position or disposition (*ethos*) of 'the Reader' is itself the subject of the narrative, for he/she has constantly to shift his/her position and expectations, as he/she shifts from one text to another. The reader, then, becomes multiple, as Calvino introduces 'other' readers of the various novels and provides dialogue and debate among them all. This multiplication of the reader is an analogue of what happens to characterization in postmodern narrative generally. All that Calvino has done is to take the initial sentence of a hypothetical text, split it up into its various component phrases, and propose each such phrase as the beginning of a new narrative, a narrative which is released by the phrase and by its introduction if not of a character, then at least of a position from which the text is understood and read. This fragmentation of a narrative, its multiplication into a series of seemingly unrelated and disconcertingly different narratives, generates at the same time a multiplicity of positions for the reading subject; but each such position is now strictly different from those that go before and after. 'The Reader', as a supposedly single, essential identity, disappears, and is replaced by a series of 'dispositions', shifts of position from which the text can be understood. The reader, then, is, as it were, released into the temporality of narrative, shifting position at every instant of reading Calvino's text. As Jip 'n' Zab suggest at the start of Brooke-Rose's *Xorandor* (1987), 'One, it's important to be two' (Brooke-Rose 1987: 7), and in this novel the 'character' of Xor7 (itself a pun on 'Exocet') also becomes multiple, hovering uncertainly between computer and Lady Macbeth whose lines it picks up and plays back.

While 'pre-modern' characterization (which also includes modernist modes) is concerned with the production of identity, postmodern narrative fractures such a homogeneity in both the 'characters' and the reading subject. Postmodern narrative seeks to circumvent the phenomenological elaboration of a definable spatial relation obtaining between a transcendent ontological reading subject and an equally fixed and non-historical object of that reader's perception, the 'character'. Earlier modes of characterization are related to the imperialist and colonialist impetus of the appropriation of space, and the grounds on which a position of intentional authority is afforded an imperial Self through its 'knowledge' of and understanding of an oppressed characterological or epistemological Other. Postmodern characterization disturbs this position by the interjection of a temporal component in the process of reading character, replacing the notion of 'position' with that of the poststructuralist displacement or 'disposition'. In short, postmodern characterization seeks to return the dimension of history which earlier modes of characterization, or of the theoretical understanding of character as 'identity' or 'essence', deny.

That denial of history in earlier theorizations of character is accompanied by a denial of politics. The bias of the novel, since its moment of inception, towards biography is obvious. The central characters of such fiction are interesting for criticism precisely to the extent that they are the locus of an anagnorisis, some moment of recognition or of turning and troping of the character. This is what passes for the supposedly temporal development of character in earlier modes of reading character. Such anagnorisis does not offer any fundamental change or 'disposition' in the reading of character; but even if it did (as earlier theory suggests), then it has the vital corollary of identifying change in the novel as something which always happens at the level of the individual rather than in the wider socio-political formation itself. Davis writes:

> Ideologically speaking . . . character gives readers faith that
> personality is, first, understandable, and second, capable of
> rational change. As part of the general ideology of middle-class
> individualism, the idea that the subject might be formed from
> social forces and that change might have to come about through
> social change is by and large absent from novels. Change is always
> seen as effected by the individual. (Davis 1987: 119)

This reduction of politics to morality is entirely in keeping with a liberalism which operates precisely on the suppression of history (replacing this with eternal, immanent 'truths' of human nature) and the elimination of politics (replaced with 'values'). Postmodern characterization offers a challenge to this, with implications that go far beyond the realm of mere aesthetic predilections.

2 A Different Economy

Postmodern characterization advances an attack on the notion of identity, or of an essential Selfhood which is not traduced by a temporal dimension which threatens that Self with heterogeneity. In short, it leads to the elaboration of 'characters' (if they can still be called such, given their confusing ontological status) whose existence (rather than essence) is characterized by *difference* (rather than identity). Postmodern figures are always differing, not just from other characters, but also from their putative 'selves'. Whereas earlier characters were present-to-themselves, or, to put this in existentialist terms, finally reduced to the status of an essential selfhood and thus reified as *en-soi*, postmodern characters always dramatize their own 'absence' from themselves.

Postmodern characters most typically fall into incoherence: character-traits are not repeated, but contradicted; proper names are used, if at all, inconsistently; signposts implying specific gender are confused; a seemingly animate character mutates into an inanimate object, and so on. At every stage in the representation of character, the finality of the character, a determinate identity for the character, is deferred as the proliferation of information about the character leads into irrationality or incoherence and self-contradiction. There is never a final point at which the character can be reduced to the status of an epistemologically accessible essential quality or list of qualities and 'properties'. What is at stake in this is the entire notion of 'representation'. As in most art-forms and cultural practices, the postmodern impetus is almost synonymous with the questioning of representation (for example, Lyotard, 1984).

Following in the wake of an existentialist philosophical tradition, many postmodern characterizations seem to argue that there is always a discrepancy between the character who acts and the character who watches him/herself acting. There is, as it were, a temporal distance between agency and self-consciousness regarding that agency, a fine example of which is Barth's fiction, 'Menelaiad' (Barth 1969). This text enacts the continual deferral of coincidence between the narrating subject and the subject narrated, even though these are ostensibly identical, 'Menelaus'; as a result, 'Menelaus', paradoxically, is 'identified' or, better, characterized as that which is always differing from himself. There is a series of confusions about the ontological presence of the character, such that at any moment in the text when it seems that 'Menelaus' *is* somewhat, immediately a difference is produced and an alternative or new narrative is released.

The voice of Menelaus (for that is all there is in this tale) begins to relate the story of his life to Telemachus, Peisistratus and a hypo-thesized listener (actually, of course, the reader). During the tale, he tells of meeting Helen, who demanded the tale of his life; within this tale, now on a different level and in a different temporal frame, he met Proteus, who asked for the tale of his life, and so on. There are, then, a number of 'hommes-récits' identified in the figure of Menelaus; but this fiction begins precisely to unravel or untangle that identity, to release all the different figures, masquerading under the identical proper name which supposedly offers them a non-temporal, non-historical identity, and produces a multi-layered narrative. In characterological terms, the result is that the consciousness that identifies itself as 'Menelaus' is always out of step or non-identical with the voice of Menelaus and with the actions which Menelaus supposedly performed. The very telling of the tale of his life, an act which is supposed to proffer and guarantee identity, in fact produces this radical *décalage* or self-difference as the constituent of 'Menelaus''s being. Menelaus is, as it were, never fully present to himself; every time he identifies himself, he has to do so by adverting to a different Menelaus, one who exists in a different temporal and narrative frame and one who exists, therefore, at a different ontological level from the narrating consciousness. Worse than this, within one of the tales Menelaus indicates his fully temporal predicament. He changes places and times every time he tries to fix or identify himself, as is fully seen in his encounter with Proteus. Menelaus is, if anything, the character as Heideggerian *Dasein*; the 'being' of Menelaus, such as it is, is endlessly deferred, endlessly seeming otherwise and reiterating itself in a different figuration. Its identity is characterized by this potentially endless differing from itself, the perpetual deferring of an essential Selfhood: 'the thing I am' is replaced or, indeed, constituted, by a 'seeming otherwise'. The character is constantly disappearing from its own surface, constantly escaping the parameters which the text implies for its figuration: in short, the character is constantly 'being there', constantly evading the fixity of a definite or identifiable and single 'place' for itself. To this extent, it becomes the merest series of instantiations of subjectivity, rather than a characterological selfhood; it has no place, but a series of *dis*positions, as the parameters of its figuration shift and metamorphose in temporal sequence.

There is a difficulty with the very notion of 'representation' of a character whose condition is that it is never present to itself in the first place but always 'ec-statically' escaping the constraints of self-presence (Docherty 1983). But it is precisely here that the politics of a 'different economy', or an economy of difference, can enter in a consideration of postmodern characterization.

Earlier theories of characterization are all dependent upon the paradigmatic dichotomy of appearance and reality, and their narratives are always 'apocalyptic' in the sense that they move from mystification to enlightenment and revelation as to the 'truth' of the character and its identity. The narrative trajectory is from the heterogeneity of different appearances to a presumed homogeneity of a real identity. It follows from this that what we can call the 'economy of identity' is based upon a supposed equality between the self of a character, on the one hand, and that character's narrative of the self, on the other; this is the 'homme' as 'récit', in Todorov's terms. The character is adequately 'represented' in the narrative; the self-presence of an identity reiterated in its mimetic relaying in the tale. Further, this 'equation' works both ways. For it is not simply the case that characters in fiction are the mimetic echoes or representations of selves in history; on the contrary, characters in fiction are, precisely to the extent that they are 'representative' of a supposed human nature, models upon whom selves in history must fashion themselves, if they are to have a claim on being a 'reasonable' or 'enlightened' individual within human nature. It is in these terms that the economy of identity assumes a political cast, for 'representation' here assumes the burden of political representation: characters, acting on behalf of selves (functioning as 'representatives', in a manner precisely akin to parliamentary representation), turn out to act as the legislators for certain kinds of political practice. As Davis indicated, the novel reduces all political action to moral action undertaken by and on behalf of individuals; character, operating according to an economy of identity whereby the character is assumed to operate as the mimetic representation of a self which is equally assumed to be fully present to itself, fully self-identical, is the means whereby this morality of individualism supplants the possibility of political praxis in narrative.

However, postmodern narrative disturbs the neat equations of the economy of identity, reversing the trajectory described by earlier narratives. In postmodern characterization, the narrative trajectory is from the assumed homogeneity of identity (as in the nameable identity of Menelaus, say) towards an endlessly proliferating heterogeneity, whereby identity is endlessly deferred and replaced by a scenario in which the 'character' or figure constantly differs from itself. Every mention of the same proper name, for instance, operates to release a new narrative, one which is at odds with the narratives previously ascribed to that proper name in the fiction. Rather than the self producing one narrative, in this postmodern model, the self disappears under a welter of proliferating narratives, 'forking paths', which never cohere or become commensurable with one another. *Vivre* does not equal *raconter* here, at least not in the sense that a life has one story: there is the production of a *surplus* of narrative, and it is this surplus which disturbs the neat equalities of the economy of identity and which calls into question the function of representation in postmodern narrative.

We have, then, a different economy, an 'economy of difference'. Postmodern narrative enacts the character as *Dasein*, the character who constantly escapes the fixity of identity by existing in the temporal predicament whereby the assumed or desired totality of a real Self is endlessly 'dispositioned', always a 'being *there*', as opposed to a being here, a being present to itself. This is not so much a character, more a series of 'appearances' which do not act as the cover for a 'deeper' reality, for it is that very notion of a material or essential reality which postmodern characterization denies. At best, the progression of a postmodern narrative cannot move from appearance to the enlightenment of a reality, but only from appearance to disappearance to *different* appearance and so on. In such characterization, the idea of a reciprocity, whereby the character is seen as a representative of the self of the historical reader, becomes impossible, since it is precisely this notion of a totalized real and essential selfhood which the texts deny. The simplicity of a seemingly 'democratic' mode of characterization, based upon a liberal individualism and the category of 'representation', is called into question. Postmodern narrative reveals that it is not simply the case that earlier modes of reading fiction reduce the political to the moral; more importantly, in their delineation of social and political formations through the medium of 'representative' characters, they confuse a political category of representation with an aesthetic mode of mimesis. Criticism has always prioritized this aesthetic component, in its endless discussion of 'well-rounded' or 'vividly realised' or 'fully depicted' characters in fiction; in short, there has been a dangerous 'aestheticisation of politics' (Benjamin 1973).

But postmodern narrative does not easily reverse this orientation. Instead, it introduces, through its mode of characterization, the category of *ethics*. The reader of postmodern narrative, as allegorized in Calvino's *If on a Winter's Night a Traveller*, is fully implicated in the proliferation of narratives. However, unlike the reader of earlier fiction, he/she is denied the possibility of producing a totalized self for the characters being processed in the reading; the totality of a supposedly enlightened truth or real essence of character is denied as a result of the proliferation of narratives which contradict such a totality. This also means that postmodern narrative attacks the possibility of the reader him/herself becoming a fully enlightened and imperialist subject with full epistemological control over the fiction and its endlessly different or altered characters. In order to read postmodern narrative at all, the reader must give up such a singular position, for he/she will be endlessly 'disposed', displaced, in figuring a number of different narratives and different characters. He/she has to be seduced from one position into many positions, has to give up a quasi-authorial position of a supposed access to the singular truth of character and move into a series of *dispositions* in trying to deal with the proliferating narratives. The reader is denied access to a totalizing narrative which will allow him/her to define and identify him/herself against the stable 'other' of a mysterious character. Rather, the reader replaces such a totalized and enlightened narrative, proposing access to a singular, monotheistic Truth, with the multiplicity of different local narratives, having no claims on truth in any absolute sense at all. The reader becomes nothing more or less than an excuse for the proliferation of further narratives, further dispositions. The reader becomes as imbricated in a temporal or historical predicament as the characters in postmodern narrative, and, like those characters, has no access to a totalized narrative of a true or essential Selfhood according to which he/she orients his/her present being. The reader's 'temporality' or historical condition in the act of reading postmodern characterization is itself characterized by the notion of disposition, of being seduced or disposed from one position to another in the construction and deconstruction of a series of narratives. In this, there is no final or overall, single position which would allow for a systematic ranging of the narratives; there is only an economy which, in its basic orientation to heterogeneity, endlessly produces more and more different narratives. Where the economy of identity produces a single totalized narrative, that of the Self, it also arrests the temporality of narrative and the notion of temporal change which is axiomatic to narrative; postmodern characterization keeps the narrative going.

In so doing, postmodern narrative lures a reader into 'disposition', a translation of the Greek word *ethos*. To this extent, the category of the ethical is introduced; and through this, which involves the reader in the search for 'the good' (as opposed to subscription to a monotheistic Truth), the political does in fact return. As MacIntyre (1967: 129) indicates, there is a distinction between the ethical and the political, but it cannot be drawn too sharply. Postmodern narrative of characterization, in attacking not only the notion of a Self but also the dichotomy on which it is based (interior 'reality' versus external 'appearance'), eradicates the distinction between the ethical and the political. To read postmodern characterization is to reintroduce the possibility of politics, and importantly of a genuinely historical political change, into the act of reading; and this reintroduction is generated from the category of the ethical, the disposition of the reading subject.

3 Seeming otherwise

What is at stake in postmodern characterization is, firstly, the confusion of the ontological status of the character with that of the reader; secondly, the decentring of that reader's consciousness, such that he/ she is, like the character, endlessly displaced and 'differing'; and thirdly, the political and ethical implication of this 'seeming otherwise', shifting from appearance to different appearance in the disappearance of a totalized Selfhood. The reading subject in postmodern characterization is, thus, exactly like Kristeva's notion of the 'subject-in-process', a subject whose very subjectivity is itself endlessly deferred, endlessly differing. The explicit political dimension of reading postmodern characterization is now clear: it involves a marginalization of the reader from a centralized or totalized narrative of Selfhood, thus rendering the reading subject-in-process as the figure of the *dissident*. Among her types of dissident, Kristeva locates both the experimental writer, working with the 'diaspora of those languages that pluralize meaning and cross all national and linguistic barriers', and, crucially, *women*: 'And sexual difference, women: isn't that another form of dissidence?' (Kristeva 1986: 299, 296) What these two groups share is the impetus towards marginalization and indefinition; they are in a condition of 'exile' from a centred identity of meaning and its claims to a totalized law or truth. Exile is itself a form of dissidence, since it involves the marginalization or decentring of the Self from all positions of totalized or systematic law (such as imperialist nation, patriarchal family, monotheistic language), and 'if meaning exists in the state of exile, it nevertheless finds no incarnation, and is ceaselessly produced and destroyed in geographical or discursive transformations' (Kristeva 1986: 298).

In experimental writing, the major source of such exile and its consequential political disposition towards dissidence is in the questioning of the system of language itself (though this is not easily distinguished from the concerns of empire, family and so on). Postmodern characterization, construed as a writing in and from exile, serves to construct the possibility, perhaps for the first time, of elaborating the paradigmatic reader of these new novels as feminized. Woman, as 'that which cannot be represented, that which is not spoken, that which remains outside naming and ideologies' (Kristeva 1986: 163), is always 'dispositioned' towards otherness, alterity. To read postmodern characterization is to begin to construct the ethics of alterity, to discover what it means to speak always from the political disposition of the Other.

References

ADLER, LOUISE, 1980, 'Historiography in Britain: "une histoire en construction" ', *Yale French Studies* 59, 243–53.

ALLEN, D. and BUTTERICK, G. F., 1982, *The Postmoderns*, New York.

ALTBACH, E. H., 1984, *German Feminism: Readings in Politics and Literature*, Albany.

ALTHUSSER, LOUIS, 1969, *For Marx*, New York (tr. from *Pour Marx*, Paris: 1965).

AMIS, MARTIN, 1978, 'The State of Fiction: A Symposium', *The New Review* (Summer), 18.

ANDERSON, PERRY, 1984, 'Modernity and Revolution', *New Left Review* 144, 96ff.

APPIGNANESI, LISA, 1973, *Femininity and the Creative Imagination*, New York.

AUERBACH, ERICH, 1953, *Mimesis*, New York.

AUSTIN, JOHN, 1962, *How to do Things with Words*, Cambridge Mass.

BACARISSE, SALVADOR (ed.), 1980, *Contemporary Latin American Fiction*, Edinburgh.

BAKHTIN, MIKHAIL, 1981, *The Dialogic Imagination*, Austin, Texas.

BARNES, JULIAN, 1985, *Flaubert's Parrot*, London.

BARRADAS, EFRAIN, 1985, 'La necessaria innovación de Ana Lydia Vega: préambulo para lectores vírgenes', *Revista Iberoamericana* 60, 132–3.

BARTH, JOHN, 1969, *Lost in the Funhouse*, London.

1980a, *LETTERS*, London.

1980b, 'The Literature of Replenishment', *The Atlantic*, January, 65–71.

1983, *Sabbatical: A Romance*, Harmondsworth, Middx.

1984, *The Friday Book: Essays and Other Nonfiction*, New York.

BARTHES, ROLAND, 1978, *A Lover's Discourse*, New York (tr. from *Fragments d'un discours amoureux*, Paris: 1977).

BAUDRILLARD, JEAN, 1976, *L'Echange symbolique et la mort*, Paris.

BAYLEY, JOHN, 1960, *The Characters of Love*, London.

BECKETT, SAMUEL, *et al.*, 1972, *Our Exagmination Round his Factification for Incamination for Work in Progress*, London (first published in 1929).

1979, *The Beckett Trilogy*, London (first published in English in 1959).

1984, *Collected Shorter Plays*, London.

BELLAMY, JOE DAVID (ed.), 1974, *The New Fiction: Interviews with Innovative Writers*, Urbana.

BELSEY, CATHERINE, 1980, *Critical Practice*, London and New York.

BENAMOU, M. and CARAMELLO, C. (eds), 1977, *Performance in Postmodern*

Culture, Madison, Wisconsin.

BENJAMIN, WALTER, 1973, *Illuminations*, ed. H. Arendt, London.

BENNETT, TONY, 1979, *Formalism and Marxism*, London and New York.

BERGER, JOHN, 1973, *G.*, Harmondsworth, Middx (first published in 1972).

BERMAN, MARSHALL, 1982, *All that is Solid Melts into Air: The Experience of Modernity*, London.

BERTENS, HANS, 1986, 'The Postmodern Weltanschauung and its Relations with Modernism: An Introductory Survey', in Fokkema and Bertens 1986: 9–51.

BHABA, HOMI K., 1983, 'Difference, Discrimination, and the Discourse of Colonialism', in *The Politics of Theory*, eds. Francis Barker *et al.*, Colchester, 194–211.

BONITA OLIVA, A. 1984, 'La transavanguardia' *Il Verri* nuova serie 1–2, 56–79.

BORGES, JORGE LUIS, 1978, *Labyrinths*, London (first published in New York in 1964).

BRADBURY, MALCOLM, 1973, *Possibilities: Essays on the State of the Novel*, London.

(ed.) 1977, *The Novel Today: Contemporary Writers on Modern Fiction*, Glasgow.

and RO, SIGMUND (eds), 1987, *Contemporary American Fiction*, London.

BRADLEY, DAVID, 1984, 'Novelist Alice Walker: Telling the Black Woman's Story', *New York Times Magazine*, 8 January, 25–37.

BROOKE-ROSE, CHRISTINE, 1986, *Xorandor*, London.

BROOKS, PETER, 1984, *Reading for the Plot: Design and Intention in Narrative*, Oxford.

BRUCE-NOVOA, J., 1984, 'La Sabina de Julieta Campos, en el laberinto de la intertextualidad', in González 1984.

BURROUGHS, WILLIAM, 1968, *The Naked Lunch*, London (first published in Paris in 1959).

BUSI, ALDO, 1988, *Seminar on Youth*, London (tr. of *Seminario sulla gioventu*, Milan: 1984).

BUTLER, CHRISTOPHER, 1980, *After the Wake*, Oxford.

1984, *Interpretation, Deconstruction and Ideology*, Oxford.

CADIOLI, A. and PERESSON, G. (eds), 1984, *Il superlibro. Conversazioni sul romanzo di sucesso*, Ancona.

CALVINO, ITALO, 1982, *If on a Winter's Night a Traveller*, London (first published in English in 1981) (tr. of *Se una notte d'inverno un viaggiatore*, Turin: 1983.).

CAUTE, DAVID, 1972, *The Illusion*, London.

CELATI, GIANNI, 1975, 'Il bazar archeologico', *Il verri*, 5a serie 12, 11–35.

1985. *Narratori delle pianure*, Milan.

CIXOUS, HÉLÈNE, 1977, *La venue à l'écriture*, Paris.

COETZEE, J. M., 1986, *Foe*, Toronto.

CONROY, MARK, 1985, *Modernism and Authority: Strategies of Legitimation in Flaubert and Conrad*, Baltimore.

CORTÁZAR, JULIO, 1975, *Hopscotch*, New York (first published in Spanish in 1963).

COWARD, R. and ELLIS, J., 1977, *Language and Materialism*, London.

COWLEY, MALCOLM (ed.), 1963, *Writers at Work: the 'Paris Review' Interviews* (Second Series), London.

CULLER, JONATHAN, 1975, *Structuralist Poetics*, London. 1983. *On Deconstruction*, London.

CUNLIFFE, MARCUS (ed.), 1975, *American Literature Since 1900*, London.

DAVIS, LENNARD J., 1980, 'Wicked Actions and Feigned Words': Criminals, Criminality, and the Early English Novel', *Yale French Studies* 59, 106–118.

1987, *Resisting Novels*, London.

DEL GIUDICE, DANIELE, 1983, *Lo stadio di Wimbledon*, Turin.

1985, *Atlante occidentale*, Turin.

DE MICHELIS, CESARE, 1986a, (Review) 'E. Palendri, '*La Pietre e il sale*', *Il Gazzettino*, 24 May.

1986b, (Review) 'C. Piersanti, *Charles*', *Il Gazzettino*, 6 September.

DERRIDA, JACQUES, 1977, *Limited Inc. abc*, Baltimore.

1979a, 'Living On: Border Lines', in *Deconstruction and Criticism*, ed. H. Bloom, New York, 75–175.

1979b, *Spurs: Nietzsche's Styles*, Chicago.

1982, *Margins of Philosophy*, Brighton.

D'HAEN, THEO, 1983, *Text to Reader*, Amsterdam.

DOCHERTY, THOMAS, 1983, *Reading (Absent) Character*, Oxford.

DOCTOROW, E. L., 1971, *The Book of Daniel*, New York.

DURAS, MARGUERITE and GAUTHIER, XAVIÈRE, 1974, *Les Parleuses*, Paris.

DURRELL, LAWRENCE, 1983, *The Alexandria Quartet*, London (first published 1957–60).

EAGLETON, TERRY, 1976, *Criticism and Ideology*, London.

1983, *Literary Theory: An Introduction*, Oxford.

1985, 'Capitalism, Modernism and Postmodernism', *New Left Review* 152, 60–73.

1986, *Against the Grain*, London.

ECO, UMBERTO, 1983, *The Name of the Rose*, London (tr. of *Il nome della rosa*, Milan: 1980)

1985, *Reflections on 'The Name of the Rose'*, London (tr. of *Postille a 'Il nome della rosa'*, Milan: 1983.)

EDGAR, DAVID, 1987, 'The New Nostalgia', *Marxism Today*, March, 30ff.

FEDERMAN, RAYMOND, 1965, *Journey to Chaos: Samuel Beckett's Early Fiction*, Berkeley.

1971, *Double of Nothing*, Chicago.

(ed.) 1975, *Surfiction*, Chicago.

1976a, 'Imagination as Plagiarism (an unfinished paper . . .)', *New Literary History* 7, 563–78.

1976b, *Take It Or Leave It*, New York.

FERRETI, G., 1981, 'Nella storia, scombinando le sue regole', *Rinascita* 38, (16, 17 April), 33.

FETTERLEY, JUDITH, 1978, *The Resisting Reader*, Bloomington.

FIEDLER, LESLIE, 1965, 'The New Mutants', *Partisan Review* 32, 505–25.

1975. 'Cross the Border – Close that Gap: Post-Modernism', in Cunliffe 1975: 344–66.

FILAR, MALVA E., 1985, 'Autorrescate e invención en *Las andariegas* de Albalucia Angel', *Revista Iberoamericana* 60, 132–3, 649–56.

FOFI, GOFFREDO, 1985, 'Ci vorrano anni', *Linea d'ombra* 11, 13–14.

FOKKEMA, DOUWE and BERTENS, HANS (eds), 1986, *Approaching Postmodernism*, Amsterdam.

FOSTER, HAL (ed.), 1983, *The Anti-Aesthetic: Essays on Postmodern Culture*, Washington.

1984, '(Post)Modern Polemics', *New German Critique* 33, 67–79.

FOUCAULT, MICHEL, 1972, *The Archaeology of Knowledge and the Discourse on Language*, New York.

1973, *Madness and Civilization*, New York.

1974, *The Order of Things*, London.

1980, *The History of Sexuality*, vol. 1, New York.

FOWLER, ROGER, 1981, *Literature as Social Discourse*, London.

1985, 'Power', in *Handbook of Discourse Analysis: Volume 1: Disciplines of Discourse*, ed. Teun A. van Dijk, London and New York, 61–82.

FOWLES, JOHN, 1977, *The French Lieutenant's Woman*, London (first published in 1969).

1985, *A Maggot*, London.

FREUD, SIGMUND, 1908, 'The Relation of the Poet to Daydreaming', in *On Creativity and the Unconscious*, New York, 1958.

GALLAGHER, DAVID P., 1973, *Modern Latin American Literature*, Oxford.

GARCÍA MÁRQUEZ, GABRIEL, 1978, *One Hundred Years of Solitude*, London (tr. of *Cien Años de soledad*, Buenos Aires: 1967).

GARCÍA PINTO, M., 1985, 'La escritura de la pasión y la pasión de la escritura: *En breve cárcel* de Sylvia Molloy', *Revista Iberoamericana* 60, 132–3, 687–96.

GASS, WILLIAM H., 1985, *Habitations of the Word*, New York.

GONZALEZ, PATRICIA ELENA, *et al.*, 1984, *La sárten por el mango*: encuentro de escritoras latinoamericanas, Río Piedras.

GRAFF, GERALD, 1975, 'Babbit at the Abyss: The Social Context of Postmodern American Fiction', *Triquarterly* 33, 305–37.

1979, *Literature Against Itself*, Chicago.

1983, 'The Pseudo-Politics of Interpretation', *Critical Inquiry* 9, 3, 597–610.

GUGLIELMI, ANGELO, 1985, 'Quel bel romanzo italiano sembra tradotto dal cirillico', *Paese sera*, 25 April.

HAMON, PHILIPPE, 1977, 'Pour un statut sémiologique du personnage', in *Poétique du recit*, ed. Roland Barthes, Paris.

HARVEY, W. J., 1965, *Character and the Novel*, London.

HASSAN, IHAB, 1980, *The Right Promethean Fire: Imagination, Science, and Cultural Change*, Urbana.

1987a, *The Postmodern Turn*, Ohio.

1987b, 'Making Sense: The Trials of Postmodernism', *New Literary History* 18, 2, 437–59.

and HASSAN, SALLY (eds), 1983, *Innovation/Renovation: New Perspectives on Modernism*, Madison.

HAYMAN, DAVID, 1974, 'Sollers Interview', *Iowa Review* 5, 4, 101–5.

HEATH, STEPHEN, 1972, *The Nouveau Roman*, London.

HEBDIGE, DICK, 1986/7, 'A Report on the Western Front: Postmodernism and the "Politics" of Style', *Block* 12, 4–26.

HERMANN, CLAUDINE, 1976, *Les Voleuses de langue*, Paris.

HOLUB, ROBERT C., 1984, 'Politicizing Post-Structuralism', *German Quarterly* 57, 1, 75–90.

HUTCHEON, LINDA, 1977, 'The outer limits of the novel: Italy and France', *Contemporary Literature* XVIII, 2, 198–216.

1980, *Narcissistic Narrative*, London.

1988, *A Poetics of Postmodernism*, London.

HUYSSEN, ANDREAS, 1984, 'Mapping the Postmodern', *New German Critique* 33, 5–53.

1986, *After the Great Divide: Modernism, Mass Culture, Postmodernism*, Bloomington and Indianapolis.

JAMESON, FREDRIC, 1983, 'Postmodernism and Consumer Society', in Foster 1983.

1984a, 'Postmodernism, or The Cultural Logic of Late Capitalism', *New Left Review* 146, 53–92.

1984b, The Politics of Theory: Ideological Positions in The Postmodernism Debate', *New German Critique* 33, 53–67.

JEFFERSON, ANN, 1980, *The nouveau roman and the poetics of fiction*, Cambridge.

1983, 'Balzac and the *nouveau roman*: problems of reading', *Romance Studies*, no. 2 (Summer), 166–80.

JENKS, CHARLES, 1981, *The Language of Post-Modern Architecture*, 3rd ed., New York.

1986, *What is Post-Modernism?*, New York.

JOHNSON, B. S., 1973, *Aren't You Rather Too Young to be Writing Your Memoirs?*, London.

JOSIPOVICI, GABRIEL, 1971, *The World and the Book*, London.

1977, *The Lessons of Modernism and Other Essays*, London.

JOYCE, JAMES, 1973, *A Portrait of the Artist as a Young Man*. Harmondsworth, Middx (first published in 1916).

KENNEDY, WILLIAM, 1975, *Legs*, Harmondsworth, Middx.

KERMODE, FRANK, 1971, *Modern Essays*, London.

1988, *History and Value*, Oxford.

KINGSTON, MAXINE HONG, 1980, *China Men*, New York.

KLINKOWITZ, JEROME, 1980, *Literary Disruptions: The Making of a Post-Contemporary American Fiction*, 2nd ed., Urbana.

KRAUSS, ROSALIND E., 1985, *The Originality of the Avant-Garde and Other Modernist Myths*, Cambridge Mass. and London.

KRESS, GUNTHER, 1985, 'Ideological Structures in Discourse, in *Handbook of Discourse Analysis*, vol.1, ed. T. A. Van Dijk, London and New York.

and HODGE, ROBERT, 1979, *Language as Ideology*, London.

KRISTEVA, JULIA, 1974, *La révolution du langage poétique*, Paris.

1980, *Desire in Language*, Oxford.

1986, *The Kristeva Reader*, ed. T. Moi, Oxford.

KROKER, A. and COOK, D., 1986, *The Postmodern scene: Excremental Culture and Hyper-Aesthetics*, Montreal.

KUTNIK, JERZY, 1986, *The Novel as Performance: The Fiction of Ronald Sukenick and Raymond Federman*, Carbondale.

LAWRENCE, D. H., 1958, *Selected Letters*, ed. D. Trilling, New York.

LAWSON, HILARY, 1985, *Reflexivity: The Post-Modern Predicament*, London.

LECLAIR, T. and MCCAFFERY, L. (eds), 1983, *Mindful Pleasures: Essays on Thomas Pynchon*, Boston.

LEITCH, VINCENT, 1980, 'The Lateral Dance: The Deconstructive Criticism of J. Hillis Miller', *Critical Inquiry* 6, 4, 593–607.

LODGE, DAVID, 1971, *The Novelist at the Crossroads*, London.

LYOTARD, JEAN-FRANÇOIS, 1984, *The Postmodern Condition*, Manchester (tr. of *La condition postmoderne*, Paris: 1979). ('Answering the Question: What is Postmodernism?' also in Hassan and Hassan 1983.)

MacCABE, COLIN, 1978/9, 'The Discursive and the Ideological in Film: Notes on the Condition of Political Intervention', *Screen* 19, 4, 29–43.

McCAFFERY, LARRY (ed.), 1986, *Postmodern Fiction: A Bio-Bibliographical Guide*, Westport.

MacDONELL, DIANE, 1986, *Theories of Discourse: An Introduction*, Oxford.

McHALE, BRIAN, 1986, 'Change of Dominant from Modernist to Postmodernist Writing', in Fokkema and Bertens 1986: 329–41. 1987, *Postmodernist Fiction*, London.

MacINTYRE, ALISTAIR, 1967, *A Short History of Ethics*, London.

MADDOX, JAMES, H., JNR., 1978, *Joyce's Ulysses and the Assault upon Character*, New Brunswick.

MAGNARELLI, SHARON, 1979, 'Gatos, lenguaje, y mujer en *El gato eficaz* de Luisa Valenzuela', *Revista Iberoamericana* 108–9, 603–12.

MALRAUX, ANDRÉ, 1950, *The Twilight of the Absolute*, tr. by S. Gilbert, London.

MARTIN, RICHARD, 1983, 'Walter Abish's Fictions: Perfect Unfamiliarity, Familiar Imperfections', *Journal of American Studies* 17, 229–50.

MARTIN, WALLACE, 1986, *Recent Theories of Narrative*, Ithaca and London.

MARX, KARL, 1852, *The Eighteenth Brumaire of Louis Bonaparte*, New York.

MAZUREK, RAYMOND A., 1982, 'Metafiction, the Historical Novel, and Coover's *The Public Burning*', *Critique* 23, 3, 29–42.

MERQUIOR, J. G., 1986, 'Spider and Bee: Towards a Critique of the Postmodern Ideology', *ICA Documents 4, Postmodernism*, 16–18, London.

MINK, LOUIS O., 1981, 'Everyman His or Her Own Annalist', *Critical Inquiry* 7, 4, 777–83.

MOI, TORIL, 1985, *Sexual/Textual Politics: Feminist Literary Theory*, London.

MONDELLO, E., 1984, 'Il ragazzo del bar diventa un caso letterario', *Paese Sera*, 6 April.

MONTALE, EUGENIO, 1977, *Tutte le poesie*, Milan.

MORRISSETTE, BRUCE, 1975, *The Novels of Robbe-Grillet*, Ithaca (tr. of *Les Romans de Robbe-Grillet*, Paris: 1963 and 1971).

NAVAJAS, GONZALO, 1987, 'Retórica de la novela postmodernista española', *Siglo XX* 4, 1–2, 16–25.

NEWMAN, CHARLES, 1985, *The Post-Modern Aura*, Evanston.

NEWMAN, MICHAEL, 1986, 'Revising Modernism, Representing Postmodernism: Critical Discourses of the Visual Arts', *ICA Documents 4, Postmodernism*, London, 32–51.

O'BRIEN, FLANN, 1975, *At Swim-Two-Birds*, Harmondsworth, Middx (first published in 1939).

OPPENHEIM, L. (ed.), 1986, *Three Decades of the French New Novel*, Urbana and Chicago.

ORWELL, GEORGE, 1962, *Inside the Whale*, London.

OTERO-KRAUTHAMMER, E., 1985, 'Integración de la identidad judía en las genealogías de Margo Glanz', *Revista Iberoamericana* 60, 132–3, 867–74.

OWENS, CRAIG, 1980, 'The Allegorical Impulse: Towards a Theory of Postmodernism', *October* 12 and *October* 13.

    1982, 'Representation, Appropriation & Power', *Art in America* 70, 5, 9–21.

    1983, 'The Discourse of Others: Feminists and Postmodernism', in Foster 1983.

PALANDRI, ENRICO, 1979, *Boccalone*, Milan.

    1986, *La Pietre e il Sale*, Milan.

PAZZI, ROBERTO, 1985, *Cercando l'Imperatore*, Casale Monferrato.

    1986, *La principessa e il drago*, Milan.

PIFER, ELLEN, 1985, 'Invention and Orthodoxy', in Rainwater and Scheick 1985.

PORPHYRIOS, D., 1986, 'Architecture and the Postmodern Condition', *ICA Documents 4, Postmodernism*, London, 30.

POPE, ALEXANDER, 1975, *Poems*, ed. J. Butt, London.

POUND, EZRA, 1922, 'Paris Letter', *The Dial* (June).

PRATT, A., 1981, *Archetypal Patterns in Women's Fiction*, Bloomington.

PYNCHON, THOMAS, 1975a, *Gravity's Rainbow*, London.

    1975b, *V.*, London.

RABINOVITCH, RUBIN, 1967, *The Reaction Against Experiment in the English Novel 1950–1960*, New York.

RAINWATER, C. and SCHEICK, W., 1985, *Contemporary American Women Writers: Narrative Strategies*, Lexington.

RICARDOU, JEAN, 1967, *Problèmes du nouveau roman*, Paris.

    1971, *Pour une théorie du nouveau roman*, Paris.

    1973, *Le Nouveau Roman*, Paris.

ROBBE-GRILLET, ALAIN, 1965, *Snapshots and Towards a New Novel*, London (tr. of *Pour un nouveau roman*, Paris: 1963).

    1984, *Le Miroir qui revient*, Paris.

ROBBINS, TOM, 1972, *Another Roadside Attraction*, New York.

    1977, *Even Cowgirls Get the Blues*, London.

ROBERTSON, MARY F., 1985, 'Medusa Points and Contact Points', in Rainwater and Scheick 1985; 119–41.

RORTY, RICHARD, 1982, *The Consequences of Pragmatism*, Brighton.

    1985, 'Habemas and Lyotard on Postmodernity', in *Habemas and Modernity*, ed. R. G. Bernstein, London.

ROTHENBERG, JEROME, 1977, 'New Models, New Visions: Some Notes Towards a Poetics of Performance', in Benamou and Caramello 1977: 11–19.

ROWE, WILLIAM, 1984, 'Ethnocentric Orthodoxies in Text as Cultural Action: Some Issues in Latin-American Literature', *Romance Studies* 5, 75–90.

RUEGG, MARIA, 1979, 'The End(s) of French Style: Structuralism and Post-Structuralism in the American Context', *Criticism* 21, 3, 189–216.

RUSHDIE, SALMAN, 1983, *Shame*, London.

RUSSELL, CHARLES, 1985, *Poets, Prophets and Revolutionaries: The Literary Avant-Garde from Rimbaud through Postmodernism*, New York and Oxford.

RYAN, MICHAEL, 1982, *Marxism and Deconstruction: A Critical Articulation*, Baltimore.

SAID, EDWARD, W., 1983, *The World, The Text, and The Critic*, Cambridge Mass.

SARRAUTE, NATHALIE, 1956, *L'Ere du soupçon*, Paris.

SARTRE, JEAN-PAUL, 1977, *La Nausée*, Paris (first published in 1938).

SCHOLES, ROBERT, 1980, 'Language, Narrative, and Anti-Narrative', *Critical Inquiry* 7, 1, 204–12.

SEARLE, JOHN, 1970, *Speech Acts*, Cambridge.

SELZER, MARK, 1984, 'Reading Foucault: Cells, Corridors, Novels', *Diacritics* 14, 1, 78–89.

SHERZER, DINA, 1986, *Representation in Contemporary French Fiction*, Lincoln and London.

SHOWALTER, ELAINE, 1987, 'A Criticism of Our Own: Autonomy and Assimilation in Afro-American and Feminist Literary Theory', in *Critical Projections*, ed. R. Cohen, London and New York.

SIMON, CLAUDE, 1986, *Discours de Stockholm*, Paris.

SMYTH, E. J., 1983, 'Narrative Embedding in *Un Régicide*', *Romance Studies*, no. 2 (Summer) 18–34.

SNOW, C. P., 1958, 'Challenge to the Intellect', *Times Literary Supplement* (15 August).

SONTAG, SUSAN, 1966, *Against Interpretation*, New York.

SOSNOSKI, JAMES, 1985, 'Literary Study as a Field for Inquiry', *boundary 2* 13, v. 2–3, 91–104.

SPANOS, W. V., 1972, 'The Detective and the Boundary: Some Notes on the Postmodern Literary Imagination', *boundary 2*, 5, 421–57.

SPIVAK, G., 1980, 'Revolutions That As Yet Have No Model', *Diacritics* 10, 4, 29–49.

STANTON, DOMNA, 1987, 'Difference on Trial: a Critique of the Maternal Metaphor in Cixous, Irigaray, and Kristeva', in *Poetics of Gender*, ed. N. K. Miller, New York, 157–82.

SUKENICK, RONALD, 1973, *Out*, Chicago.
1975, *98.6: A Novel*, New York.
1979, *Long Talking Bad Conditions Blues*, New York.
1985, *In Form: Digressions on the Act of Fiction*, Carbondale.
1986, *The Endless Short Story*, New York.

SULEIMAN, S. R., 1983, *Authoritarian Fictions*, New York.

SWINDEN, PATRICK, 1973, *Unofficial Selves*, London.

SWINGEWOOD, ALAN, 1975, *The Novel and Revolution*, London.

TABUCCHI, ANTONIO, 1983, *Donna di Porto Pim*, Palermo.

TAINE, HYPPOLYTE, 1873–1908, *History of English Literature*, 4 vols., Edinburgh.

TANI, STEFANO, 1984, *The Doomed Detective: the contribution of the detective novel to postmodern American and Italian fiction*, Carbondale. 1986, 'La giovane narrativa italiana: 1981–1986', *Il Ponte* XCII, 3, 120–48.

TANNER, TONY, 1971, *City of Words*, London.

THIHER, ALLEN, 1984, *Words in Reflection: Modern Language Theory and Postmodern Fiction*, Chicago and London.

TODOROV, T., 1971, *Poétique de la prose*, Paris.

TRENNER, RICHARD (ed.), 1983, *E. L. Doctorow: Essays and Conversations*, Princeton.

TRILLING, LIONEL, 1965, 'On the Teaching of Modern Literature', in *Beyond Culture*, New York.

ULMER, G. L., 1985, *Applied Grammatology*, Baltimore.

VATTIMO, G. and ROVATTI, P. A. (eds), 1983, *Il pensiero debole*, Milan.

VATTIMO, G., 1985, *La fine della modernità. Nichilismo ed ermeneutica nella cultura postmoderna*, Milan.
(ed.) 1987, *Filosofia '86*, Bari.

VENTURI, ROBERT, 1966, *Complexity and Contradiction in Architecture*, New York.
and SCOTT BROWN, D. and IZENOUR, S., 1972, *Learning from Las Vegas*, Cambridge Mass.

VONNEGUT, KURT, 1979, *Slaughterhouse-Five*, London.

WAGSTAFF, CHRISTOPHER, 1984, 'The Neo-avantgarde', in *Writers and Society in Contemporary Italy*, eds M. Caesar and P. Hainsworth, Leamington Spa, 35–61.

WALTON, LITZ A., 1986, 'Modernist Making and Self-Making', *Times Literary Supplement* (18 October).

WASSON, RICHARD, 1969, 'Notes on a New Sensibility', *Partisan Review* 36, 460–77.
1974, 'From Priest to Prometheus: Culture and Criticism in the Post-Modern Period', *Journal of Modern Literature* 3, 1188–1202.

WATSON, IAN, 1973, *The Embedding*, New York.

WATT, IAN, 1957, *The Rise of the Novel*, Harmondsworth, Middx.

WAUGH, PATRICIA, 1984, *Metafiction*, London and New York.

WEST, REBECCA, 1986, 'Lo spazio nei *Narratori della pianure*', *Nuova Corrente* 33, 65–74.

WHEELIS, ALLEN, 1971, *The End of the Modern Age*, New York.

WHITE, HAYDEN, 1976, 'The Fictions of Factual Representation', in *The Literature of Fact*, ed. A. Fletcher, New York, 21–44.
1980, 'The Value of Narrativity in the Representation of Reality', *Critical Inquiry* 7, 1, 5–27.

WIDDOWSON, PETER (ed.), 1982, *Re-Reading English*, London.

WILDE, ALAN, 1985, 'Shooting for Smallness: Limits and Values in Some Recent American Fiction', *boundary 2* 13, v. 2–3, 343–69.

1970, *The English Novel from Dickens to Lawrence*, London.
WILLIAMS, RAYMOND, 1977, *Marxism and Literature*, Oxford.
    1986, 'The Metropolis and the Emergence of Modernism', in *Image of the City in Modern Life*, eds E. Trimms and D. Kelly, Cambridge.
WITTGENSTEIN, LUDWIG, 1953, *Philosophical Investigations*, Oxford.
WOLF, CHRISTA, 1982, *No Place on Earth*, tr. by Jan Van Heurck, New York.
WOOLF, VIRGINIA, 1929, *The Common Reader* (second series), London.
    1953, *A Winter's Diary*, London.
    1966, 'Modern Fiction', in *Collected Essays*, London (first published in 1919).
    1973, *To the Lighthouse*, Harmondsworth, Middx. (first published in 1929).
    1977, *A Room of One's Own*, St Albans (first published in 1929).
WRIGHT, STEPHEN, 1985, *Meditations in Green*, London.
WURLITZER, RUDOLPH, 1969, *The Octopus*, London.
    1970, (Interview) *Rutgers Anthologist* 41, 34–41.
ZAVARZADEH, MAS'UD, 1976, *The Mythopoeic Reality: The Postwar American Nonfiction Novel*, Urbana.
ZERAFFA, MICHEL, 1969, v

Index